Physics of Love [Y**(ZY)]

alias "A Model of Information Processing Groups"

Release version 4.4.1
Third issue, June 2003
Publisher: Celebran Verlag, Freising, Germany

ISBN: 3-89811-026-5

Many thanks for your support of this scientific publication!
Owning a material book is a privilege.

The main changes **[L]** of version 3.2.2 compared to the first issue (version 2.4.1, September 1999) are four more chapters named:

"*Quantum Physical Discussion*", "*Minimal Information Processing*", "*Gender a Property of Information Processing*" and "*A New View of Authoring*".

The last is given as an appendix following with some helping definitions of "*Rules for Reference Remarks*".

The extensions related to the second issue (version 3.2.2, September 2000) are the chapters "*Aggression and Terrorism*", "*Religious Discussion*" **[T]** and the title change. The newly included references - **(50)** based on psychological analysis and **(122)** related to cosmology - show fundamental coincidence.

Versions 4.x.y enhance the "*Basic Physics*" foundation and include multiple philosophical references. Version 4.2.0 adds an analysis of the legality of the Iraq war at "*Appendix II: Development of This Theory*".

Dedicated in love to Sigrid remembering our first holidays during 1994, when the base ideas came into my mind.

"What the world needs today is more of the optimism of the progressive and a little less of the pathological fear of the standpatter, more faith in creative evolution, more hope of reaching yet higher levels of achievement, and more of that freedom from prejudice called charity, another name for love -

– the productive passion."

Witmer, L., 1922, cited by Lotka, A., **(102)**

Thanks to my friend Gerhard Birkl for the support during book preparation.

Thanks to "Books on Demand GmbH" for the equally named service.

Many thanks to my readers of version 1.x and 2.x! Your feedback was a needed base for this publication.

More thanks to my partners of an attempted research collaboration! It was a miracle that our research proposal has been prepared in time.

Thanks to all people, who were in any way involved with this essay by reference or stimulation of ideas. There is a special appendix "*A New View of Authoring*", which is a result to all of your contributions and a self-reference to the content meaning of this essay.

This essay uses bold printed numbers for standard references, for example "**(1)**", and bold printed capital or special characters, for example "**A**", for stimulation references. Those are listed at an extra chapter after the standard references.

Title, chapters, sub-chapters and paragraphs may show a footnote like remark to standard or stimulation references inside of bold square braces, for example **[…]**. The rules for interpreting those remarks are given at the appendix: "*Rules for Reference Remarks*".

Please excuse, if you find any errors. Mistakes related to the English language may be there and can not be avoided, because I can not afford the costs for a professional translator. Mistakes related to the sociological, physical and mathematical content should not be there, but nobody is perfect.

If you find any errors, please report them to: *postmaster@celebran.de*.

Abstract

This essay discusses groups of individuals. Both are described as very abstract things. This theory is applicable to a lot of individual kinds, which tend to organise themselves to groups. Some examples are cells, animals, humans, economies, nations. The property all of them have to share is the possibility of information processing, although the minimum can be one single method of comparison. The second issue extends to quantum physical deductions and a detailed, fermionic explanation of gender. The theory uses mainly quasi-static description, but has at least revealed a standard thermodynamic law:

$$d\mathbf{H} = \mathbf{T}\,d\mathbf{S} + \mathbf{V}\,d\mathbf{p}$$

The two terms at the right side display the two main parts of the following content. The properties derived from the axioms show similarity to real thermodynamic gases. Publications of social science in the past had left well-known problems unsolved. One of them is feedback of experience another are unselfish individuals, a third one is diversity. The three named problems and probably others are vanished in the models of this theory.

From this theory one can deduce those <u>spontaneous</u> actions.

- Dialogue without former voluntariness by analysing the environment,
- symbiosis derived even from parasitism by some established dialogue,
- learning by optimisation of costs after communication,
- hunting ground protection and marking derived even by communication benefits,
- leadership established by competence and following analysis of diversity,
- fractal group structure meaning sub- and super-grouping caused by leadership,
- rise of constitution after experience of destructive leaders.

With the help of this theory one can explain:

- why humans are generalists compared to animals,
- why an attraction between individuals occurs,
- why "intelligence" is something not only in us but <u>between</u> us, too,
- why cloning can reduce the efficiency of groups,
- why dictatorial and totalitarian regimes have a smaller lifetime than democracy but "good" monarchs raised flourish states in history,
- why radicalism and extremism are forcible by propaganda and radical and extreme people are very unselfish,
- why a plebicitic democracy tends not to join super-structures,
- why a single indirect representation of people is optimal,
- why constitutional institutions raise instability of the whole system by blocking others,
- why super-structuring of nations needs modern communication possibilities to succeed,
- why the fight for female rights is close related to the fight for free birth control,
- why artificial life will never show any creativity, if authors try to use their artificials completely without letting them get own benefits.

This theory has not yet been quantitatively verified related to most details, although the coincidences with the experiences of the reality seem to be very good. But quantitative efforts will be an important future task. The needed but not yet granted financial support prevents the quantitative verification until this issue.

Possible expendabilities are:

- mathematically defined gender specific attraction and repulsion,[1]
- repulsion between individuals at small distances,
- change of individual number by birth and death rates or competition of species[2],
- social level optimisation at first class groups (as later defined),
- calculation of fractal dimension of theoretic and real structures,
- quantum physical formulation by wave functions and operator methods **[#]**.
- dropping simplifications and examination of results by this way changed conditions.

---

[1] The gender free, mathematical part and the explanatory, gender-describing part have been not unified yet. For many circumstances the gender property can be neglected. For a better understanding the separation seems to be an opportunity by reduction of complexity. But unification including quantum wave functional description will be an important future task.

[2] Explaining the interaction of species by information processing excludes independent competition for the same food, energy or other resources from the frame of this essay. **(42)** shows that true selective extinction of species is only possible, if there is independent competition. The possible prevention of die out of species caused by human acting on the environment is therefore at most dependent on the scientific and popular knowledge of their existence. Other papers have included a description of competition for example: **(49)**.

How to Read This Essay?

This essay may have readers with several different levels of understanding and information need. Because of this only reading from the beginning to the end may not be applicable in every case.

Types of readers may be:

- social scientists
- natural scientists and engineers
- politicians
- people without academic knowledge
- Dr. Sheldrake´s fan community

The last type may cover all previous types, too. They have knowledge about phenomena, which can be better understood with this theory, as I hope. Because of this pre-education starting directly with the chapter: "*Appendix I: Dr. Sheldrake´s Publications*" may be reasonable. Further reading may be dependent to the covered other reader type.

The essay has three main parts: some verbal introduction first, mathematical formulation second and verbal conclusion and following at last. The pure verbal parts at the beginning and at the end are recommended for all readers, who want information first. Going into mathematics is needed, if verbal declarations should be logically validated. The mathematical part starts with: "*Basic Communication Benefit Formula*" and ends before: "*Minimal Information Processing*". The most difficult part, which includes complex (but not solved) integrals, is: "*Common Accounts of Benefits (**pV**)*". All other mathematical parts should be understandable by using the four arithmetic base operations and techniques for rearrangement of equations and relations. This means that typically all people with mathematical base education, as taught at schools leading to academic study capability, should have the possibility to logically validate the theory. But capability is less important as reading time. Logical validation will need much time surely, because of the length of the deductions. Although some of the readers may have the time, most will not have it.

If one is not satisfied by the verbal parts or is stimulated to receive more information, reading a little careless about the mathematical parts may be reasonable. It is not always needed to check the dependence of one formula to the next. But the following conclusions after deduction will give the needed further information. This approach may be very good suited for natural scientists and engineers, because their education will give them the capability to understand much only by overlooking.

The main addressed readers are social scientists and politicians, who may be not very attracted by mathematics. But the verbal information given along with the mathematical deductions should be of interest for them, too. Spending more time pays off!

Content

Definitions and Axiomatic Foundation

Clear definitions are essential for understanding. Important are differences to definitions that have been used before by other publications.

Individuals **(144)** are single entities, which can build a group. Because of the abstract theory many kinds of individuals could be described this way. Examples are cells, animals, humans, economies, nations. The only property that all individuals have to share, is the capability of information processing. The minimal information processing needed is the comparison of two signals. The source of one signal must be external to the individual.

Benefit is an abstract result of behaviour of an abstract individual trying to stay alive and further trying to live optimally. The increase of benefit is the origin for group building and further structures of individuals.[3] It is very important that this definition is abstract! Keeping the benefit abstract as long as possible is the only needed simple method letting every thinkable and unthinkable feedback of experience get entrance into theory. The physical relation is possible and will identify benefit as a numerically negative effect.[4] See chapter: "*Basic Physics*".

Intelligence is "the capability to generate benefits". This definition is narrower than the not fixed common interpretation of this term. "Intelligence" is a widely used property of individuals and groups in this essay. The physical relation is as well possible and will identify intelligence as negative energy - in other words: an energy saving. See chapter: "*Basic Physics*".

Activity is the part of time[5] an individual or group spends for generating a benefit for a specific job. Activity is a number without dimension and can be normalised in the way that the whole activity is 1, which any individual or group spends for everything it is doing. Every specific job can only have a fraction of activity.

$$1 = \sum_{i=1}^{n} \mathbf{A}_i$$

n: number of jobs

---

[3] Coincident importance of benefit are stating: **(7)**, **(15)**, **(32)**, **(34)**, **(78)**, **(81)**, **(83)** and **(147)**.

[4] The sign is a matter of definition and of geometry of an applied physical "effect" described by some transport. The explosion of a house by a bomb has a numerically positive effect for physical calculations, but you would not accept it as beneficial, if you are the owner. For the reconstruction of the destroyed house you would accept this property, if you do not have to pay the energetic effort. The reverse definition would be principally possible, but the historical facts of development of the physics science have defined it this way. The renaming above allows a positively defined discussion. **[#]**

[5] The important factor of time is referenced at: **(9)**, **(10)**, **(21)**, **(45)**, **(71)**, **(72)**, **(84)**, **(107)**, **(111)**, **(139)** and **(173)**.

Communication is a super-term of "information processing". The last is commonly meant to be something solitary. But the first has the same characteristics and is commonly meant to need partners. The essay will show that a complete understanding of communication includes solitary information processing and therefore includes any kind of interaction with reality an individual might have **(13)**.

Groups are communities of individuals. Later we shall recognise that building a group is only possible, if individuals communicate[6] with each other. In this context individuals and groups are models. This means that certain properties of the real individuals and groups could probably not be described by this theory.[7] [8] [9]

---

[6] Here one should recognise the equal root of the words "community" and "communication" in the English language, which tells my definition of groups! There is no such similarity in German, where "Kommunikation" is a loan-word.

[7] At this position I have to criticise: **(121) Olson, M: The logic of collective action**, because his definition of the meaning of organisation is much less abstract. Defining the equal trials to reach some goods (if collective or not) as a base for group structure can not be useful over time. Because individuals aiming every time into the same direction must have their feet cemented. A better definition is cited in the same book: **(7) Aristoteles: Nikomachic ethic.** The philosopher tells us: "Because of the benefit 'polis' has emerged…". The group definition above differs from Olson´s. My opinion is that only because of the equal interests one can not talk of groups. Building a group needs interaction of individuals and Olson´s theory itself has told us that big, abstract, non interacting "groups" are unstable and do not exist. Small groups could be stable this way, but not because of the collective goods that they reach, instead, as I think, because of their possible interaction. Forcing individuals to contribute to a group like trade unions or national states is nothing but a communication system. This way Olson´s theory can be modified and integrated and is this way very helpful for understanding.
Why is this explanation needed? Looking at recent study results like: **(105)**: *"…a more systematic approach is still badly needed, both in terms of conceptual and theoretical frameworks, and in terms of the object of study…"*,
One can find the "interest groups" as often used and always understood term. It is "always" understood, because Olson´s theory had big influence until today in social science. But all well known limitations of Olson´s theory and the told wish for the "badly needed", overcoming theory arose because of Olson´s use of concrete benefits (equal to interests) and abstract groups, where instead abstract benefits and concrete groups would have been much more applicable.

[8] One should recognise that all game theoretical approaches have the same problem of fixed interests or forced conditions like the famous "prisoners dilemma" tells. Thank God for your freedom related to most circumstances of life!

[9] It seems that one can not define a group and the derivable benefit exactly at the same time. There seem to be an uncertainty relation like Heisenberg´s in physics. One should consider **(79)**, because there was told the existence of something like that for another relationship. Probably uncertainty relations are something common, but the question is: How to define them by formula**?** **[I]** See the chapter "*Quantum Physical Discussion*" for an attempt.

<u>Structure</u> is the total result of:

- Dependence of individuals to leaders and vice versa.
- The behaviour of other groups acting as individuals or leaders of super-groups.

<u>Gender</u>[10] is a complementary property of information processing. The definition of the complementary states “female” and “male” is done only by considering energy accounts.[11] This is uncommon but conforms at most to nature’s behaviour. The sometimes resulting deviations to the common attributes are as well interesting.

<u>Female</u>: The less energy consuming, complementary information processing device.

<u>Male</u>: The more energy consuming, complementary information processing device.[12]

<u>**(pV)**</u> will be used to declare that something belongs to the grouping and volume dependent part of the equation:

$$d\mathbf{H} = \mathbf{T}\,d\mathbf{S} + \mathbf{V}\,d\mathbf{p}$$

<u>**(TS)**</u> will be used to declare that something belongs to the structuring and diversity dependent part of the equation above.

There are more definitions around but with less common importance. So the definitions will be done where the term is used first.

---

[10] Philosophical relations are: **(26)** and **(99)**.

[11] Nature seems to show in seldom cases a multiplicity of gender. Such behaviour is analysed in this book only, if a super-structuring and this way level dependent simple gender modelling is obviously possible. Neuter and hermaphroditic states are considered, too.

[12] Are those gender definitions something arbitrary? In fact they are, but I think this is truer for the standard use of gender attributes. If one would like, female and male can be exchanged and used reversed related to energy consumption. Even the words themselves are an example. Because sometime human males including myself seem to eat twice as much as their wives, the definition conforms well to human behaviour.

Axioms are needed in every theory **(39)**, **(52)**, **(174)**. We have to be thankful that we have to use them, because the need for axioms is the guarantee for freedom of thinking, too **(34)**. If someone tries to hurt this theory essentially, the axioms will be her/his target. Here the axioms are stated by words, not by mathematical formulas. Later in the mathematical chapters the first two axioms can be found again by using formulas.

{**1**} The first axiom is named "Capability of Association" (**pV**).[13]

Communication as defined above can raise association, if the partner is capable of doing so. Looking at a dialogue, the first partner has to give some benefit to the other (voluntariness is not a prerequisite). With the help of the external benefit and the internal comparison and information processing capability the second partner is able to increase her-/hisself "intelligence". Therefore the second partner is able to generate more benefit as without the dialogue.[14]

{**2**} The second axiom is named "Benefit from Diversity" (**TS**).[15]

The part belonging to grouping and volume dependence (**pV**) will show that individuals with more competence (intelligence and association capability) than other group members have time to other operations. If they use it to analyse the diversity of the group, they can generate even more benefit for themselves and for the group.

{**3**} A last axiom is named "Learning by Trial and Error".

If the only interaction with reality is communication and information processing, interests, aims but as well groups and structures are something that are results of comparison and calculation. Because of no applicable common truth experience needs trial and error **(35)**. Changing conditions force new trials. Here this axiom has not a mathematical formula yet, but inputs some disturbance into the group and individual operation over time in the way that a found optimal process and structure may be inadequate later. For specific systems one can probably implement some disturbance by mathematical formulation.

---

[13] The multiple semantic of "association" for the English language needs the clarification that at first associations in mind are meant. One can talk about stimulation of ideas, too. But one will understand by the following chapters that association in mind leads to social association. This justifies the multiple semantic.

[14] There are other papers describing association in mind **(81)**, **(97)**, **(100)**, **(101)**, **(102)**, **(114)**, **(115)**, **(137)**, **(156)** and non-linear effects leading to co-operation: **(19)**, **(33)**, **(49)**, **(68)**, **(87)**, **(126)**, **(132)**, **(134)**, **(140)**. Neural networks act the same way: **(125)**, **(127)**. Further there are already done "Artificial Life" experiments showing this behaviour by simulation **(167)** as well as for robotic circumstances: **(24)**, **(110)**.

[15] Papers describing such behaviour are **(8)**, **(14)**, **(35)**, **(42)**, **(67)**, **(87)**, **(132)**, **(138)**, **(140)**, **(153)**, but the quantitative results of **(154)** are striking **[L]**!

Benefit, Intelligence and Activity

The basic relation between benefit, intelligence and activity is the formula:

$$\frac{d\mathbf{B}}{d\mathbf{t}} = \mathbf{I}(\mathbf{t}) \cdot \mathbf{A}(\mathbf{t})$$

The variables mean:

t: time

B: benefit

I: intelligence[16]

A: activity

$\frac{d}{d\mathbf{t}}$: differentiation regarding the time variable

As stated above the activity of individuals is spread about various jobs that have to be done. One should notice that intelligence might depend on the single job[17]:

$$\mathbf{I} = \mathbf{I}(\mathrm{i}) = \mathbf{I}_{\mathrm{i}}$$

i fixed and an element of 1 to n

n: number of jobs

The benefit relation changes to:

$$\frac{d\mathbf{B}}{d\mathbf{t}} = \sum_{\mathrm{i}=1}^{\mathrm{n}} \mathbf{I}_{\mathrm{i}} \cdot \mathbf{A}_{\mathrm{i}}$$

The strategy to get the optimal benefit for a species would be to increase the intelligence of the individuals regarding the jobs that need the most activity.

If multiple jobs have to be done during the same time, the activity for all has to be shared and every job that is worked out in a parallel manner can reach only a fraction of activity. It is obvious that the same results can be achieved, if all jobs are done in a serial manner with the maximum activity of 1 applied to them. Working by this way means dividing time and not activity. This will reduce much the effort for calculation of advantageous benefits, but surely it is not how individuals act, because there are different job priorities **(38)**. Scheduling of priorities is a job like others and has to be counted as others. This tells further that this job is not something special, which one have to consider special, if one is only interested in total accounts as is the case in all following chapters.

---

[16] Please remember the narrow definition for intelligence equal to "capability to generate benefit".

[17] A vector interpretation may be reasonable during future works.

With this serial approach every benefit of job activity can be replaced by this integral:

$$\mathbf{B} = \int I(\mathbf{t})\,d\mathbf{t}$$

The integration boundaries are the times of starting and ending the job by serial job order. Activity is replaced because she evaluates to 1.

Later one can frequently recognise terms like this:

$$\mathbf{B} = \mathbf{I} \cdot \mathbf{t}$$

The common, simplificating assumption is that **I** is timely constant during the integration and **t** is the integration period resulting from end time minus start time.

Communication as Information Processing

Looking at communication one can find several kinds, which can be reduced to two different behaviours. The following examples have information flow to both sides:

a dialogue of two partners,
a work group communicating with each other.

The last example can be divided into multiple dialogues. Dialogues can emerge spontaneously and stabilise themselves as shown below.

reading a book,
looking television,
listening to a lecture

are examples that show information flow only to one side. There is no cause that pure monologues can be stable over time. Typically there will be some price the reader, watcher or listener has to pay for the service. Including the payment into the description results to a dialogue.

One can as well find mixed systems like:

panel discussion,
seminar,
television accompanied with advertising and channel quoting

they can be divided into one part that is describable by dialogues and another part that is describable by monologues.

To complete the definition of communication as read above, we look at behaviours like searching for food, what an animal or a cell may need. One can find that sensing reality, comparing results in any way, which is equal to raising association, and generating benefit out of the results is exactly what happens too to people reading a book, looking television or listening to a lecture. In this way any experience of nature can be described at least as a monologue.

Using nature purely in monologic ways is something that can not be done over time. The increasing benefit out of this behaviour will raise the population of the individuals. By emptying the resources this parasitism of nature will be stopped. So every monologic communication will have a price that one has or others have to pay for the service. Because of the last it is true that there is no real monologic communication, if one includes paying of prices as an information flow back to the first partner. On the other hand describing something as a monologue is a simplification that should be allowed for many cases and finite times.

Parasites and Symbiosis

A common behaviour of individuals is consuming and therefore loosing goods during live. Working against this, individuals derive benefit from their environment by taking new goods. Taking and consuming at the same rate would be the only very unstable system, which do not need storage of goods. Little disturbance of the taking rate will cause the individual to malfunction and die. Therefore any real individual has some storage for goods, which it needs for living.[18] By this property individuals will be as well goods for other individuals that find the stored resources useful, too. Parasitism is something very common in reality and needs no special parameters to occur **(143)**.

The parasited individual has three alternatives to react. The first is dying, because parasitism is complete and not enough resources are left for its own use. The second is working against the parasite, what needs some effort and therefore consumes extra resources. The third possibility is letting the parasite do his actions without any reaction against him, because the efforts would be higher than the loss by parasitism. Mainly the last alternative could tend to change of behaviour of both spontaneously, if at least one of both has the following minimal information processing capability.

As stated above communication can be described as: sensing reality, comparing results in any way, which is equal to raising association, and generating benefit out of the results. The simplest way for achieving this are two different sensor signals that are compared. In terms of a microprocessor the sensor values are only stored in the processors registers. The benefit of the calculation could be direct reaction like position change. For example the parasited individual can measure its resources, and therefore can estimate the loss of them. The second signal could be the concentration of food external to the individual. Looking at the parasite we probably will find a sensor, which measures external concentration of food. A second sensor signal could be the concentration of metabolic products.

If both individuals are capable of association, the following could happen. The parasite will find some food resource and during consuming this, metabolic products concentration does not increase harmful. The parasited individual will detect increased loss of resources, but it will find more external food, too.

[18] These reserves are a prerequisite for unselfish benefit contribution, too, and therefore as well for communication as described later. It tells further that any living individual has the possibility to communicate.

Symbiotic Attraction:

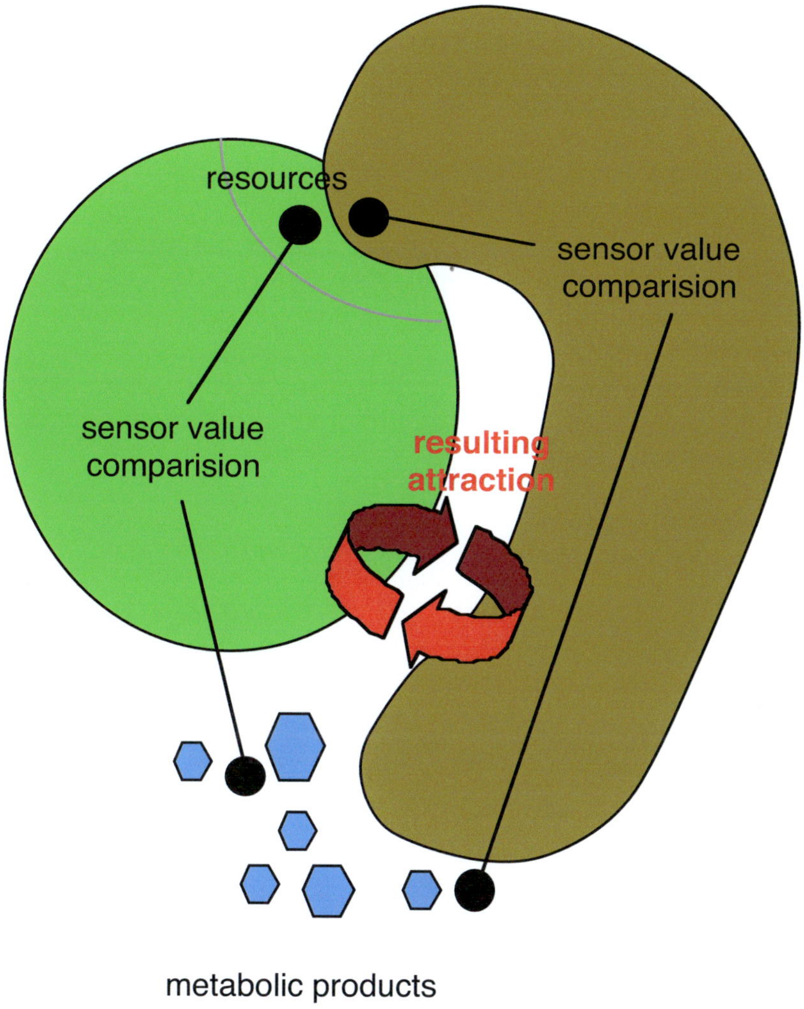

Figure 1 . Symbiotic Attraction

The calculations upon the sensor signals[19] can tell both of them that staying close together is an opportunity, if position change is the result of either calculation. Producing more or optimised food for the partner could be an alternative result. This way spontaneous symbiosis can emerge. The former parasite is now a partner and the feelings, which are equal to associations, have changed from repulsive to attractive.

One can recognise and mathematics below will show that the resulting benefit given by a dialogue, will be more than both individuals together can generate alone.[20]

If jobs of a species are mostly some dialogic communication, optimising this capability will result to more benefits than any specialisation for monologic jobs can ever reach. This is the cause, why humans can be described as generalists able to run, climb and swim, but all this not very good.

The superior benefit out of communication regarding other specialisation's has lead evolution to build more and more complex cell systems and more and more animals with communication capability until humans have been developed **(1)**, **(150)**. They carry evolution forward by building more and more complex structures of humans until nations and unions of nations are constructed.

---

[19] For experiments showing similar behaviour but without starting at parasitism take a look at: **(24)**, **(108)**, **(110)** and **(130)**. Some experiments including parasitism are: **(49)** and **(87)**. Some social science description is: **(172)**.

[20] I had first found a verbal formulation of this regarding human groups at: **(25)**.

Learning as Data Storing and Post Processing

At the examples above storing data was not needed. But having this capability will even more help individuals during the association process of their brain. Out of one sensor signal and internal data recording one can construct a system that is able to examine its environment like the individual above with two sensors but no data storage. The source of the second value that has to be compared to the sensor signal, would then be generated out of the stored data. For the example of parasitism the parasited individual could be changed in the way of being only capable of measuring food concentration and recording the values. If its positioning system makes normally random walk, the decrease of food concentration can lead to undo the last step, which would result to going to the local concentration maximum. In this way symbiosis can emerge as before, but the parasited individual will never notice that it is parasited.

Reading internal data is like reading a book and can be described like other monologic communications. Learning means storing data and calculation algorithms and using them as appropriate.

Comparing both examples tells further that direct dialogic communication can be replaced by post processing of stored data **(4)**. If all parameters are equal and fixed, the benefit from using learned behaviour should be equal to the benefit from direct reaction to communication in this case. This is not evident, if parameters can change. Therefore communication can not be replaced by learning. On the other hand using (internal) learned behaviours will give mostly optimal results very likely with less effort than (external) communication. Because of the more effective use of resources by being capable of learning, this possibility will emerge spontaneously.

Symbiotic Attraction by Learned Behavior:

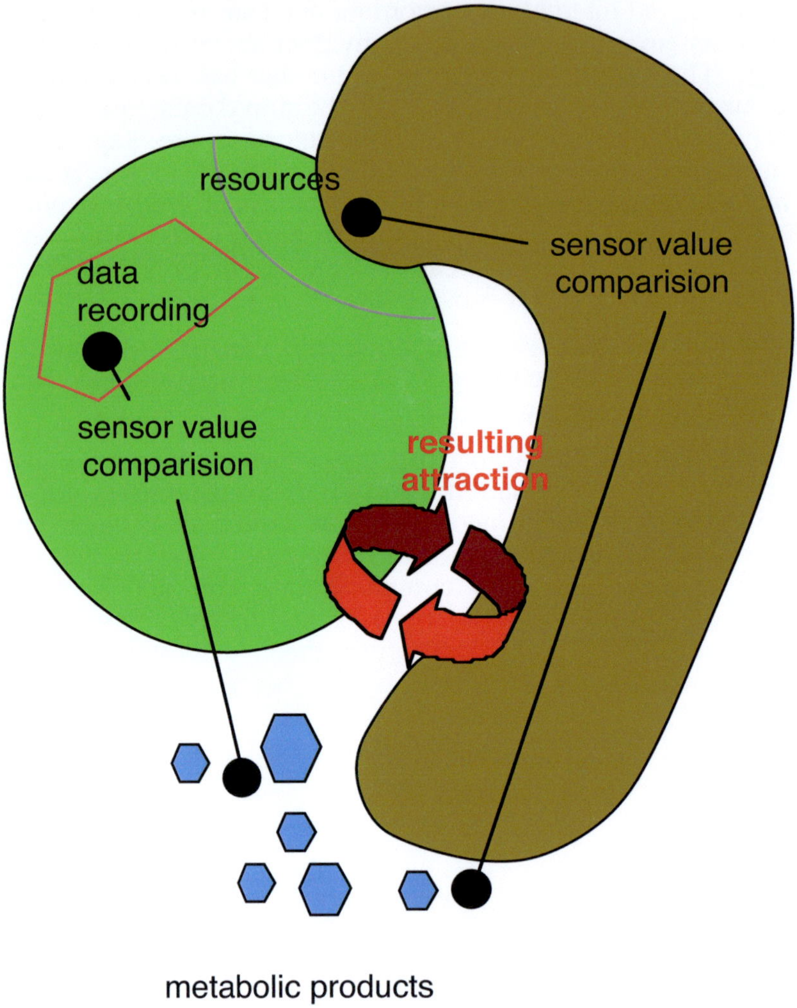

Figure 2. Symbiotic Attraction by Learned Behaviour

Leadership and Structure

Prior to symbiotic behaviour there has to be some benefit, which is given to a potential partner unselfishly **(18)**. Although voluntariness was not a prerequisite, one can assume that species with long experience of communication measured in terms of evolution, will have some instinctive tendency to unselfishness (for the first step).[21] The symbiotic offer followed by back flow of benefit and even more benefit as partners can generate together solely is the cause for group building. The mathematical formulation can be found below. There we shall find that every one of a stable social group has to contribute unselfishly to the group, but can recognise a back flow of benefit that equals at minimum the former contributed benefit.

Differences of intelligence and association capability lead to different times an individual has to contribute benefit to the group. Because of this there will be individuals with some time left for other operations. One possibility is recording the behaviour or opinions or other properties of the other group members. Doing this there will be an extra benefit that can be generated only using the diversity of the group members[22]. The leader can use this extra benefit for support of her/his leadership. In this way leadership emerges out of groups spontaneously. Having established leadership structure has been established, too, because the leader is an additional property.

---

[21] This assumption is not needed for the theory. It may be not true for humans. If it is not true, humans would have to learn it after birth only by experience. For cells building complex systems it is likely that this behaviour is already programmed in DNA or elsewhere, because of the relative short life time of a single cell compared with the complex cluster. But doubts are allowed, because different states of ontogenesis of cells are known starting from yeast as the simplest and as single cells organised eukaryonts **(42)**. Probably both is true, because only eukaryonts may have the possibility of Lamarckian inheritance of learned behaviour by object-oriented DNA program structure including data **(1)**, **(92)**, **(93)**, **(136)**. The data seems to be the best place for enquired change resulting to different individual DNA introns, as observed, without destroying functional program code. Darwinian mutation and selection **(36)** including the Baldwin effect **(116)** seems to be a very good proven way of evolution, but pure randomly done evolution may be not true – see **(55)**. Changes of behaviour are not explained in this essay by looking at specific, including genetic algorithms. For an artificial eukaryontic system compare **(20)** and **(130)**. For a mixture of thermodynamical and biological optimisation take a look at **(8)**.

[22] The base for this statement, which is the same as axiom {**2**}, is simple mathematics. A fine explanation can be found at: **(67)**. A very easy understandable hint is given by the question: What is the information a number can carry? It is obvious that the amount of information a number can carry is proportional to the amount of digits the number shows and this amount is proportional to the logarithm of the number.

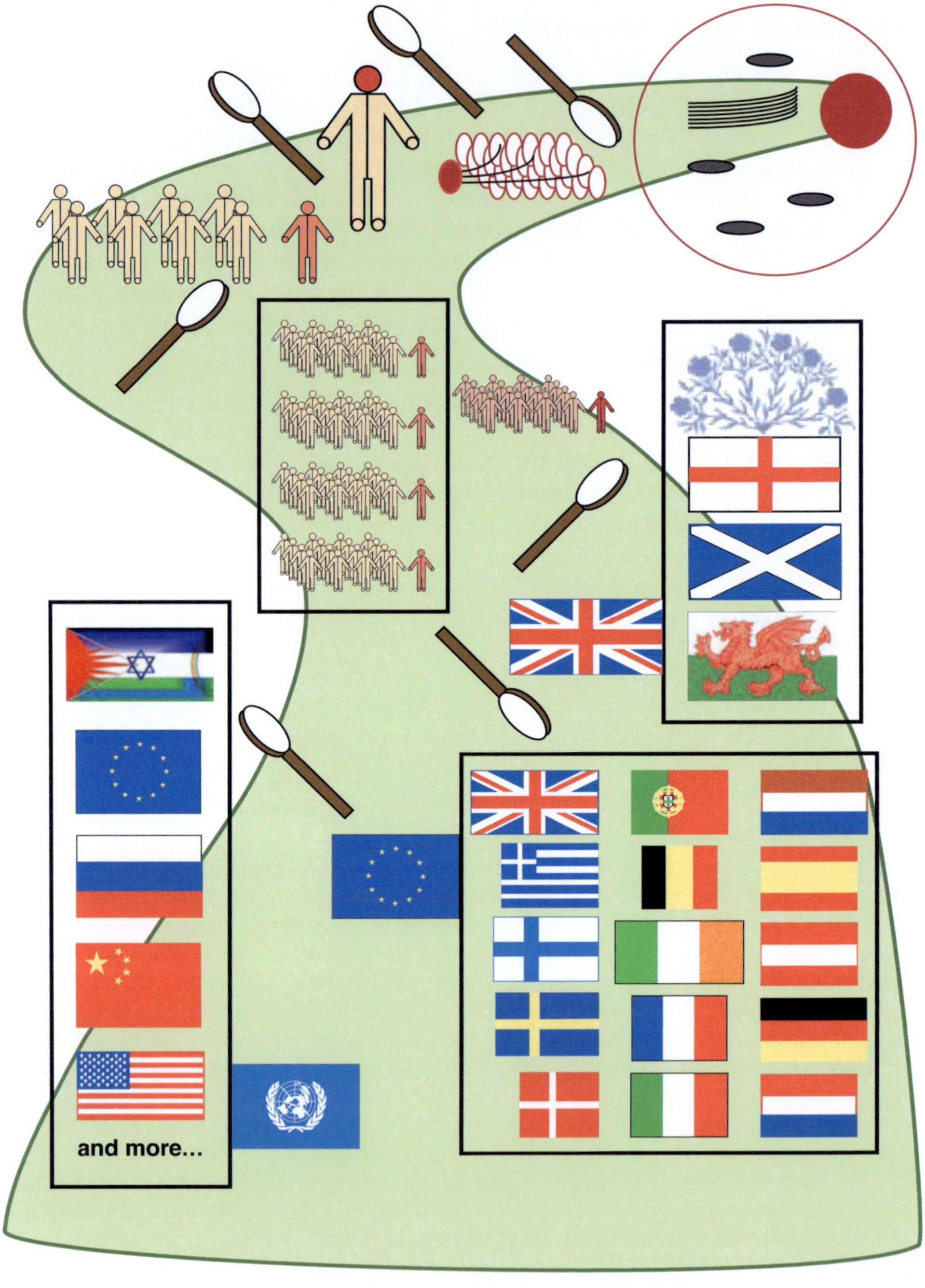

Figure 3. The Structure of the World

More complex systems have individuals build from sub-groups but as well leaders that are groups of individuals. As mentioned at the abstract individuals could be cell clusters known as animals or economies build from companies and so on. This way a thorough fractal structure from cell organelles to nations and unions of nations could be build and described with the same methods. Complexity is gone for methods but is nevertheless there regarding the uncountable parameters and fine structures one can find in reality.[23]

Pursuance of her-/his leadership could mean directly consuming more benefits compared to others of the group. Because differences of intelligence and association capability should be recognisable by other group members, the group can recognise rivals of leadership, too. Supporting her/his leadership would then lead to contribution of benefits from the extra (**TS**) part to the group, if rivals were around. As long as the group estimates that benefits from rivals would be less than from the leader, the group members will support the leadership. If they hope for more benefit form another leader, the first will not be supported anymore. Probably even membership will be cancelled. Because of the wider resources that the elder leader can use, only cancelling all benefits derived from the group can hurt her/him essentially to resign[24].

If there are no recognisable rivals around, the leader will tend not to give any of the extra benefit to the group members. This opportunity on the other hand will lead others to rivalry. Probably it is not easy to difference benefit of diversity (**TS**) from benefit of group communication (**pV**). This way an absolute (no rivals) leader can get into trouble, too, if she/he tries to consume more benefits as the stability condition for the group allows. The unstable group will push badly contributing members out or will be completely reformed. Loosing leadership and as well membership is very likely by those conditions.

The statements above show that leadership is as well an attractive position as a dangerous one. Not well behaving leaders have to focus not only loss of leadership, but loss of membership, too. The last could be followed by loss of live, if group membership and communication benefits are essential for it.

This problem has lead to several leader strategies to stabilise the own position. One is violence, terrorism and restricted information flow. One can look at this as a special kind of communication, which keeps the stability condition of the group valid by forcing the members to contribution without voluntariness. The problems of this strategy are that communication is mainly only established as a dialogue between the leader and the single group member.

---

[23] Although super-structuring of nations and merging to "global players" is on fashion today, there are old in- and foresights: (**14**), (**30**), (**69**), (**97**), (**99**), (**106**), (**119**). For recent insights take a look at (**19**), (**23**), (**49**), (**62**), (**63**), (**86**), (**95**), (**108**), (**121**), (**134**), (**165**) and (**166**).

[24] Only one male leads a group of hyenas. He is the only male that is allowed to copulate with the female members. After changing the male leader the elder one is excluded from the group and can not have the needed hunting succession after fall. Therefore he is bound to die.

The group member does not recognise much or any benefit and would leave the group if she/he could. The stability condition decreases therefore from first class to second class or even less, if the system reaches parasitic behaviour.

As we shall recognise at the mathematical formulas below the stability condition of second class gives less benefit as the first class condition. If the system is parasitic, all communication benefits have gone, although leadership has been derived from the former group benefit. This strategy does not make sense in terms of benefit but may be seductive, if forcing contribution is always needed for leading bigger groups like nations **(121)**. Violent expansion of the group will further lead to better benefit (for the leader) out of the (**TS**) part because logarithm of the number of group members is a multiplied parameter.

Because of the essential meaning of benefit for grouping and structuring the violent leader behaviour can not have long lifetime. The error rate will rise, because group and structure intelligence is low. The leader has last her/his position for a while but breakdown will occur. Probably the leader can die peacefully before this event. This will be her/his only hope.

A better strategy of stabilisation of a leaders position is raising constitution. After some experience of violent leaders groups will tend to declare constitutions not only to give rules for interaction but as well to let leaders re-enter the group as normal members without having to focus loss of membership after resigning. Although constitution may not come easy, one has the right to say that she will emerge spontaneous after enough experience. For cell clusters the information about constitution has to be distributed to any cell. By this way DNA or another ancient information recording and distribution system has emerged spontaneously.

Mixed approaches to stabilisation of leadership, which have aspects as the first strategy and as well as the second are monarchism and feudalism. For this strategy one needs some kind of constitution, which does not need to be some written law. But the constitution has to be something to what most group members would agree. Because any experience of reality raises standard group behaviour, reality is not a good base for stabilising leadership. Therefore transcendental ideology known as religion works best to solve this requirement. Another good property of religions is that all (or most?) of them try to expand their members by communication. If leadership and religion use symbiosis to benefit from each other, it is likely that religion will tell people that leadership is something procured by God. Religion will then be supported and protected by leaders.

The last approach has worked well over centuries as long as people had not much external information sources that were not controlled by leaders or religion. The complained fall of importance of religion during our days comes along with the raising importance of democracy and free individual communication. On the other hand we should not under estimate the importance of religion for setting up communication, group constitutions and support of unselfishness, which had lead to stable and well behaving structures in the past. By every synagogue, church, mosque and alike in the centre of a town it is shown that religion was (and is?) a centre of communication. Even without symbiosis to leadership this properties of religions are the cause for their spontaneous emerging. This parts religion can play with success now and in future, too. But if the group structures of religions themselves are not well defined (democratic), it is likely that other more well defined systems create more benefit for their members as the religion can. More loss of importance can be foreseen then. Another problem of religions in our days is the dependence to words of prophets or God that are many centuries old. Most religions have solved this by interpretation change over time. But this was a very slow adaptation. As change in all parts of live seems to be more rapid today as in the past the traditional behaviour of religions could brake them out of race.

Looking back to the abstract, we have to define the "good" monarch, who sets up a flourish state: If she/he gives much of the structure benefit (**TS**) to the group, the group is able to bloom up and individuals would appreciate this **(32)**. If the cause of doing so is not rivalry to other potential leaders but morality or religiosity or some feeling of rationality, people would appreciate this more, because it is something, what they would not expect. **[J]**

The "good" behaviour is something very rational in terms of group benefit, because there are indirect, iterative effects of an increased benefit in this way. The won benefit could be used to do more unselfish communication steps, to increase communication therefore, to increase association effects and at least increase benefit again. This benefit increase (**pV**) would reach the leader, too. A typical concomitant of group blooming is the increasing number of individuals by reducing the "hunting ground"[25] area a single individual needs (mathematical formula follows below). This increases the structure benefit (**TS**) by the increased logarithm of the number of individuals. This part was the source for leadership and gives directly benefit back to the leader after some times.

Although this "good" behaviour is very rational, until this theory no mathematical formulation was there to show this directly. Therefore "feelings" for rational behaviour were needed to give leaders the capability to behave this way in the past. Because feelings are nothing but complex calculations[26] without step by step consciousness, the likelihood to have those ideas of rational behaviour was not equal to zero during the past. On the other hand the very indirect benefit increase caused by this behaviour was the cause for people not to expect it and for most absolute leaders not to use it.

The strategy of monarchism and feudalism uses one single person as leader. This is only sufficient, if this person can effectively analyse the diversity. As number of group members and sub-structure increases, this efficiency will become low.

---

[25] I would much more appreciate the German term "Revier" but the English "hunting ground", but I had not found a better English term. Let me know, whether you know something sounding better.

[26] **(129)** tells a contrary opinion.

Then sub-structured leadership by parliaments and government groups are needed to do the job.

The statements above apply to economies and companies, too. If a company is small, having a "good" owner like a "good" monarch will raise prosperity. If a company gets bigger and multiple sub-structured, this will not be true any more. Having many shareholders and a leading group may help. But less money is spend for shareholder income as for employing. This means that better influence of employees should result to more prosperity and shareholder income, too. Defining some constitution for influence of employees is a good idea.[27] Probably something like this is established for every big (and small) company, even if there is no written description. **[J]**

At human structures leaders are often defined by the super-structure and not by the group members. This is a way to reduce fights caused by rivalry for leadership. Further it reduces the likelihood of leadership by "competence" and increases the likelihood of leadership by "analysis of diversity", as both defined below. But rivalry can not be totally avoided by this strategy and the new leader needs acceptance by the group in the same way, as it would result by direct emergence of leadership out of the group itself. Such externally placed leaders have to focus some conflict of loyalty. They think that they have to be thankful to the super-leader for their position and may really be kept dependent to her/him. But if they want to keep the position, the group should have the experience of opportunities given by the leader. If the super-leader is as well subjected to such sub-group dependence, a conflict should be much better avoidable as it is possible, if the super-leader assumes to be an independent dictator. Only communication over all structure levels can avoid the conflicts of loyalty.

Problems of exploitation, which one has seen in the past and until today, can be identified as violent and terroristic leadership as described above. All limitations to benefit and timeline apply. Unfortunately revolutions may as well create propagandistic and dictatorial regimes. This way nothing has been won.

[27] One may consider the German law: "Betriebsverfassungsgesetz".

Propaganda and Extremism

The symbiosis between leadership and religion and the controlled individual information sources of feudal structures can be interpreted as some kind of propaganda. Propaganda is well known for other political systems of the past and today. If we look at the activity of a free communicating individual, we shall recognise many partners and many directions. We can stay abstract, if we identify "directions" as special defined activities, which are trials to get maximal benefit. Being more concrete one could define multiple "interests". Regarding free communication we can find that an individual has a cut or intensity reduced number of partners and directions of activity, if it is subject to propaganda. Therefore benefit will be reduced.[28] Let me repeat the formula, where benefit rate is the sum of special intelligence and activity:

$$\frac{d\mathbf{B}}{d\mathbf{t}} = \sum_{i=1}^{n} \mathbf{I}_i \cdot \mathbf{A}_i$$

During propaganda individuals would try to maximise benefit as well as during free circumstances. But they would recognise that the cut or intensity reduced parts of the sum would have less weight for optimisation than before. Because of this they would try to get more "intelligence" out of the areas, which are left unreduced.

If an individual does not like politics during freedom or bound to propaganda, she/he would increase by education and communication her/his intelligence in the left unpolitical areas. If propaganda has chosen this areas well in the way that they have very low dependence to politics, people behaving this way would get even less interested in politics than without propaganda. The decision between maximising political or non-political intelligence is like a bifurcation in chaos theory. **[(67)]**

If an individual is much interested in politics, she/he will recognise a reduced offer of possibilities at areas with lower regards to politics. She/he will then try to increase intelligence using political areas. If she/he has sympathy with the political direction preferred by propaganda, she/he will not feel much restricted in this way. Best adaptation to the preferred direction would then give best benefit (during short times).

If she/he has antipathy to the preferred political direction, the individual will feel much restricted by propaganda and leaders behaviour. Because of this the indi-

---

[28] **[KK]** has stimulated/contributed the following extension: There are many filters an individual may be subjected during free operation. It may be education, social relations, own preferences and alike. It is not possible and often not an opportunity to drop all filtering. But the quality difference to propaganda is the principle ability to use the information source and rearrangement or reduction of filtering by the individual itself. Whether this is always possible even for democratic systems may be of question. Optimisation of this capability for all will be always a target of politics of today and of future.

vidual will tend to find ways for getting the lost benefit from restricted areas. This causes breaking the law and building or supporting prohibited sub-groups. A decrease of benefit will be seen by this behaviour, but the individual probably will go this way, because she/he hopes for much more benefit, after overcoming the restrictions. The two possibilities can be understood as a bifurcation, too.

The short time decrease of benefit is the cause that the adaptive behaviour will describe the majority of people and the people going into resistance are the minority. For people, who have no extra resources for living but focus some fight for survival every day, it will be very unlikely that they go into resistance. If people feel antipathy to the propagandistic government but have not enough "feeling" of rationality (compare the "good" monarch above), they would tend to leave politics and would act as some one with low political interest, what will leave them at least completely without political interest as shown above.

People, who are acting adaptive, would not hear much about contrary opinions, which propaganda suppresses. But much about the propaganda contents. Because of this they have only associations with this content and can increase their (political) intelligence only in the direction, where propaganda leads. This effect stabilises propagandistic and ideological systems, although benefit generation is low.[29]

During propagandistic circumstances radicalism and extremism will bloom. The cause for this is first polarisation of political direction the way described above. Second there is another influence coming from social level at first class groups as defined later. If an individual wants to be part of a first class group, she/he has to contribute some benefit for the group. Members with higher intelligence have to spend less activity for the group as individuals with a lower value. One can describe this as a difference of unselfishness and valence. Individuals, who estimate their valence for the group as low, would be very unselfish and would spend much activity for the group, if they unconditionally want to be members. The trick of propaganda will be to tell individuals that being a group member is something very worth for aspiring it, the trick of dictatorial and totalitarian systems is further that always only a small number of individuals are really a part of the group as defined above. Therefore the very unselfish, hard and radical working individuals will either never have a chance to be a member or would reach only very low positions of a more complex structure or both will be true, if some of them should be shown as positive examples. This leads at maximum to extremists, who will blow up themselves unselfishly by bombing others, who they estimate as enemies to the group, to which they want to belong. This helps the regime not to give them any group membership, because they are extin-

[29] Harmless situations of live show equivalent adaptations. For example couples tend to behave similar after years of living together. Other examples are told by two German proverbs, which mean in English that group members tend to adapt to leaders behaviour. The first goes: "Wie der Herr, so das Gescherr." This means translated: As the master so the bridle. But the semantic means not only inanimate subjects to mastership. Living ones are included, too. The second tells: "Wes Brot ich es, des Lied ich sing." This means translated: I sing the song, of whom´s bread I eat.

guished. Using war in this way is very effective, even with coincidence to generating more benefit (**TS**) by group expansion as shown later.

Declaring some other individuals or groups as enemies is helpful for propagandistic systems, because the unreal group, which propaganda describes, has to be defined in a certain way. As the group itself is unreal, describing it is difficult. An easier way is describing, who is not part of the group. More likely is describing, who is an enemy, because it raises the need for unselfish protection of the unreal group by individuals.[30]

If propaganda is established as well at the groups, who are in resistance to the majority, extremism is very likely to occur there, too. If not, one will find a significant less radical behaviour as shown by some of the individuals belonging to the majority.

Remember the footnotes to communication having the same root as community and to association having multiple semantic as given before. Those linguistic identities to definitions and deduction results of this theory would tell that people speaking a Roman language have a better understanding, what a group really is, and are better protected against propagandistic abuse, if this theory would describe reality well.[31]

It is no question that the propagandistic behaviour gives less benefit as a relative free system could produce. On the other hand absolutely free systems could not exist, because the base interaction between individuals would raise communication, association of ideas, grouping, structuring and at least constitution spontaneously. Even at the lowest level, there are rules implied for differentiation between parasitic and symbiotic behaviour.

---

[30] This chapter is clearly inspired by the German history and by the holocaust. There is a possible misunderstanding, which I like to prevent. Describing something like the holocaust as a logical result may hurt Jewish people and other victims of this tragedy again. But if you alternatively think that this was a never understandable catastrophe, as some philosophers do, all the killed people would be senseless wasted, because we can not learn anything about it. Knowing how things happen biologically or sociologically and how illness hurts is needed to heal wounds, whether they are beaten physically or in mind. Some acing during healing may occur and I apologise for that. [/]

[31] The tight connection between language and mind are told as well by other papers: (**33**), (**34**), (**80**) and (**89**).

Relative free systems are characterised by some kind of constitution and by very many bifurcation's along the trail, at which one can decide to do things, and which directly lead to a so called "chaotic" behaviour. The chaotic behaviour can be described as a status continuum. Only in this way the local and probably the global optimum can always be found, even if parameters are changing.[32]

Political and economic structures have changed from fixed by ideology to constitution based freedom at developed countries. One problem of this situation is loss of leading through live, what probably young and minor experienced people may feel. The only way to help them is letting them build groups and structures their way. The possible active help is giving them some understanding of unselfishness, of leadership and constitution, some time and place for communication and some resources, so they can give benefit unselfishly to their groups. But the helping elder people should focus that the results are very likely not what they would expect. If this happens, it would be the best success, because of the rise of intelligence and creativity. Communication between elder people and youngsters should secure that the new groups are integrated into the whole fractal system by keeping symbiotic behaviour on this level, too.

Intelligence and creativity do not mean the same, because freedom of ideas and behaviour, which might result to optimal creativity, may not be very intelligent, if constitutions rules are broken. This way people, who seem to have lower creativity, but behave like guards of constitution, help maximising intelligence of groups and structures as well as more creative ones. The interaction of those different people would give best benefit. **[(34)]**

[32] Today this is not evident out of this theory, but I am very sure that one will show that in future.

Aggression and Terrorism [+][33]

The analysis before lacks the view at aggression as a standard behaviour of living beings. It can be recognised for animals, too, and it seems that for example poison-producing plants can not be excluded. The animal view is helpful for understanding and a translation to human behaviour will be easily possible. As an example we are looking at the species "wolf":

If a foreign lonely wolf likes to get accepted and a member of an already existing mob of other wolfs, she/he needs to get into communicative contact. The sure reaction of the mob will be an attack. There needs to be some reason, to change this repulsive, standard behaviour. If the attacked foreign wolf behaves strong, she/he will reject the attack. Another strategy may be to start an attack first. If she/he shows some co-operation later, the behaviour of the mob will surely change. Why?

First the mob recognises the possible new member as strong and the attacks are the needed communicative tools to measure and exchange the relative value of the strength. A strong and co-operative member will be surely a benefit for the mob, because it will raise the hunting succession. The opposite is true, if the new member seems to be weak. If she/he gets accepted, the result will be some benefit decrease, because earnings need to be divided by one more, but the likelihood to increase the hunting succession is low. The same is true, if the new member is very strong but not co-operative. The member may keep most earnings for her-/himself and use the others as slaves. Therefore there will be no acceptation of weak or uncooperative individuals.

Strong and co-operative are the need properties for acceptance. Weak and unco-operative behaviour results to secure repulsion. The membership to a social group was an implicit benefit (by using their information and unselfish contribution and saving costs or increasing earnings this way). Trying to be a member and attacks to the existing members are therefore not contradictory.

Acceptance of foreign individuals is a principal benefit to the group, because the differences of experience and genetic deviations totally named diversity result to benefits, which the former group members can not produce themselves. Rejecting the week and marrying the strong - this is a basic principle. [34]

---

[33] Few days before the attack at the USA, which destroyed the World Trade Centre in New York, I had prepared a letter to [+]. Deadly aggression was already analysed and the terroristic act is for sure a typically example.

[34] This seems to contradict to the chapters below related to “unselfishness”. But it depends on the amount or estimated amount of available resources, whether unselfishness will occur. In any case it is more likely that it happens first related to members of the own group. If sub-groups of a more complex system seem to reject foreigners, they may estimate their own resources as few and may really need care (information, education, social relations) by others of the complex system including care by the “foreigners”.

Related to humans you will find this principle starting at classes of children up to professors. Surely you find it all over. For example the professors behaviour show a very high wall of repulsion, because their social group is close related to the subjected groups of assistants and students, which have to be educated. If this succeeds, there may be not very much difference between professors and subjected individuals any more. Therefore the likelihood to produce rivals to the own position is high.[35]

If you recognise this behaviour all over the range of species, it is likely that many human conflicts are based on this. For example look at the migration of Arabian people to the south of Spain.

There is an implicit parameter related to wolfs including the foreign one, which is a base of the conflict and would be a base of the arrangement of rank after acceptance. The steps of attack, defence and co-operation lead to some measurement of individual parameters: physical fitness, completeness and operating faculty of teeth, knowledge of rules of community behaviour like submission but including attacking.

Our implicit assumption was that those measurement principles were the same at the mob of wolfs and at the foreign one. This results to right operations of the foreigner and of the mob and to some implicit agreement to the fitness estimation. If the foreign wolf was estimated weak, she/he will agree to this and will stop attacking after some time and will go her/his way. If she/he was estimated strong, she/he will estimate the same and will take the right place at the rank of animals of the mob, which will stop further attacks, too.

For increasing the understanding one can use an experiment in mind to produce a deadly conflict of wolfs:

We change the measurement principles, which were implicitly assumed as identical, to be different. This results to different estimations of relative strength. If both the foreign wolf and the mob estimate their own behaviour as relative weak, both will go their way. They will not benefit from each other, but will not hurt each other, too. If both estimate their own behaviour as relative strong and will therefore estimate the opponent as relative weak, the conflict may reach a deadly level. The mob will not accept the foreigner but the foreigner will not stop attacking. It is very likely that the foreigner will be hurt efficiently, if she/he will not be killed. This misbehaviour supports definition of an identical measurement system, because deviating systems will be extinguished related to the distinct species. Different species construction may be supported this way, too. If they are not predators, it is likely that they respect other species individuals as strong and estimate themselves as weak and keep distance therefore.

---

[35] This behaviour adds to the disadvantages coming from the sub-optimal measuring method for scientific results, which needs to be overcome. Refer to "*Appendix III: A New View of Authoring*" for details.

This example shows multiple things. First it describes a bifurcation of species membership. Second it shows how important **[=]** the measurement principle is and how easy it is not to think about it, because it is typically assumed to be something already implicitly defined.

If we now turn our view again to human relations, we can clearly identify the same problems. Different language, culture, religion, ideology, trading and political system could not be avoided because of the separated development during history. But now different groups and individuals do not use the same strength measurement principle. Some conflicts are truly deadly as you know and all terroristic acts are examples.

Communication always increases information-processing capabilities by stimulation, but using non-violent communication will be much more effective, because violence instead reduces information-processing capabilities by destroying of technical equipment and hurting or killing of people (the most effective equipment to information processing). Who shall understand the reason for the aggression, if the information can not be processed any more? But even for a non-violent world verbal aggression will still be needed to break emerged walls of group bordering.

One advice to all opponents can be given right from this chapter:

Assuming to be strong is always the needed base for a bloody conflict. If you start by assuming to be weak **(174)** any hurting of others can be avoided. Reflection and confession of the own weakness leads others to helping acts, if they really take care. Unfortunately it is not true that nations do this confession and care as needed. Instead even those, who tell or assume that they are the strongest, probably care few. This may be a cause of conscious exploitation as during imperialism or simply a matter of ignorance or a result of a psychological inferiority complex as told by terror acts. The last is typically found at victims of previous tragedies and tends to continue the devils circle. This emphasises the need for a culture of weakness, care and communication. Only if <u>others</u> praise the single individual to be strong, the value is real (as later deduced). For example any entering migration pressure to nations is a praise, but thanksgiving for charity and economic investments, which let people stay at their home country, would indicate a higher value. A cool, intellectual and just reaction instead of emotional eruption would show that people or nations could stand the aggression and have resources left to take care. Using them for starting non-violent communication would indicate this strength to others.

Please check the following mathematical methods, whether they can be used as a globally acceptable measurement principle **(58)**. May be one can not avoid all ideology at the textual content, but the very abstract, axiom based, mathematical deductions are the same strategy as all natural sciences use and you will agree that this strategy has no relation to political ideology and was globally very successful.

Let me end this chapter by confessing my own weakness:

Assuming that I can give the world a globally acceptable measurement principle sounds strong. But I have no scientific reputation, agreement, title, rank or position, which can tell you that the content of this essay has any worth. My financial situation was bad, but it has already turned better. Only you and all other readers will provide, whether the proposed methods will have an effect to the world or not.

Curing conflicts of the world needs globally distributed communication possibilities as important prerequisites, which fortunately are available already.

Communication a Problem of Distribution?

Today communication of humans at developed countries is global. This was a dream in the past. Someone will await serious changes of life by the extended possibilities. Some others will not even get conscious about globalisation. Is there any serious change? The answer is that there was even serious change in the past and global communication is only a logical further extension.

As shown below the communication is much dependent to the kind of distribution of individuals. Most often a 2-dimensional area describes distribution of them well. Looking at cells in an organism 3-dimensional distribution is much more applicable. Having humans in mind a 2-dimensional distribution seems to be right, is not it? This opinion was true during Stone Age. First high cultures had first reductions of dimension by invention of characters and rivers travel (Assyrians, Egypt's and Babylonians), by sea travel (Greeks and Romans) and by road travel (Romans and Chinese). Invention of the book press was a further cut. The coincidence of invention of newspapers and telegraphy to first democratic ideas should be remarked. With telephone, fax, television, and air travel democratic nations seem to be out of fashion. Super-structures like the European union are build and are in some trouble, too, as nations were before.[36] Who will care about that after mobile telephony, eMail and Internet and not yet known techniques will have led to a global structure?

The serious change and the most important invention, which is valid to all above mentioned, is the capability to distribute communication tools as well as individuals are distributed **(172)**. The effect is that dimension, which describes human communication distribution best, has changed from 2-dimensional to lower than 1-dimensional![37] Implementing nervous systems has the same result for cell clusters. Because of the distributed tools, reaching some partner does not depend on her/his geographical position any more. This way geographical distribution does not represent communicative distribution any more. If no costs would have to be paid for communication, the dimension would be zero as for a singularity. All partners would seem to be there without effort, if one wishes. As long as communication costs depend on connection time, what is true for most examples, this simple proportionality raises a single dimension.[38]

---

[36] The cause for the trouble of spring 1999 of the European commission was already discovered by my work in 1995. The problems are not solved today, so I have to state that only single indirect representatives of people should build up this structure and similarity to nations constitutions is badly needed. See the chapter: "*Structures of 3rd Degree*".

[37] There is probably some fractal dimension left, because of different zones of geographical distance with different connection costs, if telephone calls are considered.

[38] The metric for defining communication radii depends as well on dimension of distribution space as on costs. See the chapter: "*Simplified Accounts of Benefits (**pV**)*".

Communication radii have been much extended this way during the last century. Although nobody has recognised this change of dimension as a serious thing, the following expansion of group structures close behind extension to communication radii is very remarkable. But this can be understood using the following physics methods, which show that freezing into structure is caused by long distance communication forces between individuals.

Basic Physics

The right to use physics is first success of reaching a higher level of abstraction, but second because even cosmology tells that the following is really an extension to standard physics. **[((122)#)]**

The term "benefit" is a synonym to "effect" **(157)**, if one means a positive one. Physics defines the effect as energy multiplied by time.

$$\mathbf{W} = \mathbf{E} \cdot \mathbf{t}$$

One can therefore set the dimension[39] of benefit to be the dimension of the physical term "effect". Looking at the simple relation:

$$\mathbf{B} = \mathbf{I} \cdot \mathbf{t}$$

where **t** is some time period, one recognises that with the statement above intelligence has the same dimension as energy[40].

Because systems generating more benefit are more stable and this is for physical systems true, if energy content is less, one can identify intelligence as negative energy and energy content is proportional to the temperature of a system:

$$\mathbf{I} = \mathbf{-E} \sim \mathbf{-T}$$

A common but undeclared axiom of standard physics is that mass and kinetic **[N]** energy is always positive. This contradicts to classical transport equations, the "tunnel" effect and the possible negative formulation of Schrödinger´s equation, which is typically, solely interpreted as invariant behaviour regarding time reversal **(9)**. This axiom has not any justification. The mistake comes from the assumption that mass and energy are independent from other properties. Instead of this it is not allowed to separate them from exchange operations as for example described by transport equations.

The equation told first:

$$d\mathbf{H} = \mathbf{T}\,d\mathbf{S} + \mathbf{V}\,d\mathbf{p}$$

describes some thermodynamic energy exchange. This formula is deduced at the chapter: "*Thermodynamic Discussion*".

Below we shall find some intelligence of groups and some intelligence of structures, which could be identified as the parts of the equation and one of them will show a description using diversity or entropy: **S** and the other will show a description using group interaction equal to suction or (negative) pressure: **p** and group volume: **V** dependence.

---

[39] The measurement unit of a physical variable defines the physical dimension.

[40] One should recognise that as well preparation of information (memory) as well as information processing (arithmetic) are dissipative, energy consuming operations.

If description of reality is successfully done, using the laws and deductions is justified. The application to reality will be a future task, but there are already many experiments, which are mostly related to "Artificial Life" research and which seem to be in very good coincidence. The thermodynamically describable energy input delivered by nature for keeping information processing running and thermodynamic behaviour described by this theory have the complement sign. The first can be understood as the "outside" and the last as the "inside" of our system derived from production and consumption of energy.[41]

The negative values contradict to the main rules of thermodynamics. But those foundations really break, because the closed system model, to which they belong, has to be extended by observers. It is possible to make evident by complete induction that any closed system becomes open by observing it.[42] Further something that is not observed has to be estimated as not existent **(107)**! This means that a constant energy content (1. rule) is in any case invalid. Further the relation (2. rule): "$\Delta S > 0$" is a "Gödel"ian paradoxon **(79)**, because it describes its own negation: The pixels, which form it, are surely not equally distributed on the page. This does not mean that it is a wrong statement. It only tells that its truth content is not decidable.

Descriptions of classical and quantum physical, "free" particles define a "closed" = not observable = not existent system, because there is no interaction, and show a lack of a clearly defined system of relation. Not only the method of recognition is undefined, the method of production is undefined, too. The better ways to describe physical processes are the already mentioned transport equations. There are at least two terms with complementary sign and the sum results to zero. Further there is an area in space defined as a clear system of relation. The last can be identified with the reception area of a sensing organ or of a measurement apparatus in the case of recognition or with the limiting surface of a reservoir in the case of production. Even the free particle can be described with the help of a surface, through which it travels. But as well in this case there are two terms of the description with complementary sign. The abstract differential formula is:

$$\frac{d\boldsymbol{\rho}}{d\mathbf{t}} + \vec{\nabla}\boldsymbol{\rho} \cdot \vec{\mathbf{v}} = 0$$

[41] This point is a dialectic description. It seems that every dialectic view on a special behaviour of reality owns its correlated "Gödel"ian paradoxon **[!]**. The following inside view becomes later extended by an outside view. See: "*Quantum Physical Discussion*". Other descriptions of different view methods are: **(39)** and **(47)**.

[42] You may do it yourself by using energy accounts including loss to the observer, integration of the observer loss into the next level of iteration and repeated observer application. Even for a limit to infinity the loss does not vanish but keeps some finite value. A philosophical rejection of closed systems is: **(88)**.

We consider for example some energy flow from a source to a target and change to the equivalent integral description:

The integrated energy flow over time results to some effect:

$$\mathbf{W}_{\text{Production}} = \int_0^{t} E(\mathbf{t})\,dt = \mathrm{E}_0 \cdot \mathbf{t}$$

The last term is received by the simplification of a constant production. This represents the left part of the abstract formula.

At another part of space the sent energy becomes consumed:

$$\mathbf{W}_{\text{Consumption}} = \int_0^{\mathbf{t}} \oiint_{r(\mathbf{t})} \vec{\nabla} E(\mathbf{r})\,d\vec{A}\,dt$$

Its bordering area defines the partition. This represents the right term of the abstract formula. To prepare a better understandable example, one may identify the both formulas as the energy production of the sun and the surface of the earth as the receiving border in space. For this example one can easily use polar co-ordinates for calculations, because the earth shows a clearly defined angular of space to the sun. We get:

$$\mathbf{W}_{\text{Consumption}} = -\mathrm{E}_0 \cdot \mathrm{A}_0 \cdot \mathbf{t} \cdot s(\boldsymbol{\theta}) \cdot (\mathrm{d}-1) \sum_{\mathrm{i}=1}^{\mathrm{d}} \mathbf{x}_{\mathrm{i}}^2 \cdot \left(\sum_{\mathrm{i}=1}^{\mathrm{d}} \mathbf{x}_{\mathrm{i}}^2 \right)^{-\frac{\mathrm{d}+1}{2}}$$

$$\mathbf{W}_{\text{Consumption}} = -\mathrm{E}_0 \cdot \mathrm{A}_0 \cdot \mathbf{t} \cdot s(\boldsymbol{\theta}) \cdot (\mathrm{d}-1) \left(\sum_{\mathrm{i}=1}^{\mathrm{d}} \mathbf{x}_{\mathrm{i}}^2 \right)^{-\frac{\mathrm{d}-1}{2}} = -\mathbf{W}_{\text{Production}} \cdot \frac{s(\boldsymbol{\theta}) \cdot (\mathrm{d}-1)}{\mathbf{r}^{\mathrm{d}-1}}$$

$$\mathbf{t} > 0,\ s(\boldsymbol{\theta}) > 0,\ \mathbf{E}_{\text{Production}} > 0 \Rightarrow \mathbf{E}_{\text{Consumption}} < 0$$

d = 3: is the space dimension in case of the example.

It is obvious that the sign of the flow is geometry and view dependent. From the point of the sun one can define as well a positive production as a negative loss. From the point of the earth one can define a positive income or a negative consumption. If the sign is chosen for one point viewing to the other side changes the sign by the transport through the area in space:

(+Production) + (-Consumption) = 0

(-Loss) + (+Income) = 0

If we assume a positive advance of time, it becomes impossible to tell a distinct sign of the above considered, surely kinetic energy as the matter of the flow without defining the distinct situation regarding the area of relation.

Comparing the current definitions of science, then one of the terms can be viewed as the already know physical world (res extensa **(39)**), but the complementary view (res cogitans **(39)**) with complementary sign can be described as well by neglecting the standard physical view. The standard approach as the outside view (relative to the observer) and the new approach as the inside view are therefore both simplifications. This tells that standard physics is not something bad. It has lead to much success of science and technology and is half of the truth, but has reached its limits. This blindness **(28)** to methods of thinking have to be overcome.

The following chapter examines information related transports known as communication of individuals.

Basic Communication Benefit Formula (pV) [J]

The assumption for the following formulas is that acting occurs in a serial manner. One can transform all parallel actions to a serial description as shown above.

We now try to describe a dialogue (which is not needed to be human) by dividing it into single segments. Those segments can later be summed up again.

Looking at two individuals with equal rights and similar properties we find that they may be exchangeable if all parameters are exchanged, too. The partners are identified by index a and b. The dialogue begins with some news the first (a) tells to the second (b). The serial manner of action guarantees that during this time no other benefit can be produced. The news told to the second partner are some benefit, which is given unselfishly and completely to her/him:

$$\mathbf{B}_1 = \mathbf{I}_{a1} \cdot \mathbf{t}_1$$

It is not needed that this benefit is given to the partner voluntarily (compare "*Parasites and Symbiosis*"). The index 1 is placed to all variables because it is the first step of the dialogue.

Figure 4. The First Offer

At this position **axiom {1}** has to be used. It is derived by assuming some association, which has been stimulated by the unselfish contributed benefit coming from (a) and which is proportional to the "intelligence" meaning "capability to generate benefit" of the partner (b). The capability to association is described by a multiplying parameter χ. Now the axiom is defined by mathematical formula:[43]

$$\boxed{\mathbf{S}_{b2} = \chi_{b1} \cdot \mathbf{I}_{b1} \cdot \mathbf{B}_1}$$

[43] A first try for a calculation of thought combinations was: (**104**).

$$\mathbf{s}_{b2} = \chi_{b1} \cdot \mathbf{I}_{b1} \cdot \mathbf{I}_{a1} \cdot \mathbf{t}_1$$

Figure 5. Result of Association

The dimension of $\boldsymbol{\chi}$ is equal to the dimension of:

$$\frac{1}{\mathbf{I} \cdot \mathbf{t}}$$

The resulting intelligence of partner b during the second step is then:

$$\mathbf{I}_{b2} = \mathbf{I}_{b1} + \mathbf{s}_{b2}$$

$$\mathbf{I}_{b2} = \mathbf{I}_{b1} + \chi_{b1}\mathbf{I}_{b1}\mathbf{I}_{a1}\mathbf{t}_1$$

Now partner b answers and is generating this benefit to partner a:

$$\mathbf{B}_2 = \mathbf{I}_{b2} \cdot \mathbf{t}_2$$

$$\mathbf{B}_2 = \left(\mathbf{I}_{b1} + \chi_{b1}\mathbf{I}_{b1}\mathbf{I}_{a1}\mathbf{t}_1\right) \cdot \mathbf{t}_2$$

Figure 6. The Answer

Now situation changes, because partner a can then associate:

$$\mathbf{B}_3 = \left(\mathbf{I}_{a1} + \chi_{a2}\mathbf{I}_{a1}\mathbf{I}_{b2}\mathbf{t}_2\right)\cdot \mathbf{t}_3$$

Figure 7. The Group Building by Association

To get further results we have to use some simplifications, which as well can be defined partly in another way or which may not be defined for other circumstances. The other possibilities have to be examined during future tasks. The simplifications are:

$\chi(t)$ is a step function in the way that:

$$\chi(\mathbf{t}) = \chi_i$$

$$\chi_i = \chi \mid i = j-1$$

$$\chi_i = 0 \mid i < j-1 \text{ (all other i)}$$

This means that all associations, which have been there before the last step of the dialogue, have been forgotten immediately. Another formulation is that only the one step directly before raises association. The same result is produced, if one assumes that all steps before sum up only to a maximum of association capability. After some steps one would find a balance of stimulation and forgetting. The difference to the assumption above would be only a constant, which can be multiplied to the variable $\boldsymbol{\chi}$, but because $\boldsymbol{\chi}$ is not defined by value the formula result is the same.

We define that the whole communication time of the dialogue shall be Ω. For the communication steps the following is valid:

$$\Omega = \sum_{j=1}^{n} \mathbf{t}_j$$

Every step of partner a shall be of equal length. This shall be true for partner b, too. Setting up all steps of both partners to equal length will be too much simplification, because different communication quantities of the partners are likely. We define for big n and independent of even or odd number:

$$\Omega_{aP} = n \cdot \mathbf{t}_{aP}$$

$$\Omega_{aS} = n \cdot \mathbf{t}_{aS}$$

$$\Omega_{bP} = n \cdot \mathbf{t}_{bP}$$

$$\Omega_{bS} = n \cdot \mathbf{t}_{bS}$$

The extra index P defines the period of time, during which benefit is produced for the partner. The extra index S defines the period of time, during which benefit is generated for selfish use.

$$\Omega = \Omega_{aP} + \Omega_{aS} + \Omega_{bP} + \Omega_{bS}$$

$$\mathbf{t}_D = \mathbf{t}_{aP} + \mathbf{t}_{aS} = \mathbf{t}_{bP} + \mathbf{t}_{bS} = \frac{\Omega}{2n}$$

The special part of the first step is neglected. This is possible, if many steps are found. Very short dialogues can be influenced by this speciality.

The results are the following benefit formulas arranged by producer dependence, if simplifications are valid:

$$\mathbf{B}_i = (\mathbf{I}_a + \chi_a \mathbf{I}_a \mathbf{I}_b \mathbf{t}_{bP}) \cdot \mathbf{t}_a$$

$$i = 1, 3, 5, 7, \ldots, 2n\text{-}1$$

$$\mathbf{B}_j = (\mathbf{I}_b + \chi_b \mathbf{I}_b \mathbf{I}_a \mathbf{t}_{aP}) \cdot \mathbf{t}_b$$

$$j = 2, 4, 6, 8, \ldots, 2n$$

$$\mathbf{B}_i = (\mathbf{I}_a + \chi_a \mathbf{I}_a \mathbf{I}_b \mathbf{t}_{bP}) \cdot (\mathbf{t}_{aP} + \mathbf{t}_{aS})$$

$$\mathbf{B}_j = (\mathbf{I}_b + \chi_b \mathbf{I}_b \mathbf{I}_a \mathbf{t}_{aP}) \cdot (\mathbf{t}_{bP} + \mathbf{t}_{bS})$$

First Conclusions Derived from The Benefit Formulas

The dialogue results to a benefit increase, which can not be generated by single acting of any partner. This increase of benefit is the cause of attractiveness of dialogues and partners. Like for standard physics one can define a force between partners. The benefit formulas show high similarity to those found at standard physics (for example: electrostatic or gravitational attraction). This tells that physical methods are helpful. But the found attraction can be asymmetrically, what is contrary to the standard physical examples.

Monologic Communication as Special Case

One of the communicating partners will not receive extra benefit by the other partner for the special case of monologic communication. It can be deduced out of the common dialogic case by setting:

$$\mathbf{t}_\mathrm{P} = 0.$$

The following formulas result, if b does not give benefit to a:

$$\mathbf{B}_\mathrm{a} = \mathbf{I}_\mathrm{a} \cdot (\mathbf{t}_\mathrm{aP} + \mathbf{t}_\mathrm{aS})$$

$$\mathbf{B}_\mathrm{b} = (\mathbf{I}_\mathrm{b} + \chi_\mathrm{b}\mathbf{I}_\mathrm{b}\mathbf{I}_\mathrm{a}\mathbf{t}_\mathrm{aP}) \cdot \mathbf{t}_\mathrm{bS}$$

In this case attraction is as well single sided and in the contrary direction to communication.

Mixed Systems

Mixed systems can be identified as having some dialogic part and some monologic part, too. They can completely be described by dialogic formulas, because only the periods of time have to be defined deviated.

Formulas of Whole Benefit

For a better understanding the formulas have been rearranged by consumer dependence.

$$\mathbf{B}_\mathrm{b} = \sum_{i=1,3,\ldots}^{2n-1} \mathbf{B}_\mathrm{iP} + \sum_{j=2,4,\ldots}^{2n} \mathbf{B}_\mathrm{jS}$$

$$\mathbf{B}_\mathrm{b} = \mathrm{n} \cdot (\mathbf{I}_\mathrm{a}\mathbf{t}_\mathrm{aP} + \chi_\mathrm{a}\mathbf{I}_\mathrm{a}\mathbf{I}_\mathrm{b}\mathbf{t}_\mathrm{bP}\mathbf{t}_\mathrm{aP} + \mathbf{I}_\mathrm{b}\mathbf{t}_\mathrm{bS} + \chi_\mathrm{b}\mathbf{I}_\mathrm{b}\mathbf{I}_\mathrm{a}\mathbf{t}_\mathrm{aP}\mathbf{t}_\mathrm{bS})$$

$$\mathbf{B}_\mathrm{a} = \sum_{j=2,4,\ldots}^{2n} \mathbf{B}_\mathrm{jP} + \sum_{i=1,3,\ldots}^{2n-1} \mathbf{B}_\mathrm{iS}$$

$$\mathbf{B}_\mathrm{a} = \mathrm{n} \cdot (\mathbf{I}_\mathrm{b}\mathbf{t}_\mathrm{bP} + \chi_\mathrm{b}\mathbf{I}_\mathrm{b}\mathbf{I}_\mathrm{a}\mathbf{t}_\mathrm{aP}\mathbf{t}_\mathrm{bP} + \mathbf{I}_\mathrm{a}\mathbf{t}_\mathrm{aS} + \chi_\mathrm{a}\mathbf{I}_\mathrm{a}\mathbf{I}_\mathrm{b}\mathbf{t}_\mathrm{bP}\mathbf{t}_\mathrm{aS})$$

Those formulas can be split into partner part and selfish part, if partners are described as an entity:

$$\mathrm{B}_\mathrm{P} = \mathrm{n} \cdot (\mathbf{I}_\mathrm{a}\mathbf{t}_\mathrm{aP} + \chi_\mathrm{a}\mathbf{I}_\mathrm{a}\mathbf{I}_\mathrm{b}\mathbf{t}_\mathrm{bP}\mathbf{t}_\mathrm{aP} + \mathbf{I}_\mathrm{b}\mathbf{t}_\mathrm{bP} + \chi_\mathrm{b}\mathbf{I}_\mathrm{b}\mathbf{I}_\mathrm{a}\mathbf{t}_\mathrm{aP}\mathbf{t}_\mathrm{bP})$$

$$\mathrm{B}_\mathrm{S} = \mathrm{n} \cdot (\mathbf{I}_\mathrm{a}\mathbf{t}_\mathrm{aS} + \chi_\mathrm{a}\mathbf{I}_\mathrm{a}\mathbf{I}_\mathrm{b}\mathbf{t}_\mathrm{bP}\mathbf{t}_\mathrm{aS} + \mathbf{I}_\mathrm{b}\mathbf{t}_\mathrm{bS} + \chi_\mathrm{b}\mathbf{I}_\mathrm{b}\mathbf{I}_\mathrm{a}\mathbf{t}_\mathrm{aP}\mathbf{t}_\mathrm{bS})$$

Stability of a Group (pV)

If a group should be stable, the basic assumption is that the benefit from communication has to have more value than the benefit that can be generated in another way during the same time.

Examination of symmetries:

Let us look at the difference of benefit of partners:

$$\mathbf{\Delta B} = \mathbf{B}_b - \mathbf{B}_a$$

$$\mathbf{\Delta B} = n \cdot \begin{pmatrix} \mathbf{I}_a\mathbf{t}_{aP} + \chi_a\mathbf{I}_a\mathbf{I}_b\mathbf{t}_{bP}\mathbf{t}_{aP} + \mathbf{I}_b\mathbf{t}_{bS} + \chi_b\mathbf{I}_b\mathbf{I}_a\mathbf{t}_{aP}\mathbf{t}_{bS} \\ -\mathbf{I}_b\mathbf{t}_{bP} - \chi_b\mathbf{I}_b\mathbf{I}_a\mathbf{t}_{aP}\mathbf{t}_{bP} - \mathbf{I}_a\mathbf{t}_{aS} - \chi_a\mathbf{I}_a\mathbf{I}_b\mathbf{t}_{bP}\mathbf{t}_{aS} \end{pmatrix}$$

This is equal to:

$$\mathbf{\Delta B} = n \cdot \begin{pmatrix} \mathbf{I}_a\mathbf{t}_{aP} - \mathbf{I}_b\mathbf{t}_{bP} \\ +(\chi_a - \chi_b)\mathbf{I}_b\mathbf{I}_a\mathbf{t}_{aP}\mathbf{t}_{bP} \\ +\mathbf{I}_b\mathbf{t}_{bS} - \mathbf{I}_a\mathbf{t}_{aS} \\ +(\chi_b\mathbf{t}_{aP}\mathbf{t}_{bS} - \chi_a\mathbf{t}_{bP}\mathbf{t}_{aS})\mathbf{I}_a\mathbf{I}_b \end{pmatrix}$$

The left and right positions in the brace are related to the b and a individual. The parts of the sum can be identified as:[44]

Asymmetry of unselfishness
Asymmetry of capability to use association
Asymmetry of selfish solitary consumption
Asymmetry of selfish communication benefit consumption

[44] Probably one can define gender asymmetry by special parameters. This is a work that has to be done in future.

Calculation of the benefit surplus for each single individual

$$\mathbf{B}_a = n \cdot \begin{pmatrix} \mathbf{I}_b \mathbf{t}_{bP} + \chi_b \mathbf{I}_b \mathbf{I}_a \mathbf{t}_{aP} \mathbf{t}_{bP} \\ + \mathbf{I}_a \mathbf{t}_{aS} + \chi_a \mathbf{t}_{bP} \mathbf{t}_{aS} \mathbf{I}_a \mathbf{I}_b \end{pmatrix}$$

$$\mathbf{B}_b = n \cdot \begin{pmatrix} \mathbf{I}_a \mathbf{t}_{aP} + \chi_a \mathbf{I}_b \mathbf{I}_a \mathbf{t}_{aP} \mathbf{t}_{bP} \\ + \mathbf{I}_b \mathbf{t}_{bS} + \chi_b \mathbf{t}_{aP} \mathbf{t}_{bS} \mathbf{I}_a \mathbf{I}_b \end{pmatrix}$$

For comparison we write the formulas for "solitary" benefit generation, which as well means pure selfish generation even during the P-time:

$$\mathbf{B}_{aS} = n \cdot \left(\mathbf{I}_a \mathbf{t}_{aP} + \mathbf{I}_a \mathbf{t}_{aS} \right)$$

$$\mathbf{B}_{bS} = n \cdot \left(\mathbf{I}_b \mathbf{t}_{bP} + \mathbf{I}_b \mathbf{t}_{bS} \right)$$

The benefit surplus by communication is then:

$$\mathbf{B}_a - \mathbf{B}_{aS} = n \cdot \begin{pmatrix} \mathbf{I}_b \mathbf{t}_{bP} + \chi_b \mathbf{I}_b \mathbf{I}_a \mathbf{t}_{aP} \mathbf{t}_{bP} \\ + \chi_a \mathbf{t}_{bP} \mathbf{t}_{aS} \mathbf{I}_a \mathbf{I}_b - \mathbf{I}_a \mathbf{t}_{aP} \end{pmatrix}$$

$$\mathbf{B}_b - \mathbf{B}_{bS} = n \cdot \begin{pmatrix} \mathbf{I}_a \mathbf{t}_{aP} + \chi_a \mathbf{I}_b \mathbf{I}_a \mathbf{t}_{aP} \mathbf{t}_{bP} \\ + \chi_b \mathbf{t}_{aP} \mathbf{t}_{bS} \mathbf{I}_a \mathbf{I}_b - \mathbf{I}_b \mathbf{t}_{bP} \end{pmatrix}$$

Here it seems difficult to advance. Therefore we do the following:

Calculation of the benefit surplus generated altogether

Because of the multiple possible asymmetries that were discovered above, and because benefit difference could be of reasonable value, it is best to look at the partners as if they are an entity. The parts of the sum have been arranged to display the relation to the consuming partner. The left sum parts are related to a, the right are related to b:

$$\mathbf{B}_a + \mathbf{B}_b = n \cdot \begin{pmatrix} \mathbf{I}_b \mathbf{t}_{bP} + \mathbf{I}_a \mathbf{t}_{aP} \\ + (\chi_b + \chi_a) \mathbf{I}_b \mathbf{I}_a \mathbf{t}_{aP} \mathbf{t}_{bP} \\ + \mathbf{I}_a \mathbf{t}_{aS} + \mathbf{I}_b \mathbf{t}_{bS} \\ + (\chi_a \mathbf{t}_{bP} \mathbf{t}_{aS} + \chi_b \mathbf{t}_{aP} \mathbf{t}_{bS}) \mathbf{I}_a \mathbf{I}_b \end{pmatrix}$$

For comparison we write the formulas for "solitary" benefit generation, which as well means pure selfish generation even during the P-time. The arrangement applies as above:

$$\mathbf{B}_{aS} + \mathbf{B}_{bS} = n \cdot \begin{pmatrix} \mathbf{I}_a \mathbf{t}_{aP} + \mathbf{I}_b \mathbf{t}_{bP} \\ + \mathbf{I}_a \mathbf{t}_{aS} + \mathbf{I}_b \mathbf{t}_{bS} \end{pmatrix}$$

The benefit surplus by communication is then:

$$\mathbf{B}_{a+} + \mathbf{B}_{b+} = n \cdot \begin{pmatrix} (\chi_b + \chi_a)\mathbf{I}_b\mathbf{I}_a\mathbf{t}_{aP}\mathbf{t}_{bP} \\ +(\chi_a\mathbf{t}_{bP}\mathbf{t}_{aS} + \chi_b\mathbf{t}_{aP}\mathbf{t}_{bS})\mathbf{I}_a\mathbf{I}_b \end{pmatrix} > 0$$

The surplus greater zero is needed, if communication shall make any sense. If it is less, communication will not be established during reasonable time. Negative association variables (χ) can not occur (by axiomatic definition). In this case communication would give intelligence reduction[45]. Because of this the positivity of the surplus is secure.

If selfishness of individuals is needed for rational behaviour **(121)**, we have to compare the selfish used parts of the communication benefit to the complete solitary and pure selfish benefit. Again the left sum parts are related to a, the right are related to b:

$$\Delta\mathbf{B}_r = n \cdot \begin{pmatrix} \mathbf{I}_a\mathbf{t}_{aS} + \mathbf{I}_b\mathbf{t}_{bS} \\ +(\chi_a\mathbf{t}_{bP}\mathbf{t}_{aS} + \chi_b\mathbf{t}_{aP}\mathbf{t}_{bS})\mathbf{I}_a\mathbf{I}_b \\ -\mathbf{I}_a\mathbf{t}_{aP} - \mathbf{I}_b\mathbf{t}_{bP} \\ -\mathbf{I}_a\mathbf{t}_{aS} - \mathbf{I}_b\mathbf{t}_{bS} \end{pmatrix}$$

$$\Delta\mathbf{B}_r = n \cdot \begin{pmatrix} (\chi_a\mathbf{t}_{bP}\mathbf{t}_{aS} + \chi_b\mathbf{t}_{aP}\mathbf{t}_{bS})\mathbf{I}_a\mathbf{I}_b \\ -\mathbf{I}_a\mathbf{t}_{aP} - \mathbf{I}_b\mathbf{t}_{bP} \end{pmatrix}$$

Comparing self-generateable benefit and benefit by partnership one gets:

$$\Delta\mathbf{B}_r = n \cdot \begin{pmatrix} (\chi_a\mathbf{I}_a\mathbf{t}_{aS} - 1)\cdot\mathbf{I}_b\mathbf{t}_{bP} \\ +(\chi_b\mathbf{I}_b\mathbf{t}_{bS} - 1)\cdot\mathbf{I}_a\mathbf{t}_{aP} \end{pmatrix}$$

The whole partnership will be an advantage, if the following is true:

$$\chi_i\mathbf{I}_i\mathbf{t}_{iS} > 1 \qquad \text{or} \qquad \mathbf{t}_{iS} > \frac{1}{\chi_i\mathbf{I}_i}$$

The last relation defines the minimal time needed for selfish use, if an individual should recognise partnership as an advantage. This time depends only on the intellectual properties of the individual itself. As better they are as shorter the needed selfish time is.

[45] Probably one can recognize such reduction in reality, if someone is stressed and overloaded by communication, but this has not to be examined here.

On the other hand the last formula is given by crossing over of consumer relations: A part belonging to a is compared to one belonging to b and vice versa. This means that this relation can not be easily evaluated by one individual itself. This shows, why self-assurance depends to interaction with others, although faculties are own properties.

Comparing terms belonging to the same Partner one gets:

$$\Delta \mathbf{B}_r = n \cdot \begin{pmatrix} \mathbf{I}_a(\chi_a \mathbf{I}_b \mathbf{t}_{bP} \mathbf{t}_{aS} - \mathbf{t}_{aP}) \\ + \mathbf{I}_b(\chi_b \mathbf{I}_a \mathbf{t}_{aP} \mathbf{t}_{bS} - \mathbf{t}_{bP}) \end{pmatrix}$$

For this direct comparison between selfish benefit with and without communication it is likely that both kinds of benefit, can be measured with the same kind of sensors. Because selfish benefit generation needs an action, which is internal to either individual, one can extract two relations regarding either individual, which describe obvious benefit:

$$\chi_a \mathbf{I}_b \mathbf{t}_{bP} \mathbf{t}_{aS} - \mathbf{t}_{aP} > 0$$

$$\chi_b \mathbf{I}_a \mathbf{t}_{aP} \mathbf{t}_{bS} - \mathbf{t}_{bP} > 0$$

The influence of the partner is there during the communicative part, but this was unselfishly delivered:

$$\chi_a \mathbf{I}_b \mathbf{t}_{bP} > \frac{\mathbf{t}_{aP}}{\mathbf{t}_{aS}}$$

$$\chi_b \mathbf{I}_a \mathbf{t}_{aP} > \frac{\mathbf{t}_{bP}}{\mathbf{t}_{bS}}$$

or as a common derivation:

$$\chi_i \mathbf{I}_j \mathbf{t}_{jP} > \frac{\mathbf{t}_{iP}}{\mathbf{t}_{iS}}$$

Looking back to the benefit surplus for each single individual those relations save a positive surplus in this case, too.

This condition for obvious group benefit can be named as <u>stability condition of first class</u> for groups. Alternatively one can talk about a "first class group". This condition is derived only by social relationship. Any external conditions like communications costs have no influence to its meaning.

The common stability condition for a group is derived from the benefit surplus:

$$\mathbf{B}_{b+} + \mathbf{B}_{a+} = n \cdot \begin{pmatrix} (\chi_a + \chi_b) \mathbf{I}_b \mathbf{I}_a \mathbf{t}_{aP} \mathbf{t}_{bP} \\ + (\chi_a \mathbf{t}_{bP} \mathbf{t}_{aS} + \chi_b \mathbf{t}_{aP} \mathbf{t}_{bS}) \mathbf{I}_a \mathbf{I}_b \end{pmatrix} > 0$$

by introduction of m partners, which results to:

$$\frac{1}{2}\sum_{i=1}^{m}\sum_{j=1;\,i\neq j}^{m}\left(\left(\chi_i+\chi_j\right)\mathbf{t}_{iP}\mathbf{t}_{jP}+\chi_i\mathbf{t}_{jP}\mathbf{t}_{iS}+\chi_j\mathbf{t}_{iP}\mathbf{t}_{jS}\right)\cdot\mathbf{I}_i\mathbf{I}_j>0$$

This condition for possibly not obvious group benefit can be named as <u>stability condition of second class</u>. Alternatively one can talk about a "second class group". This condition is always fulfilled, but some extension to external influences as communication costs will produce more meaning.

What tells the stability condition of first class?

$$\chi_i\mathbf{I}_j\mathbf{t}_{jP}>\frac{\mathbf{t}_{iP}}{\mathbf{t}_{iS}}$$

This relation has many variables, so possibilities to fulfil it are manifold. To get more information, we shall look at different scenarios:

<u>Unselfish contribution is timely dominating</u>

$$\mathbf{t}_{iP}\gg\mathbf{t}_{iS}$$

This means then:

$$\chi_i\mathbf{I}_j\mathbf{t}_{jP}\gg 1$$

It can only be fulfilled, if the association capability of individual i is very high or the unselfish delivered benefit from individual j is very high or both.

A high association capability may be the case for leaders using competence for group support. A high delivered benefit from partners may be the case for less fitted individuals, which have to be withdrawn. Although acting unselfishly for the group may be timely dominating, generation of group benefit by individual i may be low.

A different behaviour of other individuals is needed, because having only leaders is unusual, produced benefit has to be consumed and there has to be someone to withdraw others.

<u>Selfish use is timely dominating</u>

$$\mathbf{t}_{iP}\ll\mathbf{t}_{iS}$$

This means then:

$$\chi_i\mathbf{I}_j\mathbf{t}_{jP}\ll 1$$

It can be fulfilled, if the association capability of individual i is low or the unselfish delivered benefit from individual j is low or both.

Pure parasitic behaviour may have:

$$\chi_i = 0$$

This will be a stupid consuming of delivered goods without analysing their meaning, but is very selfish of course. Baby's are close to this category.

As more association capability is there as less consumption of others goods is allowed for the selfish use. At maximum of no use of others goods pure selfish behaviour is allowed, too. But group membership has to be estimated as not existing.

A different behaviour of others is needed, because parasites need parasited counterparts and low fitted individuals need benefit sources.

<u>Selfish use and unselfish contribution are approximately equal</u>

$$\mathbf{t}_{iP} \approx \mathbf{t}_{iS}$$

this gives a first class condition of:

$$\chi_i \mathbf{I}_j \mathbf{t}_{jP} > 1$$

If group members have similar properties, which means similar $\chi_i \mathbf{I}_j \mathbf{t}_{jP}$ terms, then dominating unselfish contribution or selfish consumption can not be the case, because this will lead to differences as shown above. The equal time distribution is a good assumption for the similar case. For later calculation it will be a simplification.

<u>Some Answers</u>

Exceeding differences of benefit generation or consumption beyond the limits discussed at the scenarios above will lead to group reformation and to exclusion of not well behaving members. The found differences above can be recognized as withdrawing of weaker by fitter individuals, what will lead to a more balanced system after some time. Withdrawing, forcing contribution and exclusion will lead to approximately equal[46] social level and to the last discussed symmetrical first class condition.[47]

The assumption of approximately equal properties can be written as:

$$\frac{\mathbf{I}_j \mathbf{t}_{jP}}{\mathbf{I}_i \mathbf{t}_{iP}} = \frac{\chi_j}{\chi_i}$$

This shows that asymmetry of unselfish benefit contribution is proportional to the association capability ratio.

---

[46] There is a German proverb, which describes this: "Gleich und Gleich gesellt sich gern." This means translated: "Equal and equal (people) gladly build communities."

[47] The buddhistic religion emphasises the importance of symmetry.

The Meaning of χ

Now we have to consider, what the meaning of χ really is. The discussion of pure parasitic behaviour above tells that χ is somehow like a filter function operating on the received associative benefit. External loss of benefit has not been defined so far and has not to be considered here. Internal loss regarding association may have multiple causes. Considering intellectual properties, one may be a little unsure, whether this properties are already described by the intelligence factors **I**. If this would be true, then χ has to be independent of intellect. But I disagree to this opinion. One has to look at the steps of information processing during the benefit generation. There can be identified the base functionality, which produces benefit out of internal individual data and methods. With no external communication that is all and intelligence increase is not the case. But those internal data and methods define some intelligence and this is the factor **I**, which can be found at the mathematical formulas. Considering communication at the next step the association capability is surely some internal intellectual property. But one has to assume some methods and data from experience, which is a capability independent from the first mentioned intelligence. If benefit outcome for a special individual capability shall increase by communication, the association process has to combine external delivered benefit with the internal base intelligence by using the associative intelligence. This way both intelligence factors and the association variable are multiplied factors of the mathematical formula, although χ depends to intellectual properties, too. Looking at the development of children the intelligence of for example manual capabilities increases parallel with the communication capabilities. If the mathematical formulas above describe reality well, one has to assume some quadratic increase of intelligence at least during childhood. Further some interrelations between the base capabilities and the associative capabilities should be found. Then χ itself would be dependent of **I**. At this time such considerations are neglected and have to be done during future tasks. The dependence of **I** to χ is defined by the benefit sum formulas.

Further effects may be there, because of the very likely durable increasing of intelligence by communication, which was neglected. But other possible dependencies can be considered. Although they are intellectual properties, too, they can be assumed as independent of the base intelligence for the focused benefit generation. Typically we find special names for such dependencies for example: <u>will</u> and <u>force</u>. If will has any influence, then a high variability of χ dependent to time may be the case. Force ducts the same way, but may be some more stable influence.

Although approximately equal association capability variables χ do not have to be the case for all stability scenarios above, assuming a global constant has some attraction. The assumption seems to be well suited looking at those kinds of cells, which show no childhood and seem to have all capabilities of the parent after partitioning. This may be at special scenarios a considerable simplification. A more exact description regarding the variability could be introduced by defining:

$$\chi_i = \chi + \Delta\chi_i$$

The stability relation above can be changed to:

$$\mathbf{I}_j \mathbf{t}_{jP} > (\chi + \Delta\chi_i)^{-1}$$

$$\chi \mathbf{I}_j \mathbf{t}_{jP} > \frac{\chi}{\chi + \Delta\chi_i} = \left(1 + \frac{\Delta\chi_i}{\chi}\right)^{-1}$$

$$\chi \mathbf{I}_j \mathbf{t}_{jP} > 1 - \frac{\Delta\chi_i}{\chi} + \left(\frac{\Delta\chi_i}{\chi}\right)^2 - \left(\frac{\Delta\chi_i}{\chi}\right)^3 \ldots$$

This leads to the estimation:

$$\chi \mathbf{I}_j \mathbf{t}_{jP} > 1 - \frac{\Delta\chi_i}{\chi}$$

which can be identified as some variance of the stability condition given by the assumption of a global constant $\boldsymbol{\chi}$. The variance can be interpreted as an equivalent difference to the time ratio:

$$\frac{\mathbf{t}_{iP}}{\mathbf{t}_{iS}}$$

of unselfish and selfish communication parts.

<u>More Answers</u>

Everyone of a stable group of first class must be willing (or forced) to give any other group member a minimum account of self-generated benefit unselfishly. Further everyone should have the will (or has to be forced to) and the capability to use benefit coming from partners. If association variables $\boldsymbol{\chi}$ are approximately equal, then every one has to contribute approximately the same benefit. If association variables differ reasonable, then individuals with lower association variables must get more of other benefit. Individuals with higher association variables may need less care.

For this case weaker individuals have to be withdrawn, if the group wants to keep the first class condition. Alternatively weak or consciously bad behaving individuals can been pushed out and then will loose membership to keep the group more easily stable. Probably one can find an optimum between withdrawing and exclusion. Those calculations have to be done at future tasks.

Emergence of Leadership

If the symmetrical first class condition is the case, we can look at the following ratio:

$$\frac{\chi_i \mathbf{I}_j}{\chi_j \mathbf{I}_i} = \frac{\mathbf{t}_{iP}}{\mathbf{t}_{jP}}$$

Assuming some approximately equal intelligence **I** (focusing on some special benefit), individuals with higher association capability have to contribute more time unselfishly to the group! But more likely is that the selfish to unselfish time ratio will differ for such individuals and the symmetrical assumption becomes invalid.

Assuming some approximately equal association capability χ, this tells that members with high intelligence (equal to capability to generate benefit) only have to contribute an inversely proportional long time unselfishly to the group. Individuals with high intelligence have more time to do other things compared to others with lower intelligence.

Both possibilities give the base for potential leadership. The first assumption will break symmetry. With the (in calculations neglected) durable increase of intelligence dependent to χ the potential leader can get more intelligence increase as the others can. Then time difference of unselfish contribution will represent the asymmetrical intellectual properties.

If will is of influence, then a higher will of using other members contributions can be a typical leaders property. If an individual has occupied a leaders position, it can analyse the diversity of the group and generate more benefit out of this information (**TS** - see chapters below). With the conditions above spontaneous leadership will emerge. With the extra **TS**-benefit rivalry of potential leaders will emerge.

Leaders can generate more benefit surplus to the group by spending a longer period of time for the group, which one can identify as benefit from "competence". Or they can "analyse diversity" and give the resulting benefit to the group. The last possibility is more appreciated by other group members, because the properties of them define diversity. This benefit could be recognised as a product of the group and not as a leaders product, which in contrast would be the case for leadership by competence.

This shows that "Peter's priciple" **[K]**: "People move up in hierarchy until they have reached maximum of incompetence." may apply. But this will be not important, if the leader uses the diversity of her/his group members efficiently. Because of this people with high technical competence are seldom at high management positions, and people with high communicative competence reach those positions more easily. The same applies for cells, because nervous cells are the most communicative species.

How likely is the stability condition of first class?

Important to estimation of likelihood for the first class condition is the correctness of the statement above that only at those circumstances group benefit is obvious to all members. The statement seems to be right that the selfish benefits for either case are likely to be measured with the same sensors. But important is further that looking at the communication benefit surplus:

$$\mathbf{B}_{a+} + \mathbf{B}_{b+} = n \cdot \begin{pmatrix} (\chi_b + \chi_a)\mathbf{I}_b\mathbf{I}_a\mathbf{t}_{aP}\mathbf{t}_{bP} \\ +(\chi_a\mathbf{t}_{bP}\mathbf{t}_{aS} + \chi_b\mathbf{t}_{aP}\mathbf{t}_{bS})\mathbf{I}_a\mathbf{I}_b \end{pmatrix} > 0$$

the benefit part:

$$(\chi_b + \chi_a)\mathbf{I}_b\mathbf{I}_a\mathbf{t}_{aP}\mathbf{t}_{bP}$$

can be recognised as existing much worse. This part is caused by an associative intelligence increase and the resulting benefit has been contributed unselfishly. This part of the benefit surplus has not been used in any way before to calculate the first class condition!

Recognising capability to association needs self-regarding knowledge, which only humans may have. Probably recognising benefit out of such functionality was not possible at all in the past without existence of ideas found in this essay even for humans. Because of the common usability of those conclusions to all kinds of communicating species it is clear that this effect is really difficult to recognise especially for non-human species. Second there is no selfish benefit, because the benefit is unselfishly delivered to the partner. This way the benefit seems to be only of second level quality for the generating individual.

Because of those arguments, one has to assume that the stability condition of first class is a <u>needed property of all social groups</u>.

Some of the unstable latent groups described by **(121)** could probably be identified as groups that fulfil stability of second but not of first class. The not communicating groups defined at **(121)** are never meant in this essay (compare definitions above).

Advantage of Unselfishness

If we look back at the communicative benefit surplus of each single individual:

$$\mathbf{B}_a - \mathbf{B}_{aS} = n \cdot \begin{pmatrix} \mathbf{I}_b \mathbf{t}_{bP} + \chi_b \mathbf{I}_b \mathbf{I}_a \mathbf{t}_{aP} \mathbf{t}_{bP} \\ + \chi_a \mathbf{t}_{bP} \mathbf{t}_{aS} \mathbf{I}_a \mathbf{I}_b - \mathbf{I}_a \mathbf{t}_{aP} \end{pmatrix}$$

$$\mathbf{B}_b - \mathbf{B}_{bS} = n \cdot \begin{pmatrix} \mathbf{I}_a \mathbf{t}_{aP} + \chi_a \mathbf{I}_b \mathbf{I}_a \mathbf{t}_{aP} \mathbf{t}_{bP} \\ + \chi_b \mathbf{t}_{aP} \mathbf{t}_{bS} \mathbf{I}_a \mathbf{I}_b - \mathbf{I}_b \mathbf{t}_{bP} \end{pmatrix}$$

and input the stability conditions of first class:

$$\chi_a \mathbf{I}_b \mathbf{t}_{bP} \mathbf{t}_{aS} - \mathbf{t}_{aP} > 0$$

$$\chi_b \mathbf{I}_a \mathbf{t}_{aP} \mathbf{t}_{bS} - \mathbf{t}_{bP} > 0$$

then we can delete each last line in braces for a lower estimation:

$$\mathbf{B}_a - \mathbf{B}_{aS} = n \cdot \left(\mathbf{I}_b \mathbf{t}_{bP} + \chi_b \mathbf{I}_b \mathbf{I}_a \mathbf{t}_{aP} \mathbf{t}_{bP} \right)$$

$$\mathbf{B}_b - \mathbf{B}_{bS} = n \cdot \left(\mathbf{I}_a \mathbf{t}_{aP} + \chi_a \mathbf{I}_b \mathbf{I}_a \mathbf{t}_{aP} \mathbf{t}_{bP} \right)$$

As a result benefit surplus only depends to unselfishly delivered terms.

The second term of each sum is the "hidden" part as shown above.

Now we input the stability condition of first class groups with similar properties with the minimal values:

$$\chi_a \mathbf{I}_b \mathbf{t}_{bP} = 1 \text{ and } \chi_b \mathbf{I}_a \mathbf{t}_{aP} = 1$$

Then we find:

$$\mathbf{B}_a - \mathbf{B}_{aS} = 2n \cdot \mathbf{I}_b \mathbf{t}_{bP}$$

$$\mathbf{B}_b - \mathbf{B}_{bS} = 2n \cdot \mathbf{I}_a \mathbf{t}_{aP}$$

as direct plus hidden benefit.

Every partner receives the same amount of benefit again indirectly by the other as he/she has received directly. But the advantage may be asymmetric. The benefit asymmetry is proportional to the asymmetry of unselfishness. For a global constant $\boldsymbol{\chi}$ asymmetry is not the case, because the unselfish delivered benefit parts are equal as calculated above. This way both partners give similar benefit to the other in the direct case as well as in the hidden case.

Other Scenarios (as Above)

The other scenarios have shown some asymmetry of selfish to unselfish time distribution, which result to some asymmetry of partners regarding contribution. Now we want to understand, what effects result considering the communication benefit.

If we assume a dialogue, which means only two partners are there, then one has to play a timely dominating unselfish part and the other has to show a timely dominating selfish use. Those time relations can be defined as:

$$\frac{\mathbf{t}_{aP}}{\mathbf{t}_{aS}} \cdot \frac{\mathbf{t}_{bP}}{\mathbf{t}_{bS}} = 1 + \Delta, \; |\Delta| < 1$$

with

$$\chi_a \mathbf{I}_b \mathbf{t}_{bP} > \frac{\mathbf{t}_{aP}}{\mathbf{t}_{aS}} \gg 1 \;\text{ and }\; \chi_b \mathbf{I}_a \mathbf{t}_{aP} > \frac{\mathbf{t}_{bP}}{\mathbf{t}_{bS}} \ll 1$$

as a lower estimation it results:

$$\chi_a \mathbf{I}_b \mathbf{t}_{bP} \cdot \chi_b \mathbf{I}_a \mathbf{t}_{aP} = 1 + \Delta$$

This calculation is possible, too, if similar properties are the case where:

$$\chi_a \mathbf{I}_b \mathbf{t}_{bP} < 1 \;\text{ and }\; \chi_b \mathbf{I}_a \mathbf{t}_{aP} > 1$$

But this is not our focus at this point. After input of the Δ-equation into the unselfish communication benefit surplus:

$$\mathbf{B}_a - \mathbf{B}_{aS} = n \cdot \left(\mathbf{I}_b \mathbf{t}_{bP} + \chi_b \mathbf{I}_b \mathbf{I}_a \mathbf{t}_{aP} \mathbf{t}_{bP} \right)$$

$$\mathbf{B}_b - \mathbf{B}_{bS} = n \cdot \left(\mathbf{I}_a \mathbf{t}_{aP} + \chi_a \mathbf{I}_b \mathbf{I}_a \mathbf{t}_{aP} \mathbf{t}_{bP} \right)$$

we get:

$$\mathbf{B}_a - \mathbf{B}_{aS} = n \cdot \left(\frac{1}{\chi_a \chi_b \mathbf{I}_a \mathbf{t}_{aP}} + \frac{1}{\chi_a} \right) \cdot (1 + \Delta)$$

$$\mathbf{B}_b - \mathbf{B}_{bS} = n \cdot \left(\frac{1}{\chi_b \chi_a \mathbf{I}_b \mathbf{t}_{bP}} + \frac{1}{\chi_b} \right) \cdot (1 + \Delta)$$

or further:

$$\mathbf{B}_a - \mathbf{B}_{aS} = n \cdot \left(\frac{1}{\chi_b \mathbf{I}_a \mathbf{t}_{aP}} + 1 \right) \cdot \frac{(1+\Delta)}{\chi_a}$$

$$\mathbf{B}_b - \mathbf{B}_{bS} = n \cdot \left(\frac{1}{\chi_a \mathbf{I}_b \mathbf{t}_{bP}} + 1 \right) \cdot \frac{(1+\Delta)}{\chi_b}$$

Now again lower estimations are possible, if both behave extremely different as above assumed:

$$\mathbf{B}_a - \mathbf{B}_{aS} \approx n \cdot \frac{1}{\chi_b \mathbf{I}_a \mathbf{t}_{aP}} \cdot \frac{(1+\Delta)}{\chi_a}$$

$$\mathbf{B}_b - \mathbf{B}_{bS} \approx n \cdot (0+1) \cdot \frac{(1+\Delta)}{\chi_b}$$

refined as:

$$\mathbf{B}_b - \mathbf{B}_{bS} \approx n \cdot \frac{1+\Delta}{\chi_b}$$

$$\mathbf{B}_a - \mathbf{B}_{aS} \approx n \cdot \frac{1+\Delta}{\chi_a \chi_b \mathbf{I}_a \mathbf{t}_{aP}} = \frac{\mathbf{B}_b - \mathbf{B}_{bS}}{\chi_a \mathbf{I}_a \mathbf{t}_{aP}}$$

The benefit surplus of the very selfish acting individual b is mainly defined only by its own parameter $\boldsymbol{\chi}$. The behaviour is very similar to a monologue as defined in the former chapter. It could be that the individual does not recognise others as partners by those circumstances and therefore does not recognise unselfish behaviour as an advantage, although the benefit surplus was only given by unselfish contributions (of others).

The benefit surplus of the very unselfish partner a may be low but it is mainly defined by its own parameters, too. Better as for b is the possible influence regarding the unselfish time contribution. If unselfishness does not seem to be advantageous any more, this partner has the possibility to cancel such behaviour, if she/he is not forced to contribute. Further one can recognise that the benefit surplus of the unselfish contributing partner is proportional to the benefit of the more selfish partner, so withdrawing pays off.

This behaviour of both partners at an asymmetric situation is something typical for parents and children. The estimations above allow some understanding of psychological problems[48] during the mature of children. It is a needed condition that the parent is the unselfish contributing partner over a long time starting with the child as a baby. As we have seen the unselfish contributing partner has the

[48] References related to psychology are: **(22)**, **(41)**, **(50)**, **(76)** and **(101)**.

control about the system. This is true from the start for an acting parent in reality. Another effect of this asymmetry is dependence of the selfish acting to the more unselfish contributing partner. Problems arise, if the selfish acting partner gets conscious about the dependence. For human childhood this could be an early event, but might be different for any individual.

There are two possible directions for a resulting reaction of the child. The first direction is a tendency to behave more selfishly as before hoping for a reduced control in this case. I would like to name this behaviour "natural". For explanation one should consider individual relations only described by short time benefit maximisation strategies and with the possibility to change partners freely. A more and consciously selfish behaving partner will receive lower unselfish contribution by others probably until complete cancelling of group membership. But the wanted effect of reduced dependence to others contributions will result.

For the child unfortunately the "natural" prerequisites are not the case, because it is very unlikely that parent's contributions really decrease efficiently. They have a long time experience of unselfish contribution to the child and a free change of contribution to others is not possible, if the number of children is small. The only possibility to reach the release of control is consciously cancelling of group membership by the child itself. This can be found for seldom cases of the reality.

If there is any communication and therefore group membership to the family left, the result of the first direction may be the opposite of the wanted result, if parents increase their contribution and therefore increase unconsciously their control to keep the child in the family. If any dependency to other group members is needed for survival, asymmetric groups are kept more stable as well as more symmetrical ones by this functionality. Because of this leaving the family is less likely for young children, although some feeling of unhappiness caused by realisation of dependency and following inefficiency of "natural" behaviour may be there from the start.

The second possible direction to go for a child is decreasing selfishness and increasing its unselfish behaviour (including increasing communication). If this is possible, then brothers, sisters and parents will get controlled by the unselfish acting child and being itself controlled by others can be accepted much better. If all are acting this way, the family reaches a more symmetrical behaviour. The common problem for this possibility is that parents have to empower **[(25)]** their children and have to reduce their own power equivalently. Further some justly competence distribution between the children of a family has to be managed. Erroneous results of children's actions have to be accepted, analysed altogether and better actions have to be taught. Primitively keeping of power is a much easier job at first look. But better benefit contribution of the children will reach the parents and the whole family at least. The experience of effects of unselfish contribution and of a symmetric family is of high importance for the individual development regarding general social community.

The same can be found looking at couples with a high degree of asymmetry. Sometimes one lover reduces or prohibits standard communication but keeps a minimal level for example by body talk **(123)**. This way the second lover can be forced to increased contribution even by reduction of contributions of the first. If a liaison is established and kept using those asymmetrical conditions, there will be one, who feels dependent and controlled and therefore unhappy, although the other may tell: "But I do everything for you!" The partner, who has acted tactically all the time, may get the wanted result of increased love of the other, but will stay unhappy. Behaving this way may be only an opportunity during start of the liaison, but has to be cancelled and replaced by symmetrical contribution later. The last may include the risk of loosing the partnership, if true communication would show bad personal attributes. Therefore keeping such behaviour has as origin typically some lack of self-assurance of the tactically acting partner, which may be not even justified. **[(@|<)]**

In any case of asymmetric or symmetric group conditions some communicative benefit surplus is there as long as the stability conditions of first class are fulfilled. For those conditions there is never loss by unselfishness. The conclusion is that communication opens a lot of benefit generation possibilities. Even if no partner can find some benefit surplus by direct comparison of selfish benefit, there would be some value, if communication were a real act. Communication can stabilise itself therefore. The attraction to communicative behaviour comes from the associative part, which gives always some benefit surplus, even if individuals would recognise a balanced account at first. Pure rational behaviour as demanded by **(121)** will nevertheless and even lead to communication and symbiosis! A high degree of unselfishness that on the other hand **(121)** can not describe, is in this theory very well possible. Regarding rational behaviour unselfishness is not a common benefit renunciation. Unselfishness only supports feedback and benefit surplus is the result at least. "*Ethic is accepting a knowledge and motive above selfishness.*", as Lotka **(102)** tells, is not needed but will emerge. But be sure that this is not paradox.

In following calculations the symmetric properties are often assumed, because extreme scenarios always need partners of the other extreme relation. Considering a group as a whole will then result to balanced effects of extremity. Replacing the extreme counterparts by symmetrical behaving individuals will not change the whole group accounts. Therefore the symmetrical assumption is a good simplification.

"Hunting Ground" Behaviour and Communication Costs

The calculations above used implicit simplifications that we have not told before. The first is that there are resources, from which every individual can take the needed unselfish contribution. The second is that individuals can always communicate without effort. Both simplifications are unreal assumptions and have to be dropped now.

As seen above at "*Communication as Information Processing*" it is shown that all real experience can be described by dialogic communication. Some of those communication kinds could be simplified by an assumption of monologes If we want to analyse some communication behaviour of a special kind, the monologic assumption can mostly easily be applied to all other exchange that we not focus on. Analysing the interaction of individuals of one species may need to fix other communication behaviours, which could be identified as not belonging to the same species. For example analysing the interaction of individual cows would lead to fix the cow - grass interaction.

This can be systematically applied by defining some "hunting ground" and neglecting all communication, which belongs to it. But what not should be neglected is that benefit generation comes out of the hunting ground.

The following shows that this use of hunting grounds is allowed, if the intrinsic communication behaves monologic. This was defined by:

$$\mathbf{B}_a = \mathbf{I}_a \cdot (\mathbf{t}_{aP} + \mathbf{t}_{aS})$$

$$\mathbf{B}_b = (\mathbf{I}_b + \chi_b \mathbf{I}_b \mathbf{I}_a \mathbf{t}_{aP}) \cdot \mathbf{t}_{bS}$$

It can be written as:

$$\mathbf{B}_a = \mathbf{B}_{aP} + \mathbf{B}_{aS}$$

$$\mathbf{B}_b = (1 + \chi_b \mathbf{B}_{aP}) \cdot \mathbf{I}_b \mathbf{t}_{bS}$$

The benefit derived from the last formula can be identified as some offer given to the individual by nature and some parameters internal to the individual, which describe its capability to use the offer optimally. This special intelligence and association capability can be assumed to be independent to similar variables found during the following focused not hunting ground like communication. Although this may be a simplification, assuming the independence shows that the benefit rate will be constant.

Hunting ground benefit is correlated to some area in the way that the individual can not derive benefit always from the same point. Typically there will be some benefit at some point, which could be consumed, but afterwards the consumed area part needs some time for regeneration. If hunting ground benefit should be constant over time, the individual needs an area that is big enough to deliver always the benefit and which is able this way to regenerate along with consumption.

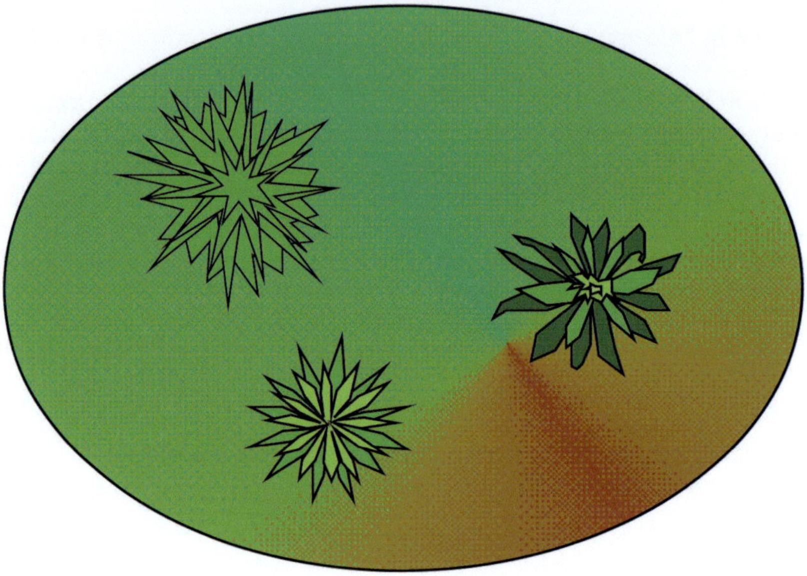

Figure 8. The "Hunting Ground"

Figure 9. The Potential Pot of the Hunting Ground

This area parameter is a parameter of communication, too, because individuals will not be close together. Therefore communication needs some kind of movement to the partners, which would raise communication costs.

The distribution of individuals about some area could be commonly described as some n-dimensional volume. Because of this the formulas of this theory, which are depending to volume wear the "(**pV**)" sticker. For animal relations the volume dimension can be assumed to be 2, therefore the term area describes it well. For cells in an organism a dimension of 3 may be mostly a better assumption. As later explained, modern human communication can be identified by having individuals only distributed in less than a single dimension!

In the formulas always **V** is used as symbol for this n-dimensional volume, although the term "area" may be found in the describing text.

If we can assume a homogenous distribution of individuals, the second parameter to define the hunting ground area is the distance between individuals.

We now assume that environment offers per time difference $\mathbf{\Delta t}$ an area $\mathbf{\Delta V}$, then the needed hunting ground area divided by regeneration time gives this area ratio. For a circle in two dimensions it gives:

$$\frac{\mathbf{\Delta V}}{\mathbf{\Delta t}} = \frac{\mathbf{V}}{\mathbf{t}} = \frac{\pi \cdot \mathbf{r}_R^2}{\mathbf{t}_R}$$

with:

$\mathbf{r}_R$: radius of the hunting ground area
$\mathbf{t}_R$: regeneration time

It is obvious that the radius of the hunting ground area may be longer as the radius of the individual itself. In this case movement should be an individual possibility. If these both are not true, the direct contact enables communication.

In the (inner) areas of hunting grounds the typical requirement is that no other individual may exist. This situation should be described by some repulsive force between individuals at low distances, but this expansion is not yet included in this essay.

If individuals have experience of communication, they would know about the benefits. It is more likely that they actively search for communication partners. This may be an extra effort and may lead into areas, where hunting ground conditions do not apply or taking benefits form others areas are prohibited by causing repulsion. Therefore active partner search needs reserved resources, which can be consumed during movement. The origin of those resources may be hunting ground benefit, which was generated before or former communication benefit. Repulsion of others out of the own hunting ground will occur extremely, if no communication benefit can be found by interaction of individuals. As more as communication results to benefits as less intensive repulsion will be. At least one can recognise effective hunting ground area reduction and increase of individuals, if communication benefits would allow this.

It is unlikely that communication benefit will always give enough resources to keep communication running, because of the other kind of hunting ground benefit. Going back into the own hunting ground is then a needed procedure after communication. In this way communication can be described as a sum of single steps out of the own hunting ground.

It is seldom possible that individuals have no own hunting ground. With little restrictions regarding their monastery buddhistic monks do not have one. They can only generate benefit by communication. This is the job religion gives them. This way keeping them bound to communication is an optimal strategy for spreading. It only operates well, if there is another "species", which behave symbiotic to them: the farmer and majority of people.

It is unsure, whether distance between individuals is really the minimal radius in terms of hunting ground area. A weaker occupation of positions would lead to longer distances. The average distance is recognisable, if an individual has some understanding for its own hunting ground area. This is true, if one can assume that searching for partners gives experience about the average distance (and about the own hunting ground area, too). If there is no special property that let distinguish quality of communication partners, the average distance to other individuals will be the average step length for communication.

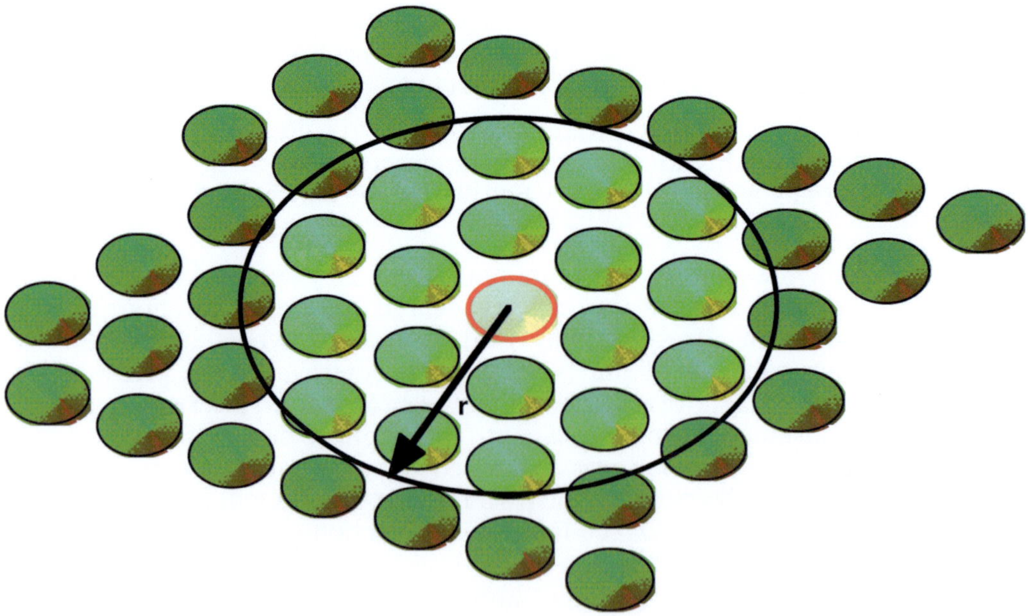

Figure 10. Communication Radius and "Hunting Grounds"

If radius of communication is much longer as radius of the individual itself, species will develop tools to support finding a communication partner inside its own hunting ground (smell markers, singing etc.). In literature such tools are often only declared regarding hunting ground bordering, but supporting communication is often underestimated. With this circumstances reaching the hunting ground can be set equal to reaching the individual. The optimal step radius is then the average distance of individuals, too.

Clear hunting ground areas can be described by a potential pot with benefit > 0 inside and benefit = 0 outside the radius. On the other hand it is likely that not all positions inside can be protected from others use. But in this case the individual would have the possibility to nibble at others grounds, too. This leads to a less steep potential pot but with the same volume, if other parameters are unchanged. The average distance of the individuals does not change by those circumstances.

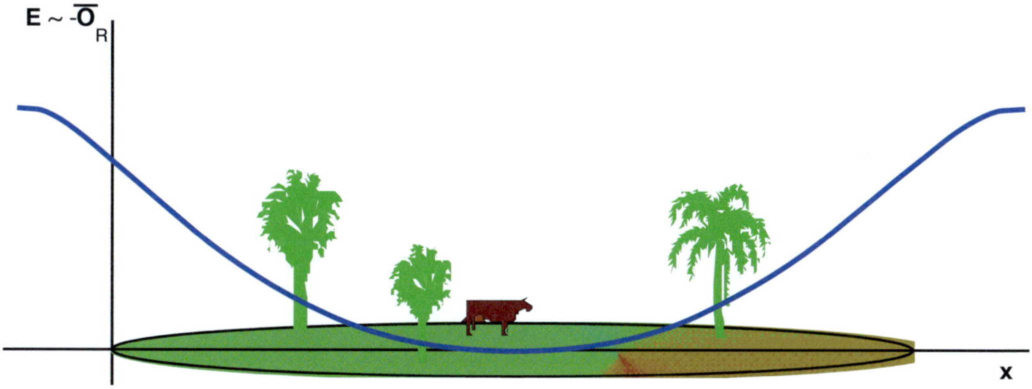

Figure 11. A Less Steep Potential

If an individual can always fill its resources on the way to communication for example by nibbling enough around at others hunting grounds, then no hunting ground can be related to the individual. If all individuals behave this way and communication delivers further benefit surplus, individuals will stay close together. They will as long getting closer as long as the first condition will be valid. After some time too much individuals will occupy non-communicative benefit areas and spontaneous hunting ground behaviour will emerge.

Parts of The Individual Potential Pot

The own hunting ground forces some attraction to the individual. Others grounds force repulsion. Both effects can be described with one common potential. Communication raises attraction between individuals. Movement to communication and normal live consumption are the reasons for the loss of resources.

Changes of Phase

If costs of communication are higher than the generateable benefit, there will be no cause for communication and active movement steps. Using physical terminology this status can be described as gaseous. Individuals would behave repulsive by random meeting.

If benefit surplus is enough for reaching individuals of the neighbourhood, but costs of communication would be too expensive to reach more far individuals, one can describe the status as liquid.

If benefit surplus is enough for far effects to individuals beyond neighbourhood, one will find some structure made out of communication. Using physical terminology one would describe this status as solid. There will be sub-structures, which will have fractal properties. One may think about snowflakes for picturing this.

There are other descriptions of multiple phases: **(2)**, **(68)**, **(86)**, **(125)**. One essay describes a fractal systematic of economies: **(166)**.

Common Accounts of Benefits (pV)

If the accounts of benefits are positive, an individual can use this surplus as follows:

It can increase its own biomass, generate descendants or pay communication costs. The last would include all social behaviour.

If the balance of benefit is negative, the individual can reduce its own biomass, generate descendants of inactive mode (for blooming during the next raining period), die, decrease of communication efforts, if the benefit is not important, increase communication efforts, if the benefit is important (emergency signals).

The individual benefit account is:

$$\mathbf{B}_{\mathrm{i}} = \mathbf{I}_{0\mathrm{i}}\mathbf{t}_{0\mathrm{i}} + \mathbf{I}_{\mathrm{Xi}}\mathbf{t}_{\mathrm{Xi}} - \mathbf{U}_{\mathrm{Mi}}\mathbf{t}_{\mathrm{Mi}} - \mathbf{U}_{\mathrm{Li}}\Omega$$

i is the index of the individual,
0 indexes the benefit of hunting ground and

$\mathbf{t}_0$ means: period of time spend at the hunting ground area.
$\mathbf{U}_L$ is the loss by metabolism (regularly life). This loss lasts over the whole analysed, representative time period $\mathbf{\Omega}$.
X indexes the benefit from communication and

$\mathbf{t}_X$ means: communication period.
$\mathbf{U}_M$ is the loss by movement and

$\mathbf{t}_M$ means: movement period

The whole period $\mathbf{\Omega}$ shall be representative in the way that the periods of the single benefit generation or consumption functions should show the same average values, as if one would do all time analysis.

In all further formulas the metabolic loss is not included, because it can be distributed to the other parts resulting to deviated potentials but equal formula, as if metabolic loss would be zero:

$$\mathbf{B}_{\mathrm{i}} = \left(\mathbf{I}_{0\mathrm{i}} - \mathbf{U}_{\mathrm{Li}}\right) \cdot \mathbf{t}_{0\mathrm{i}} + \left(\mathbf{I}_{\mathrm{Xi}} - \mathbf{U}_{\mathrm{Li}}\right) \cdot \mathbf{t}_{\mathrm{Xi}} - \left(\mathbf{U}_{\mathrm{Mi}} + \mathbf{U}_{\mathrm{Li}}\right) \cdot \mathbf{t}_{\mathrm{Mi}}$$

$$\mathbf{B}_{\mathrm{i}} = \mathbf{I}_{0\mathrm{i}}{}' \mathbf{t}_{0\mathrm{i}} + \mathbf{I}_{\mathrm{Xi}}{}' \mathbf{t}_{\mathrm{Xi}} - \mathbf{U}_{\mathrm{Mi}}{}' \mathbf{t}_{\mathrm{Mi}}$$

We do not look at the special benefit consumption, but we know that there is a need to have a benefit production rate bigger than zero most of the time, if metabolic loss is not already included in the formulas. If there is any surplus, it can be spend for all life effects: regularly (stable) consumption, increase of biomass, increase of descent individuals. If there is any real loss caused by metabolism, decrement of biomass could occur, too.

Communication will occur only if this is valid:

$$\mathbf{I}_{Xi}\mathbf{t}_{Xi} - \mathbf{U}_{Mi}\mathbf{t}_{Mi} > \mathbf{I}_{0i}\left(\mathbf{t}_{0i} + \mathbf{t}_{Xi}\right)$$

This means that communication benefit minus movement loss has to be more than hunting ground benefit during hunting ground residence time plus communication time. The time sum is used, because this time will be reasonable, if no leaving for communication is the case.

It has been assumed that movement is needed, too, during hunting ground residence for optimisation of the outcome. If moving for communication is a much higher effort as moving at the hunting ground, then the movement time should be added to the sum in braces on the right side.

Now we assume that loss of resources by movement is only a function of distance of individuals. If the movement for communication would be always done with constant velocity, the movement time $\mathbf{t}_{Mi}$ would be proportional to the distance of individuals. The loss rate is constant, if the environment potential is negligible. Faster velocity would raise loss rate, slower velocity would decrease loss rate. Such loss ratios depending to velocity can be found at all real movements like going/running or gas consumption of cars, if moving systems operating in the optimal range. That individuals do operate at an optimal mode may be a valid assumption. If shorter movement time delivers more communication benefit, a higher loss rate by increased velocity may be reasonable.

The loss by movement is set to:

$$\mathbf{U}_{Mi}\mathbf{t}_{Mi} = k_i \cdot \mathbf{u} \cdot \mathbf{r}$$

k_i: number of communication steps
u: loss rate per distance
r: average distance of individuals

The benefit from communication shall be set to an average value for all partners. If no one has special opportunities, then this assumption is valid. If gender specific communication is the case, then this assumption is not valid. Neglecting the gender difference may be allowed, if a smaller value compared to other communicative benefits may be assumable. Doing so is at least a reduction of complexity of the description. But unification should be done during future tasks. The chapter "*Gender a Property of Information Processing*" will give a basic understanding of gender related to information processing.

The communication benefit is:

$$\mathbf{I}_{Xi}\mathbf{t}_{Xi} = k_i \cdot \mathbf{B}_X$$

k_i: number of communication steps
$\mathbf{B}_X$: average benefit from a single communication step

The hunting ground benefit is a function of outcome per area:

$$\mathbf{B}_{0i} = \overline{\mathbf{O}}_R \cdot \frac{\pi \cdot \mathbf{r}_R^2}{\mathbf{t}_R} \cdot \mathbf{t}_{0i}$$

Because this benefit may be essential for communication to support the step efforts, we describe it as benefit resource per communication step:

$$\mathbf{B}_{0i} = \mathbf{I}_{0i}\mathbf{t}_{0i} = k_i \cdot \mathbf{B}_0$$

with:

$$\mathbf{t}_{0i} = k_i \cdot \mathbf{t}_{0ø}$$

$\mathbf{t}_{0ø}$: average time the individual spends at the hunting ground per step it follows:

$$\mathbf{B}_{0i} = k_i \cdot \overline{\mathbf{O}}_R \cdot \frac{\pi \cdot \mathbf{r}_R^2}{\mathbf{t}_R} \cdot \mathbf{t}_{0ø}$$

More common as for 2 dimensions above the hunting ground area may be every n-dimensional volume, which correctly describes distribution of individuals:

$$\mathbf{B}_{0i} = k_i \cdot \overline{\mathbf{O}}_R \cdot \frac{\mathbf{V}_R}{\mathbf{t}_R} \cdot \mathbf{t}_{0ø}$$

$\mathbf{V}_R$: hunting ground area (volume).

With:

$$\mathbf{O}_R = \overline{\mathbf{O}}_R \cdot \frac{\mathbf{t}_{0ø}}{\mathbf{t}_R}$$

it results:

$$\mathbf{B}_{0i} = k_i \cdot \mathbf{O}_R \cdot \mathbf{V}_R$$

$\mathbf{O}_R$: benefit outcome per area and communication step

With:

$$\mathbf{B}_{0i} = k_i \cdot \overline{\mathbf{O}}_R \cdot \frac{\mathbf{V}_R}{\mathbf{t}_R} \cdot \mathbf{g}_{0\varnothing} \cdot \Omega$$

another formula results:

$$\mathbf{B}_{0i} = k_i \cdot \mathbf{o}_R \cdot \mathbf{V}_R \cdot \Omega$$

by using:

$$\mathbf{o}_R = \overline{\mathbf{O}}_R \cdot \frac{\mathbf{g}_{0\varnothing}}{\mathbf{t}_R}$$

$\mathbf{o}_R$: benefit outcome per area and communication time
$\mathbf{g}_{0\varnothing}$: fraction of time used for hunting ground residence
Ω: a representative period of time

The benefit sum of the individual becomes:

$$\mathbf{B}_i = k_i \cdot (\mathbf{B}_R + \mathbf{B}_X - \mathbf{B}_M)$$

$$\mathbf{B}_i = k_i \cdot (\mathbf{O}_R \cdot \mathbf{V}_R + \mathbf{B}_X - \mathbf{u} \cdot \mathbf{r})$$

This equation has the advantage not to include any visible time dependency.

The division of the complete benefit into the three parts explains, why the most developed states are placed in areas of temperate climate. One can find distinct seasons and therefore people have to store a lot of resources. During winter hunting ground benefit was small, but storage was filled and much time was there for communication. It is interesting that the highest Christian holidays are celebrated during winter (Christmas) or early spring (Easter).

One can introduce common description:

If $\mathbf{o}_R$ is a function of space and time, the following is valid:

$$\mathbf{B}_R = \int\int \ldots \int o_R(\mathbf{x}, \mathbf{y}, \ldots, \mathbf{t}) \partial\mathbf{x} \partial\mathbf{y} \ldots \partial\mathbf{t}$$

The integrations have to be done from zero to hunting ground ends in space coordinates and from start to end of $\mathbf{t}_{0i}$ in time. If the individual is able to maximise benefit, it will be found at the space and time, where

$$o_R(\mathbf{x}, \mathbf{y}, \ldots, \mathbf{t})$$

would be maximal.

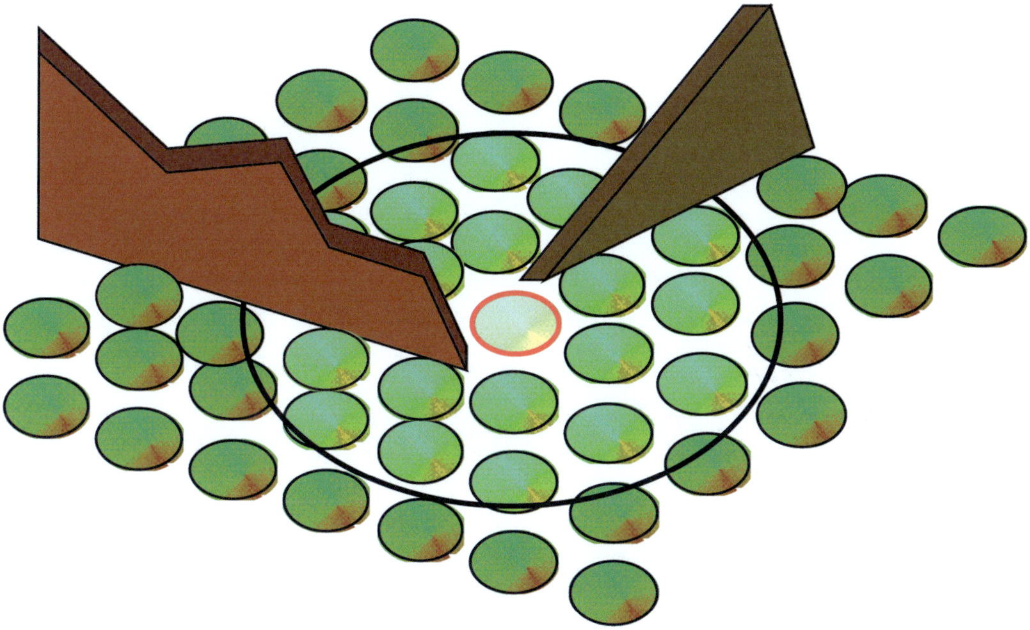

Figure 12. A Non Trivial Topology

If **U** is a function of space and time, the following is valid:

$$-\mathbf{B}_{\mathrm{M}} = -\oint U(\mathbf{x}, \mathbf{y}, \ldots, \mathbf{t})\, d\mathbf{t}$$

This is the route integral from start to end of $\mathbf{t}_{\mathrm{Mi}}$ of the spatially and timely changeable potential **U**. If the individual is able to find optimal ways, it will go through the valleys of the potential. Another communication ready individual of the same species should find the same potential. The valleys of this potential will then make finding the partner easier. The raising of towns and cities at preferred positions can be understood this way. If it is needed to climb mountains of this potential, then one will find points, where one has to decide where to go. If the decisions are not reversible, chaotic effects describable as bifurcations will be found.

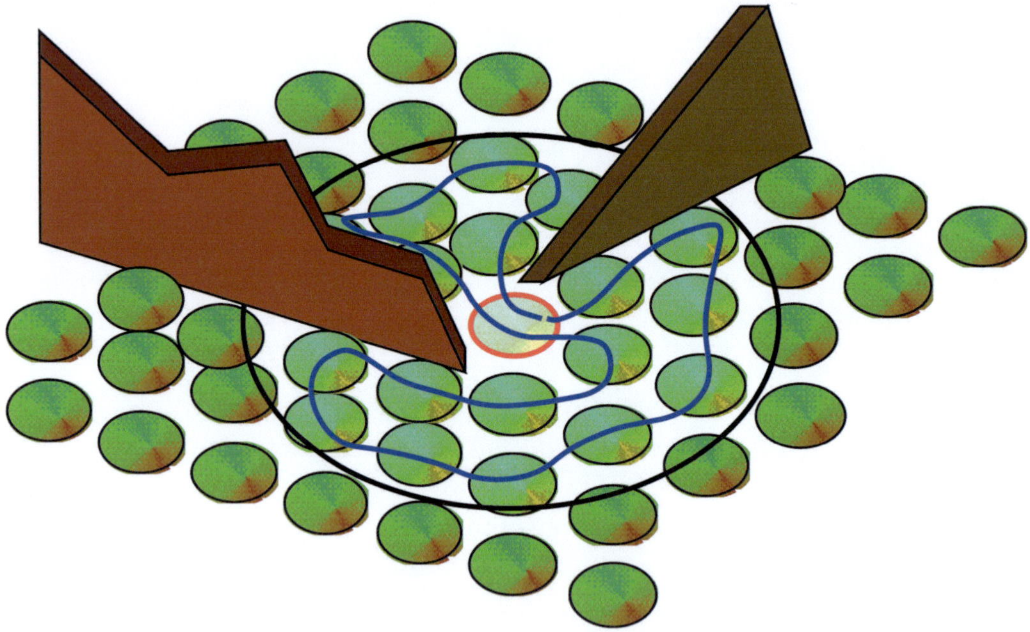

Figure 13. The Route of Communication

The Common Integral Benefit Sum of Individual and System (pV)

The benefit sum of the individual was:

$$\mathbf{B}_i = k_i \cdot \left(\mathbf{o}_R \cdot \mathbf{V}_R + \mathbf{B}_X - \mathbf{u} \cdot \mathbf{r}\right)$$

$\mathbf{B}_X$ displayed in detail is:

$$\mathbf{B}_X = \frac{\sum_{j=1;\, j\neq i}^{n} \mathbf{B}_{Xj}}{n - 1}$$

The benefit surplus of communication was for partner i during a single step talking to j:

$$\mathbf{B}_{Xj} = \mathbf{I}_j \mathbf{t}_{jP} + \chi_j \mathbf{I}_j \mathbf{I}_i \mathbf{t}_{iP} \mathbf{t}_{jP} + \chi_i \mathbf{t}_{jP} \mathbf{t}_{iS} \mathbf{I}_i \mathbf{I}_j - \mathbf{I}_i \mathbf{t}_{iP}$$

This could be lower estimated by using the stability condition of first class:

$$\chi_i \mathbf{I}_j \mathbf{t}_{jP} \mathbf{t}_{iS} - \mathbf{t}_{iP} > 0$$

$$\mathbf{B}_{Xj} \geq \mathbf{I}_j \mathbf{t}_{jP} + \chi_j \mathbf{I}_j \mathbf{I}_i \mathbf{t}_{iP} \mathbf{t}_{jP}$$

or:

$$\mathbf{B}_{Xj} \geq \left(1 + \chi_j \mathbf{I}_i \mathbf{t}_{iP}\right) \mathbf{I}_j \mathbf{t}_{jP}$$

This could be again lower estimated by using the stability condition of first class for the other partner:

$$\chi_j \mathbf{I}_i \mathbf{t}_{iP} > \frac{\mathbf{t}_{jP}}{\mathbf{t}_{jS}}$$

$$\mathbf{B}_{Xj} > \left(1 + \frac{\mathbf{t}_{jP}}{\mathbf{t}_{jS}}\right) \mathbf{I}_j \mathbf{t}_{jP}$$

With this estimation communicative benefit surplus for the individual i depends only to properties of the partner individuals.

If $\mathbf{t}_{jP} \ll \mathbf{t}_{jS}$, which means more selfish partners, then it becomes:

$$\mathbf{B}_{Xj} > \mathbf{I}_j \mathbf{t}_{jP}$$

If $\mathbf{t}_{jP} \gg \mathbf{t}_{jS}$, which means more unselfish partners, then it becomes:

$$\mathbf{B}_{Xj} > \mathbf{I}_j \frac{\mathbf{t}_{jP}^{\,2}}{\mathbf{t}_{jS}}$$

Those different scenarios show that even for very selfish behaviour of one individual others have some benefit by the group membership of the first. Further benefits of others are increasing quadratically by very unselfish contribution. The maximum of unselfishness was defined by the minimal selfish time, which the partners need:

$$\mathbf{t}_{jS} > \frac{1}{\chi_j \mathbf{I}_j}$$

Because of the former lower estimations there could be some small amount of more unselfishly producible benefit, but the following seems be a good upper bound calculation:

$$\mathbf{B}_{Xj} < \chi_j \left(\mathbf{I}_j \mathbf{t}_{jP}\right)^2$$

The continuum of possible benefit surplus can be defined by:

$$\mathbf{B}_{Xj} : \mathbf{I}_j \mathbf{t}_{jP} < 2\mathbf{I}_j \mathbf{t}_{jP} < \chi_j \left(\mathbf{I}_j \mathbf{t}_{jP}\right)^2$$

The left position is defined by very selfish behaviour of partners, the middle position is defined by symmetrical (equal selfish and unselfish) behaviour and the right position is defined by maximal unselfish behaviour of partners.

For further calculations, we use the symmetrical assumption.

The partner i communicates n - 1 times, but partner j communicates only 1 time with i. Summation results to:

$$\sum_{j=1;\, j\neq i}^{n} \mathbf{B}_{Xj} > \sum_{j=1;\, j\neq i}^{n} \left(1 + \frac{\mathbf{t}_{jP}}{\mathbf{t}_{jS}}\right) \mathbf{I}_j \mathbf{t}_{jP}$$

Symmetrically simplified:

$$\sum_{j=1;\, j\neq i}^{n} \mathbf{B}_{Xj} > 2 \cdot \sum_{j=1;\, j\neq i}^{n} \mathbf{I}_j \mathbf{t}_{jP}$$

The time factors can be defined as:

$$\sum_{j=1;\, j\neq i}^{n} \mathbf{t}_{jP} = \mathbf{f}_\Omega \cdot \Omega \;\mid\; 0 \leq \mathbf{f}_\Omega < 1$$

$\mathbf{f}_\Omega$: fraction of time, which is used for communication unselfishly.

A weighted calculation of the average $\mathbf{I}_{\varnothing}$ can be done:

$$\mathbf{I}_{\varnothing} = \frac{\sum_{j=1;\, j\neq i}^{n} \mathbf{I}_j \mathbf{t}_{jP}}{\sum_{j=1;\, j\neq i}^{n} \mathbf{t}_{jP}} = \frac{\sum_{j=1;\, j\neq i}^{n} \mathbf{I}_j \mathbf{t}_{jP}}{\mathbf{f}_{\Omega} \cdot \Omega}$$

$\mathbf{I}_{\varnothing}$: is the effective intelligence of the other individuals. The benefit sum can then be assumed to be:

$$\sum_{j=1;\, j\neq i}^{n} \mathbf{B}_{Xj} = 2 \cdot \mathbf{I}_{\varnothing} \cdot \mathbf{f}_{\Omega} \cdot \Omega$$

$$\mathbf{B}_X = \frac{\sum_{j=1;\, j\neq i}^{n} \mathbf{B}_{Xj}}{n - 1} = \frac{2 \cdot \mathbf{I}_{\varnothing} \cdot \mathbf{f}_{\Omega} \cdot \Omega}{n - 1}$$

For longer times $\mathbf{\Omega}$ and not too narrow communication radii one will find:

$$\Omega \sim (n-1)$$

Or with other words: The number of possible communication steps is proportional to the time available. We define:

$$\mathbf{t}_{\varnothing} = \frac{\mathbf{f}_{\Omega} \cdot \Omega}{n - 1}$$

$\mathbf{t}_{\varnothing}$: is the effective time of individual communication. The effective benefit is then:

$$\mathbf{B}_X = 2 \cdot \mathbf{I}_{\varnothing} \cdot \mathbf{t}_{\varnothing}$$

$\mathbf{t}_{\varnothing}$ depends on the distribution of individuals. As more dense individuals are packed as longer the time sum:

$$\sum_{j=1;\, j\neq i}^{n} \mathbf{t}_{jP}$$

of the communication will be relative to the whole time $\mathbf{\Omega}$, which has to contain hunting ground residence and movement without communication, too. If second smell markers and alike lead to instant communication by crossing hunting ground borders, we find:

$$\mathbf{f}_{\Omega} = \frac{(n - 1) \cdot \mathbf{V}_R}{\mathbf{V}_G}$$

$\mathbf{V}_G$: is a space volume of yet undefined dimension that includes all individuals of a group.

Benefit of a single step is then given as:

$$\mathbf{B}_X = 2 \cdot \mathbf{I}_\varnothing \cdot \frac{\mathbf{V}_R}{\mathbf{V}_G} \cdot \Omega$$

Because $\mathbf{\Omega}$ is the whole time, during which representative benefit can be generated from all types and can be consumed, too, one can set up the undefined benefit integral from communication regarding a single step as follows:

$$\mathbf{B}_X = 2 \cdot \mathbf{I}_\varnothing \cdot \frac{\mathbf{V}_R}{\mathbf{V}_G} \cdot \int d\mathbf{t}$$

The average communication time is then:

$$\mathbf{t}_\varnothing = \frac{\mathbf{V}_R}{\mathbf{V}_G} \cdot \Omega$$

Some expansion for short distance repulsion seems to make sense, too. This has to be done during a later task. Unclear at this time is the exponent of the **V/V**-relationship for this case.

If distribution of individuals is a function of space and time, then the following is valid:

$$W(x, y, \ldots)$$

is defined as the likelihood to find an individual at a position in space. This can be described without time dependence, if longer periods of time are focused.

$$\sum_{j=1;\, j\neq i}^{n} \mathbf{B}_{Xj} = 2 \cdot W_i(\mathbf{x}, \mathbf{y}, \ldots) \cdot W_G(\mathbf{x}, \mathbf{y}, \ldots) \cdot \int I_\varnothing(\mathbf{t})\, d\mathbf{t}$$

W_i: can be calculated for a single individual, if the route of movement is defined.

W_G: is set up by the distribution of individuals. It means group likelihood.

$$W_G = \frac{\sum_{j=1;\, j\neq i}^{n} W_j}{n - 1}$$

If n is a big number i can be included into summation.

The integration of time is now possible about any or undefined period of time. The result of the likelihood multiplication has to be:

$$W_{\mathrm{i}}(\mathbf{x},\mathbf{y},\ldots)\cdot W_{\mathrm{G}}(\mathbf{x},\mathbf{y},\ldots)=\frac{\mathbf{t}_{\varnothing}}{\Omega}$$

This is clear, if one remembers $\mathbf{t}_{\varnothing}$ as the part of time used for communication during the representative time $\mathbf{\Omega}$.

We divide the likelihood of position of the individual and of the group into three parts. One depends to hunting ground (r, R), one to topology (u, U) and one to partnership (p, P):

$$W_i(\mathbf{x},\mathbf{y},\ldots)=W_r+W_u+W_p$$

$$W_G(\mathbf{x},\mathbf{y},\ldots)=W_R+W_U+W_P$$

$$W_r(\mathbf{x},\mathbf{y},\ldots)>0,\ \ W_R(\mathbf{x},\mathbf{y},\ldots)>0$$

In the case without external contacts W_p and W_P are zero. In the case without external contact trials W_u and W_U are zero, too.

The term:

$$W_i(\mathbf{x},\mathbf{y},\ldots)\cdot W_G(\mathbf{x},\mathbf{y},\ldots)$$

can be reduced to:

$$W_i\cdot W_G=W_p(\mathbf{x},\mathbf{y},\ldots)\cdot W_P(\mathbf{x},\mathbf{y},\ldots)$$

The cause is that at the hunting ground area of partner i the likelihood to find another partner is zero per definition of hunting ground. During movement from hunting ground to the partner along in topology there is no partner already found. Communication can not take place during those phases. Therefore all likelihood's, which include W_u or W_U are zero. Another formulation is that searching partners are on divided ways.

Either W_p depends to W_P and vice versa, because the single individual will appreciate amassing others, and group distribution will define rules for individual distribution. Probably iterative methods can give approximations for real systems.

The Common Benefit Sum of The Individual

is then:

$$\mathbf{B}_i = k_i \cdot \begin{pmatrix} \int\int\ldots\int o_R(\mathbf{x},\mathbf{y},\ldots,\mathbf{t})\partial\mathbf{x}\partial\mathbf{y}\ldots\partial\mathbf{t} \\ +2\int I_\varnothing(\mathbf{x},\mathbf{y},\ldots,\mathbf{t})\,W_{pi}(\mathbf{x},\mathbf{y},\ldots)\cdot W_P(\mathbf{x},\mathbf{y},\ldots)d\mathbf{t} \\ -\oint U(\mathbf{x},\mathbf{y},\ldots,\mathbf{t})\,d\mathbf{t} \end{pmatrix}$$

We can extend the loss potential **U** all over space, if we assume that movement in the own hunting ground causes loss of benefit. Only $\mathbf{o}_R$ has to be changed to some "effective" variable, which does not include implicitly benefit loss by movement any more. All individuals should then recognise the same potential, if they are of the same species (are not distinguishable after parameter exchange).

In the same way $\mathbf{o}_R$ can be spread all over space. Its value has to be low outside of the hunting ground boundaries. Most functions need not to be chosen separately for every individual, because the "own" hunting ground is the centre of movements, too, and different communication partners are describable by different integration parameters and boundaries. The index i has been added to the likelihood above, because a general function is not obvious. For real systems one could probably find one out of the group distribution and/or hunting ground and environment potential. The possible differences of the number and kind of the communication partners lead to the assumption that generally intelligence, which is bound to individuals, is dependent to their spatial distribution. Therefore an intelligence function dependent to the space co-ordinate can be defined.

As we have used before, likelihoods without time dependency are only valid, if time integration is during a longer representative period of time. In this case $\mathbf{o}_R$ can be assumed as time independent, too. The same can be assumed for the loss potential **U**. It will be derived from topology of space. Changes of topology can be assumed to be very slow regarding representative time period. But we have to integrate the route and movement itself will be time dependent. With only small deviations of intelligence $\mathbf{I}_\varnothing$ can be assumed to be spatial independent.

Simplified we get:

$$\mathbf{B}_i = k_i \cdot \begin{pmatrix} \int\int\ldots\int o_R(\mathbf{x},\mathbf{y},\ldots,\mathbf{t})\partial\mathbf{x}\partial\mathbf{y}\ldots\int d\mathbf{t} \\ +2\int I_\varnothing(\mathbf{t})\mathbf{W}_{pi}\mathbf{W}_P\,d\mathbf{t} \\ -\oint U(\mathbf{x},\mathbf{y},\ldots,\mathbf{t})\,d\mathbf{t} \end{pmatrix}$$

As mentioned above **I** being independent from time is an often-used assumption, too. If we assume further that optimal ways in topology are always used, the route integral will be simply proportional to time. But we have to choose some other "effective" **U**-potential. If hunting ground outcome can be assumed to be a constant ratio for every single individual, some "effective" outcome **o** can be defined, which only depends on individuals spatial distribution:

Further simplified we get:

$$\mathbf{B}_{\mathrm{i}} = \mathrm{k}_{\mathrm{i}} \begin{pmatrix} o_R(\mathbf{x},\mathbf{y},\ldots)\mathbf{V}_{\mathrm{R}} \int dt \\ +2\mathbf{I}_{\varnothing}\, W_{pi}(\mathbf{x},\mathbf{y},\ldots) \cdot W_P(\mathbf{x},\mathbf{y},\ldots) \int d\mathbf{t} \\ -U(\mathbf{x},\mathbf{y},\ldots) \int d\mathbf{t} \end{pmatrix}$$

Prerequisites are: spatially fixed group individuals, known ways, average of ways, constant hunting ground outcome for every individual.

If we assume homogeneous distribution and neglect repulsing forces at small distances, one can get:

$$\mathbf{W}_{\mathrm{p}} \cdot \mathbf{W}_{\mathrm{P}} = \frac{\mathbf{V}_{\mathrm{R}}}{\mathbf{V}_{\mathrm{G}}}$$

This is the ratio of volume occupied by a single communication ready individual to the whole group volume.

The Formula of The Common Benefit Sum of The System

$$\mathbf{B} = \sum_{\mathrm{i}=1}^{\mathrm{n}} \mathrm{k}_{\mathrm{i}} \begin{pmatrix} \int\int\ldots\int o_R(\mathbf{x},\mathbf{y},\ldots,\mathbf{t})\partial\mathbf{x}\partial\mathbf{y}\ldots\partial\mathbf{t} \\ +2\int I_{\varnothing}(\mathbf{x},\mathbf{y},\ldots,\mathbf{t})\, W_{pi}(\mathbf{x},\mathbf{y},\ldots)\, W_P(\mathbf{x},\mathbf{y},\ldots)\, d\mathbf{t} \\ -\oint U(\mathbf{x},\mathbf{y},\ldots,\mathbf{t})\, d\mathbf{t} \end{pmatrix}$$

Simplified using the conditions above:

$$\mathbf{B} = \sum_{\mathrm{i}=1}^{\mathrm{n}} \mathrm{k}_{\mathrm{i}} \begin{pmatrix} o_R(\mathbf{x},\mathbf{y},\ldots)\mathbf{V}_{\mathrm{R}} \int dt \\ +2\mathbf{I}_{\varnothing}\, W_{pi}(\mathbf{x},\mathbf{y},\ldots) \cdot W_P(\mathbf{x},\mathbf{y},\ldots) \int d\mathbf{t} \\ -U(\mathbf{x},\mathbf{y},\ldots) \int d\mathbf{t} \end{pmatrix}$$

One has to use those sums with caution, because the integration parameters and boundaries have to be chosen different for every individual. Probably those parameters can be derived from some general functions for real (known) systems.

Simplified Accounts of Benefits (pV)

Because of the complex formulas above someone would like easier and more informative equations. This is only possible by much simplification. It is very sure that real systems will not behave that simple, but going back to common formulation is always an exit to reality.

Little before, we have found this communication likelihood:

$$\mathbf{W}_p \cdot \mathbf{W}_P = \frac{\mathbf{V}_R}{\mathbf{V}_G}$$

Without stability of first class the common communication benefit sum is:

$$\mathbf{B}_{X+} = \frac{1}{2}\sum_{i=1}^{n}\sum_{j=1;\, i\neq j}^{n}\left(\left(\chi_i + \chi_j\right)\mathbf{t}_{iP}\mathbf{t}_{jP} + \chi_i \mathbf{t}_{jP}\mathbf{t}_{iS} + \chi_j \mathbf{t}_{iP}\mathbf{t}_{jS}\right)\cdot \mathbf{I}_i \mathbf{I}_j$$

Now simplification using symmetric properties:

$$\mathbf{t}_{iS} \approx \mathbf{t}_{iP},\ \mathbf{t}_{jS} \approx \mathbf{t}_{jP}$$

gives:

$$\mathbf{B}_{X+} = \frac{1}{2}\sum_{i=1}^{n}\sum_{j=1;\, i\neq j}^{n}\left(\left(\chi_i + \chi_j\right)\mathbf{t}_{iP}\mathbf{t}_{jP} + \chi_i \mathbf{t}_{jP}\mathbf{t}_{iP} + \chi_j \mathbf{t}_{iP}\mathbf{t}_{jP}\right)\cdot \mathbf{I}_i \mathbf{I}_j$$

or:

$$\mathbf{B}_{X+} = \sum_{i=1}^{n}\sum_{j=1;\, i\neq j}^{n}\left(\chi_i + \chi_j\right)\cdot \mathbf{I}_i \mathbf{t}_{iP} \mathbf{I}_j \mathbf{t}_{jP}$$

Homogeneous association capability, intelligence and time distribution are now defined as follows:

$$\chi_i = \chi_j = \chi_\varnothing,\ \text{for all i, j}$$

$$\mathbf{I}_i = \mathbf{I}_j = \mathbf{I}_\varnothing,\ \text{for all i, j}$$

$$\mathbf{t}_{iP} = \mathbf{t}_{jP} = \mathbf{t}_\varnothing,\ \text{for all i, j}$$

$$\text{n - 1} \approx \text{n for big n}$$

which results to:

$$\mathbf{B}_{X+} = 2\text{n}^2 \chi_\varnothing \mathbf{I}_\varnothing^2 \mathbf{t}_\varnothing^2$$

$$\mathbf{B}_{X+} = 2\text{n}^2 \chi_\varnothing \mathbf{I}_\varnothing^2 \left(\frac{\mathbf{V}_R}{\mathbf{V}_G}\right)^2 \int d\,\mathbf{t}^2$$

If the volume **V** is 3-dimensional, this formula looks like a physical effect derived from a "**van der Waals**" potential of real gases! The extension by some repulsive potential at small distances may further lead to something very similar to the "Lennard-Jones" potential of real gases! But this has to be examined during later tasks.

The statement that groups may behave like gaseous, liquid or solid gets now a firm base! The same is true for the awaited fractal description.

<u>With</u> stability condition of first class the individual average benefit of communication was:

$$\mathbf{B}_X = \frac{\sum_{j=1;\, j\neq i}^{n} \mathbf{B}_{Xj}}{n-1} > \frac{\sum_{j=1;\, j\neq i}^{n} \left(1 + \frac{\mathbf{t}_{jP}}{\mathbf{t}_{jS}}\right) \mathbf{I}_j \mathbf{t}_{jP}}{n-1}$$

Now the homogeneous simplifications above should be valid further:

$$\mathbf{B}_X = 2 \cdot \mathbf{I}_\varnothing \cdot \mathbf{t}_\varnothing$$

$$\mathbf{B}_X = 2 \cdot \mathbf{I}_\varnothing \cdot \frac{\mathbf{V}_R}{\mathbf{V}_G} \cdot \int d\mathbf{t}$$

Then the system sum is:

$$\mathbf{B}_{X+} = \sum_{i=1}^{n} k_i \mathbf{B}_X = n(n-1)\mathbf{B}_X \approx n^2 \mathbf{B}_X$$

$$\mathbf{B}_{X+} = 2n^2 \cdot \mathbf{I}_\varnothing \cdot \frac{\mathbf{V}_R}{\mathbf{V}_G} \cdot \int d\mathbf{t}$$

Comparison of sums with and without stability condition of first class give the stability condition of first class for the whole group:

$$\chi_\varnothing \cdot \mathbf{I}_\varnothing \cdot \frac{\mathbf{V}_R}{\mathbf{V}_G} \cdot \int d\mathbf{t} \geq 1$$

or better:

$$\chi_\varnothing \cdot \mathbf{I}_\varnothing \cdot \frac{\mathbf{V}_R}{\mathbf{V}_G} \cdot \Omega \geq 1$$

In this case the communicative benefit formula of first class above is a lower estimation of the general formula.

At this time someone may estimate:

$$n\mathbf{V}_R = \mathbf{V}_G$$

as another reasonable simplification, what may be true. This implies steady communication, but this is an effect of the arbitrary assumption of instant communication after crossing of hunting ground borders, which is implicitly dropped, if always

$$n\mathbf{V}_R < \mathbf{V}_G$$

should be valid.

Simplification of Topology

Assuming a very simple topology with equal ways, flat potential and a single communication per step the loss:

$$\mathbf{B}_{Mi} = k_i\left(-U(\mathbf{x},\mathbf{y},\ldots)\int d\,\mathbf{t}\right)$$

$$\mathbf{B}_{Mi} = \sum_{j=1;\, j\neq i}^{n} \left(-U(\mathbf{x},\mathbf{y},\ldots)\int d\,\mathbf{t}\right)$$

results as:

$$\mathbf{B}_{Mi} = -\sum_{j=1;\, j\neq i}^{n}\left(\mathbf{u}_{ij}\cdot\mathbf{r}_{ij}\right) = -(n-1)\cdot\mathbf{u}_{\varnothing}\cdot\mathbf{r}_i$$

The stored resource of benefit, which individual i needs, is now defined as: $\left|\mathbf{B}_{Mi}\right|$

With the help of this the following distance can be left behind on a single step:

$$\mathbf{r}_i = \frac{\left|\mathbf{B}_{Mi}\right|}{(n-1)\cdot\mathbf{u}_{\varnothing}} = \frac{\sum_{j=1;\, j\neq i}^{n}\mathbf{r}_{ij}}{n-1}$$

This is the communication radius of i.

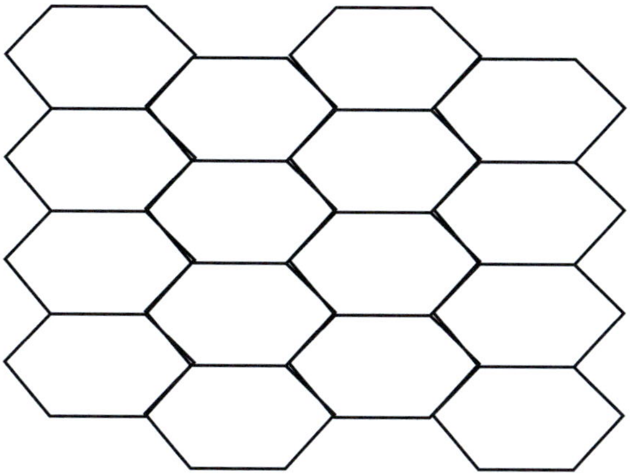

Figure 14. Parts of the Group Volume Related to Individuals

The number of partners can be calculated dependent to **r** as follows:

$$n_{max} = \frac{\int d\mathbf{r}}{\mathbf{V}_R}, \; n = \frac{\int d\mathbf{r}}{\mathbf{V}_I}$$

$\mathbf{V}_I$: volume of an individual (part of the group volume)

$\mathbf{V}_R$: hunting ground volume

The volume integral has to be done using the applicable distribution space and the applicable boundaries.

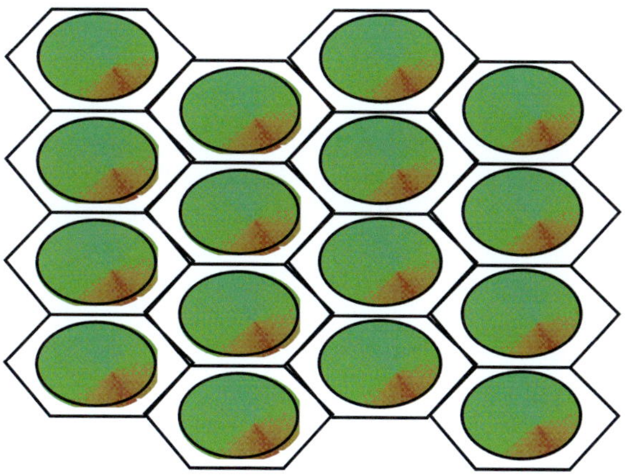

Figure 15. "Hunting Ground" Volume Related to Individuals

The group volume is received by volume integration from $\mathbf{r} = 0$ to $\mathbf{r} = \mathbf{r}_i$:

$$\mathbf{V}_G = \int d\mathbf{r}$$

$$\mathbf{V}_I = \frac{\mathbf{V}_G}{n} \geq \frac{\mathbf{V}_G}{n_{max}} = \mathbf{V}_R$$

$$n = \frac{\mathbf{V}_G}{\mathbf{V}_I}$$

For further discussion the following ratio is interesting:

$$\frac{\mathbf{V}_I}{\mathbf{V}_R} = \frac{\mathbf{B}_{0i}}{|\mathbf{B}_{Mi}|} = \frac{\mathbf{O}_R \cdot \mathbf{V}_R}{\mathbf{u}_Ø \cdot \mathbf{r}_i}$$

This ratio describes the surplus by hunting ground benefit, which allows individual communication radii to be extended beyond hunting ground radii. There is the implicit assumption that communication benefits do not help increasing the communication radii. Replacing $\mathbf{V}_I$ in the formula before results to:

$$n = \frac{\mathbf{u}_Ø \cdot \mathbf{r}_i \cdot \mathbf{V}_G}{\mathbf{O}_R \cdot \mathbf{V}_R^2} = \frac{\mathbf{u}_Ø \cdot \mathbf{r}_i \cdot \int_0^{\mathbf{r}_i} d\mathbf{r}}{\mathbf{O}_R \cdot \mathbf{V}_R^2} \sim \mathbf{r}_i^{d+1}$$

n increases proportional to the power of dimension of space plus one.

If n is fixed during change of dimension, because always the same unselfish contribution can be given to the other individuals of the group, the communication radius changes this way:

$$\mathbf{r}_i \sim n^{\frac{1}{d+1}}$$

Decreasing the dimension of distribution increases the communication radius. Modern communication tools of men change the distribution in a way that dependence only to the power of one can be assumed, if costs are defined only by connection time. The last can be interpreted as some virtual movement. This prolongs the communication radii and extends group volume. Effects of communication do not only reach next neighbours. Therefore the system behaves as described by the physical phase ”solid”. One can tell that individuals get frozen into fractal structure.

Summary of Simplifications

Benefit parts of the system for constant hunting ground benefit:

$$\mathbf{B}_{\mathrm{R}} = \sum_{i=1}^{n} \mathrm{k}_{\mathrm{i}} \left(o_R(\mathbf{x}, \mathbf{y}, \ldots) \mathbf{V}_{\mathrm{R}} \int d\mathbf{t} \right)$$

$$\mathbf{B}_{\mathrm{R}} = \mathrm{n}^2 \cdot \mathbf{o}_{\mathrm{R}} \cdot \mathbf{V}_{\mathrm{R}} \cdot \int d\mathbf{t}$$

Benefit part of communication.

$$\mathbf{B}_{\mathrm{X+}} = 2\mathrm{n}^2 \chi_{\varnothing} \mathbf{I}_{\varnothing}^2 \left(\frac{\mathbf{V}_{\mathrm{R}}}{\mathbf{V}_{\mathrm{G}}} \right)^2 \int d\mathbf{t}^2$$

The time integral results to the whole representative time:

$$\Omega = \frac{\mathbf{r}_{\mathrm{sum}}}{\mathbf{v}}$$

v: optimal velocity

$$\mathbf{r}_{\mathrm{sum}} = \mathbf{v} \cdot \int d\mathbf{t} = \sum_{j=1;\, j \neq i}^{n} \mathbf{r}_{\mathrm{ij}}$$

$$\mathbf{B}_{\mathrm{M}} = -\sum_{i=1}^{n} (\mathrm{n} - 1) \mathbf{u}_{\varnothing} \mathbf{r}_{\mathrm{i}} \approx \mathrm{n}^2 \mathbf{u}_{\varnothing} \mathbf{r}_{\mathrm{sum}}$$

$$\mathbf{B}_{\mathrm{M}} = -\mathrm{n}^2 \cdot \mathbf{u}_{\varnothing} \cdot \mathbf{v} \cdot \int d\mathbf{t}$$

<u>General benefit sum of the system (without stability of first class):</u>

$$\mathbf{B} = \mathrm{n}^2 \cdot \mathbf{o}_{\mathrm{R}} \cdot \mathbf{V}_{\mathrm{R}} \cdot \int d\mathbf{t} + 2\mathrm{n}^2 \chi_{\varnothing} \mathbf{I}_{\varnothing}^2 \left(\frac{\mathbf{V}_{\mathrm{R}}}{\mathbf{V}_{\mathrm{G}}} \right)^2 \int d\mathbf{t}^2 - \mathrm{n}^2 \cdot \mathbf{u}_{\varnothing} \cdot \mathbf{v} \cdot \int d\mathbf{t}$$

<u>Benefit sum of the system with stability condition of first class applied:</u>

$$\mathbf{B} = \mathrm{n}^2 \cdot \mathbf{o}_{\mathrm{R}} \cdot \mathbf{V}_{\mathrm{R}} \cdot \int d\mathbf{t} + 2\mathrm{n}^2 \cdot \mathbf{I}_{\varnothing} \cdot \frac{\mathbf{V}_{\mathrm{R}}}{\mathbf{V}_{\mathrm{G}}} \cdot \int d\mathbf{t} - \mathrm{n}^2 \cdot \mathbf{u}_{\varnothing} \cdot \mathbf{v} \cdot \int d\mathbf{t}$$

No End of Growth

We can define an energy relation (as for standard physics) for group benefit (**pV**). Either the energy relation for group benefit, as for individual benefit follows from the condition for a stable system:

$$\frac{d\mathbf{B}}{d\mathbf{t}} = \mathbf{I} = -\mathbf{E} = \text{const.}$$

The stability is given by a constant number of individuals, which could be supported in the case of this condition. It is not an actual stability condition in the way that the actual number of individuals is kept constant. If the number would be lower as the condition allows, further increase will be the case. If the number would be higher, further decrement will be the case. Stability is therefore only a long time effect.

Because the dimension of benefit was defined to be equal to the physical effect, this relation is an "energy" equation. From:

$$\mathbf{B} = \mathrm{n}^2 \cdot \mathbf{o}_\mathrm{R} \cdot \mathbf{V}_\mathrm{R} \cdot \int d\mathbf{t} + 2\mathrm{n}^2 \chi_\varnothing \mathbf{I}_\varnothing^2 \left(\frac{\mathbf{V}_\mathrm{R}}{\mathbf{V}_\mathrm{G}} \right)^2 \int d\mathbf{t}^2 - \mathrm{n}^2 \cdot \mathbf{u}_\varnothing \cdot \mathbf{v} \cdot \int d\mathbf{t}$$

follows the group intelligence:

$$\mathbf{I}_\mathrm{G} = \frac{d\mathbf{B}}{d\mathbf{t}} = \mathrm{n}^2 \mathbf{o}_\mathrm{R} \mathbf{V}_\mathrm{R} + 2\mathrm{n}^2 \chi_\varnothing \mathbf{I}_\varnothing^2 \left(\frac{\mathbf{V}_\mathrm{R}}{\mathbf{V}_\mathrm{G}} \right)^2 \int d\mathbf{t} - \mathrm{n}^2 \mathbf{u}_\varnothing \mathbf{v}$$

This can never be constant. There is always increasing benefit over time. Using the stability condition of first class at its minimum value one can derive from:

$$\mathbf{B} = \mathrm{n}^2 \cdot \mathbf{o}_\mathrm{R} \cdot \mathbf{V}_\mathrm{R} \cdot \int d\mathbf{t} + 2\mathrm{n}^2 \cdot \mathbf{I}_\varnothing \cdot \frac{\mathbf{V}_\mathrm{R}}{\mathbf{V}_\mathrm{G}} \cdot \int d\mathbf{t} - \mathrm{n}^2 \cdot \mathbf{u}_\varnothing \cdot \mathbf{v} \cdot \int d\mathbf{t}$$

the relation:

$$\mathbf{I}_\mathrm{G} = \frac{d\mathbf{B}}{d\mathbf{t}} = \text{const.} = \mathrm{n}^2 \mathbf{o}_\mathrm{R} \mathbf{V}_\mathrm{R} + 2\mathrm{n}^2 \mathbf{I}_\varnothing \frac{\mathbf{V}_\mathrm{R}}{\mathbf{V}_\mathrm{G}} - \mathrm{n}^2 \mathbf{u}_\varnothing \mathbf{v}$$

This is obviously true, if all variables are simplified to not depending on time. If stability condition of first class is exactly fulfilled, there will be a stable condition regarding energy relation. If the stability condition of first class is more as minimally fulfilled, one has to go back to the more basic formula above and always increasing benefit surplus results (which could be very small). If communicative benefit results are obviously more as the stability condition of first class needs, hunting ground area reduction is very likely. This way the stable energy condition is valid at most times, but always pushes of benefit increase may occur.

If the parameters above would be space and time dependent, this will result to a rough potential, where local minima and maxima could be found. But for all cases there seems to be an incessant non-equilibrium.

The energy relation for the individual can be defined by dropping one "n" for the group relation above.

Basic Structure Properties (TS)

The mathematical chapters before have shown the relations of individuals and benefit by communication. The following chapters show relations between leader(s) and group(s) and benefit by structure. The origin of benefit in the following chapters is the diversity of group members. Using this kind of benefit would be an opportunity therefore structure is needed, because someone has to analyse this diversity to dig the benefit. The emergence of leadership out of competence has been found before. For the description of the benefit by structuring we use **axiom { 2 }**, which we have to declare now in mathematical ways:

$$\boxed{\mathbf{I}_S = \mathbf{I}_L + \mathbf{q} \cdot \mathbf{I}_\varnothing \cdot ln(\mathrm{n})}$$

Later we shall find that

$$\mathbf{I}_S > \mathbf{I}_\varnothing$$

is a deduced result.

The variables have this meaning:

$\mathbf{I}_S$: intelligence of the structure
$\mathbf{I}_L$: intelligence of the leader
$\mathbf{I}_\varnothing$: average intelligence of group members
ln: logarithm to the natural base e = 2.718281828...
n: number of members
q: variable depending to constitution

This axiom has two parts. The first is the leaders intelligence, the second is the intelligence derived from analysing the group. Leaders intelligence in this concern does not have to be identically to that found before for unstructured group membership. One can look at this (**TS**) part as another job, which uses probably another intelligence (equal to capability to generate benefit). This last variable describes the relation between leader and members with regard to structure intelligence. Such a relation would be defined by some constitution. The *ln*(n) factor of the second part is pure statistical mathematics. It describes the diversity of the group.[49] If you want to know how much information a number can carry, you should recognise that the number of digits has to be proportional to this quantity. This means that the logarithm of the number is proportional to this information quantity **(67)**, **(131)**. The same rule is valid for the information a number of individuals are carrying.

[49] Other papers describe order out of disorder (entropy) as well: **(8)**, **(14)**, **(35)**, **(42)**, **(67)**, **(69)**, **(87)**, **(131)**, **(132)**, **(138)**, **(140)**, **(153)** and **(154)**.

Whether statistics are usable, may be of doubt. One can do this, if individuals are exchangeable by exchanging all parameters, too. One may agree for cells and for example ants. But are humans or nations not something much more complex? The answer is yes and no: Yes - there is more complexity. But as well: No - we always neglect complexity at every distinct fractal level by using several. Even politicians do this change of role, if they should be recognised as a private person or a nations leader by using special role protocols for either case.

This second part of the axiom includes the average intelligence of members, too. It is obvious that solutions for problems may be derived more likely, if intelligence of group members is higher. Further it is likely that different individuals have good combinable ideas, but may not have the chance to work it out by dialogue. Leadership will support this combination of ideas, but ideas would be of quality proportional to the intelligence of the contributing members.

For the common but simple formula the average intelligence is used. For special discussions of real systems describing this more exactly could be a possibility. Another hint is the tendency to equal social level of first class groups, which tells that using the average may be a good simplification even if the average is weighted calculated as shown above.

The right for using some variable as a constitution describing parameter is caused by the trivial experience that the relations between a leader and her/his group are not always equal, and that those different relations are mostly not dependent to group members intelligence.

“Intelligence” used for this essay has only meaning regarding benefit generation. Below we shall find a stability condition for the structure, which will show benefit and intelligence interrelation.

Using the logarithm to the natural base is only for better compatibility to physical equivalents. A better understanding of possible values is given later by using the logarithm to the base 10. Every other base of the logarithm would work as well. Changing the base would result to some equivalent change to the constitutional variable.

Conclusions from Axiom {2}

Democratic structures are more intelligent as totalitarian ones. If all other parameters are equal, a structure with more members is more intelligent. Totalitarian systems let most individuals not be members of any groups, which have influence. Therefore they can not contribute to the average intelligence. Further they do not contribute to the intelligence of the structure because they are not counted by *ln(*n*)*.

It is not contrary that most other papers including **(121)** tell that only small groups can exist or work properly. They are right in the way that increasing the number of members will as well raise sub-structuring spontaneously, if derived benefits exceed a level where costs of a new structure can be paid. Those sub-structures seem to divide the original group. If this succeeds, then loss of benefit may be secure. The needed behaviour is giving the super-structure its special responsibility, but leaving sub-structures their own out of former responsibilities of the base group.

One can recognise this sub-structuring as some possible effect following expansion in the way that some members would have a smaller communication radius as the super-group radius is. If this would be true for longer, then individuals with this property would get lost to the super-group. They only will be part of the system as members to the sub-group. This status is dangerous, because loosing them for the super-group means loosing intelligence of structure. Good leaders should help those individuals to get complete communication radius again. It is likely that a fall of activity for the super-group would be the case for the individuals. But this is not a problem as deduced below.

The reality tends to build up the most intelligent system, because group intelligence (**pV**) is at non-equilibrium. Therefore hunting ground reduction parallel with increase of number of individuals or increase of communication follows. This leads to sub- and super-structuring. All together they add up to increase group and structure intelligence. Always changing conditions and following trials as assumed by axiom {**3**} will make existing strategies and structures unstable and cause innovation and reformation of both.

The last together with the first paragraph results to a tendency to democracy. If one looks towards history, one would probably think that democracy and dictatorship are two possibilities. And if one belongs to either the other system would be future. This pessimism is not true as concluded above. The extreme could occur, but lifetime will be short because of the higher error rate.

Intelligence of structure can be increased as better as sub-structures have possibilities of influence (**q**) to super-structures and super-super-structures and all beyond in hierarchy.

Totalitarian regimes will show a significant decrease of number of individuals, which are members (with influence) to the structure.

As higher the structure intelligence of the leader as higher is the structure intelligence of the group. A possibility of increasing structure intelligence may be change of leadership. The <u>leader value</u> may be not of that much weight as the member dependent part. This can be possible for complex systems. Only by this asymmetry a single natural person is able to lead a structure of size of a national state.

Structured systems have the capability to be error tolerant. This means that other structure levels may correct errors at a specific level. For example erroneous acting of government can be overcome by change of behaviour of people. This way there is most times no need for structure change.

<u>Where can intelligence be found?</u>

A former common opinion were that only brains have intelligence and one can find some only there. This may tell people, who estimate their own brains as centre of the world. With individuals forced by attraction to build groups this force is an intelligence storage medium between them. As structures emerge the structures itself are storage systems of intelligence. In the microcosmic direction cells and even brain cells act as well. This way one recognises a very complex and all including system of pertinent intelligence **(51)**, which must be true, because benefit is generated overall. This may sound esoteric, but it is only deduced by axioms, which do not have any transcendent meaning.

Stability of a Structure (TS)

As more structure a system shows as more intelligence it will have. The repeated application of the group and structure intelligence will show that every thinkable sub-structure will have more intelligence as the sum of the included sub-parts. But fine structuring to the extreme will not occur, because structuring raises costs, too **(63)**. The comparison of structure benefit and cost results to a stability condition for a structure:

We define:

B: benefit
I: intelligence (capability to generate benefit)
A: time dependent activity

u: costs

$\frac{d\mathbf{B}}{d\mathbf{t}}$: benefit rate

$\frac{d\mathbf{u}}{d\mathbf{t}}$: cost rate

$$\mathbf{B} = \int I(\mathbf{t})\,A(\mathbf{t})\,d\mathbf{t}$$

The stability condition is:

$$\frac{d\mathbf{u}}{d\mathbf{t}} < \frac{d\mathbf{B}}{d\mathbf{t}} = I(\mathbf{t}) \cdot A(\mathbf{t})$$

We define further:

$\frac{d\mathbf{B}_i}{d\mathbf{t}}$: benefit rate of an individual,

$\mathbf{I}_\varnothing$: average intelligence of individuals,
$\mathbf{A}_\varnothing$: average activity of individuals.

The averaged individual benefit rate is:

$$\frac{d\mathbf{B}_i}{d\mathbf{t}} = \mathbf{I}_\varnothing \cdot A_\varnothing(\mathbf{t})$$

We have made the assumption of **I** as independent from time, what may be allowed focusing small time periods.

We set:

$\mathbf{A}_S$: activity related to the structure,

n: number of structure members,

$\frac{d\mathbf{B}_S}{d\mathbf{t}}$: benefit rate of the structure,

$\mathbf{I}_S$: intelligence of the structure

$$A_S(\mathbf{t}) = \mathrm{n}\, A_\varnothing(\mathbf{t})$$ [50]

The structure benefit is then:

$$\frac{d\mathbf{B}_S}{d\mathbf{t}} = \mathbf{I}_S \cdot A_S(\mathbf{t})$$

Basic structure intelligence is input:

$$\frac{d\mathbf{B}_S}{d\mathbf{t}} = \left(\mathbf{I}_L + \mathbf{q} \cdot \mathbf{I}_\varnothing \cdot \ln(\mathrm{n})\right) \cdot A_S(\mathbf{t})$$

Benefit surplus is:

$$\mathbf{B}_+ = \mathbf{B}_S - \mathrm{n} \cdot \mathbf{B}_i$$

Further surplus results are:

$$\frac{d\mathbf{B}_+}{d\mathbf{t}} = \left(\mathbf{I}_L + \mathbf{q}\mathbf{I}_\varnothing \ln(\mathrm{n})\right) A_S(\mathbf{t}) - \mathrm{n}\mathbf{I}_\varnothing A_\varnothing(\mathbf{t}) = \left(\mathbf{I}_L + \mathbf{q}\mathbf{I}_\varnothing \ln(\mathrm{n})\right)\mathrm{n}\, A_\varnothing(\mathbf{t}) - \mathrm{n}\mathbf{I}_\varnothing A_\varnothing(\mathbf{t})$$

$$= \left(\mathbf{I}_L + \mathbf{q}\mathbf{I}_\varnothing \ln(\mathrm{n}) - \mathbf{I}_\varnothing\right)\mathrm{n}\, A_\varnothing(\mathbf{t})$$

Benefit surplus has to be bigger than zero. With this condition one can find:

$$\mathbf{I}_L + \mathbf{q}\mathbf{I}_\varnothing \ln(\mathrm{n}) - \mathbf{I}_\varnothing > 0$$

$$\mathbf{I}_L + \mathbf{q}\mathbf{I}_\varnothing \ln(\mathrm{n}) > \mathbf{I}_\varnothing$$

$$\mathbf{I}_S > \mathbf{I}_\varnothing$$

This was formerly stated after declaring axiom {**2**} mathematically, but is now deduced by needed benefit surplus, if structuring shall make any sense.

---

[50] There may rise the question, whether the average value is a good description. The mathematical deduction of this chapter is very similar to the one found at (**121**). But this reference is more exact by letting individuals contribute differently. Comparing this my deduction is a simplification. If number of group members are high, this is likely to be allowed and results should be the same. For small groups this may not be true, but examination has to be done during future work.

The cost rate a single individual has to pay for structure is:

$$\frac{d\mathbf{u}_{\mathrm{i}}}{d\mathbf{t}} = \mathbf{U}$$

U: structure dependent variable, $\mathbf{U} \geq 0$.

The cost rate of the structure is then:

$$\frac{d\mathbf{u}_{\mathrm{S}}}{d\mathbf{t}} = \mathrm{n} \cdot \frac{d\mathbf{u}_{\mathrm{i}}}{d\mathbf{t}} = \mathrm{n} \cdot \mathbf{U}$$

The cost rate has to be smaller than benefit surplus rate:

$$\frac{d\mathbf{u}_{\mathrm{S}}}{d\mathbf{t}} < \frac{d\mathbf{B}_{+}}{d\mathbf{t}}$$

$$\mathrm{n}\mathbf{U} < \left(\mathbf{I}_{\mathrm{L}} + \mathbf{q}\mathbf{I}_{\varnothing}\, ln(\mathrm{n}) - \mathbf{I}_{\varnothing}\right)\mathrm{n}\, A_{\varnothing}(\mathbf{t})$$

$$\mathbf{I}_{\mathrm{L}} + \mathbf{q}\mathbf{I}_{\varnothing}\, ln(\mathrm{n}) - \mathbf{I}_{\varnothing} > \frac{\mathbf{U}}{A_{\varnothing}(\mathbf{t})}$$

We assume that it is approximately valid:

$$\mathbf{I}_{\mathrm{L}} \approx \mathbf{I}_{\varnothing}$$

resulting to:

$$\mathbf{q}\mathbf{I}_{\varnothing}\, ln(\mathrm{n}) > \frac{\mathbf{U}}{A_{\varnothing}(\mathbf{t})}$$

or:

$$\mathbf{q}\mathbf{I}_{\varnothing}\, ln(\mathrm{n})\, A_{\varnothing}(\mathbf{t}) > \mathbf{U}$$

This is the stability condition of a structure.

This condition can be used to define a growth law for n:

$$\mathrm{n} > \mathrm{e}^{\frac{\mathbf{U}}{\mathbf{q}\mathbf{A}_{\varnothing}\mathbf{I}_{\varnothing}}}$$

We shall use this formula later at the chapter "*Quantum Physical Discussion*".

Concluding we find that a structured group is as more stable as the left side of the stability condition increases or the right side decreases. One can tell this by words:

- If activity of group members is high, the group is more stable. If there is a reduced activity related to politics as today sometimes complained, the political system gets destabilised.
- If costs of structure are reduced, the system is more stable. Totalitarian systems may have low internal costs, because other people have to pay for such groups, to which they are not members. Therefore costs are relative low regarding produced benefit for few structure members.
- Increase of average intelligence stabilises the systems. For humans this means education and public media are stabilising opportunities.
- If the group individuals have more influence relative to leadership, the stability is better.
- If the number of individuals can be increased, the stability increases, too. This may lead to violent expansion of states.

Individual Sight on Structures Above

Looking on human structures there is the human as base individual and groups of humans, which may be individuals on higher levels. For common application the individual sight is meant as belonging to some base individuals, at what level we ever want to start.

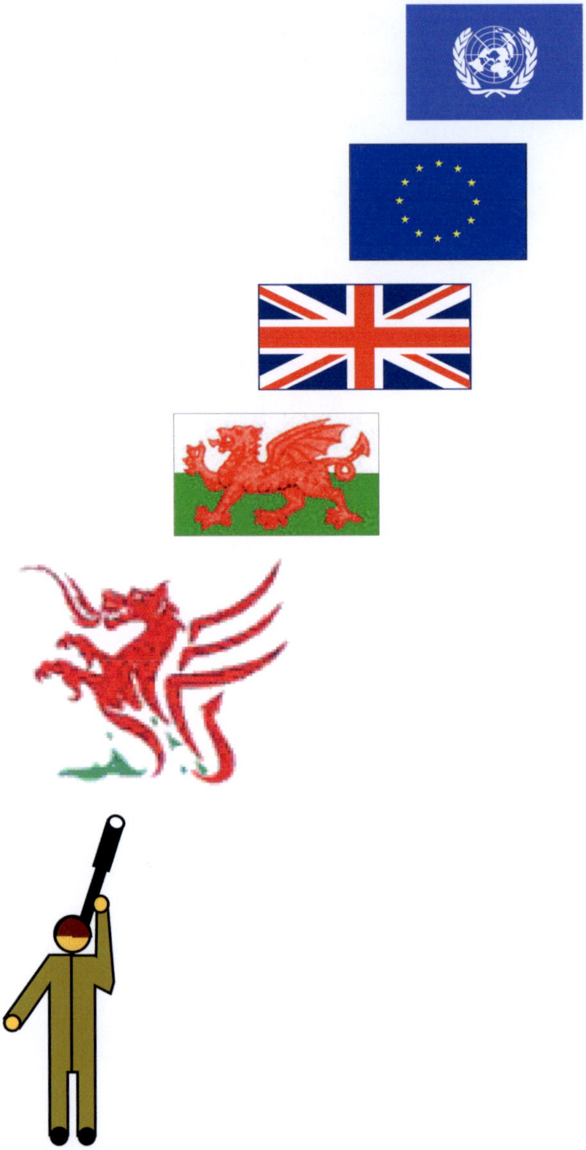

Figure 16. Individual Sight on Structures Above

The activity an individual can spend for contributing to super-structures has to be estimated as constant over time and independent of number of levels of super-structuring. If the individual is free, it may choose this activity only regarding to own interests. This is not true, if there is some forcing to contribution. The last is found at least since taxes have been invented. The individual interests will be a parameter to distribution of activity, but some externally fixed base directions can be assumed.

Distribution of activity is found either horizontally regarding different structures or vertically regarding sub- and super-groups of the same structure. Some examples for structures are:[51]

- *molecule, peptide, cell organelle, cell, organ, animal, mob of animals*
- *city, district, country, nation, nations union*
- *companies department, company, economic lobby, world trade association*
- *club, regional union of clubs, national union of clubs, world club union*

Further examinations only focus on vertical distribution. If a new level of hierarchy is added as highest super-structure, one can assume that such an operation does not change activity for the whole hierarchy. Only redistribution of the fractions of the fixed maximal value may occur. If quality of this structure does not change much by adding a level, this assumption may be true. If quality change is obvious, horizontal activity redistribution may occur, too. This possibility is neglected during the following deductions.

We look at two different structure hierarchies now. The activities are defined this way:

$A_0(\mathbf{t})$: activity, which would be there without any structure

$A_i(\mathbf{t})$: activity for structure level i

$A_j'(\mathbf{t})$: activity for structure level j after extension

$$A_0(\mathbf{t}) = \sum_{i=1}^{k} A_i(\mathbf{t}) = \sum_{j=1}^{m} A_j'(\mathbf{t})$$

The costs rate **U**, which an individual has to contribute and is able to contribute, can be assumed as constant. The last is true, because taxes can not be increased endlessly. The first is true, because some stable conditions can be assumed during not too long times.

[51] **(95)** tells by quantitative results that it is right to treat different structures equally. **[L]**

We define:

$\mathbf{U}_0$: costs rate, which could be paid for all structures

$\mathbf{U}_i$: costs rate for structure level i

$\mathbf{U}'_j$: costs rate for structure level j after extension

$$\mathbf{U}_0 = \sum_{i=1}^{k} \mathbf{U}_i = \sum_{j=1}^{m} \mathbf{U}'_j$$

If structure levels can always be described with the formula of axiom {**2**} above, then self-similarity of structures is obvious. This is a standard property of fractal systems[52]. For simplification we assume now that $\mathbf{q}$ and $\mathbf{I}_\varnothing$ are global constants of the structure. This may not be true for real structures, but this examination should be done during future tasks. The results based on simplification may not be blindly applied to real structures, but they will give first views of basic functionality.

$\mathbf{I}_\varnothing$ is surely different for any group, but letting base individuals have influence on all levels *ln*(n) is the variant parameter and $\mathbf{I}_\varnothing$ of base individuals can be used as a lower estimation for all levels. Structuring on higher levels will only increase this value by involving higher sub-structure intelligence's to averaging calculations.

The stability condition is valid for the sum of all groups of the structure, too. For individuals this sum is even more important, because the need for a structure change may only become obvious, if the sum of costs increases beyond the sum of benefit.

Now we place a new super-structure on top of an existing structure with activities named by **A**. The new structure has activities named by **A´**. The number of structure levels were k. After increase the new number of levels is:

$$k + 1 = m.$$

Placing the new super-structure has to generate benefit surplus. Therefore the following is valid by using the simplification $\mathbf{I}_L \approx \mathbf{I}_\varnothing$:

$$\sum_{i=1}^{k} \mathbf{U}_i < \sum_{i=1}^{k} A_i(\mathbf{t})\left(\mathbf{I}_L + \mathbf{q}\mathbf{I}_\varnothing\, ln(\mathrm{n}_i) - \mathbf{I}_\varnothing\right)$$

$$\sum_{i=1}^{k} \mathbf{U}_i < \sum_{i=1}^{k} A_i(\mathbf{t})\mathbf{q}\mathbf{I}_\varnothing\, ln(\mathrm{n}_i)$$

---

[52] One may recognise here that this fractal system is relative complex, because the formula for any level is identical, but variables and parameters may change at any level. This is not true for simpler fractals.

Now the next simplification is introduced: The activity for the base individual should be equal on every structure level. This assumption is naturally arbitrary. For the most cases we estimate that activity will fall with higher levels. But the following calculations shall only show that the stability condition keeps valid after placement of the super-structure with this assumption. Improving this the result will lead to another limit function for activity per structure level. It follows:

$$A_i(\mathbf{t}) = \frac{A_0(\mathbf{t})}{\mathrm{k}}$$

$$A_{\mathrm{j}}'(\mathbf{t}) = \frac{A_0(\mathbf{t})}{\mathrm{m}}$$

$$\mathbf{U}_0 < \mathbf{q}\mathbf{I}_{\varnothing} \frac{A_0(\mathbf{t})}{\mathrm{k}} \sum_{\mathrm{i}=1}^{\mathrm{k}} ln(\mathrm{n}_{\mathrm{i}})$$

$$\mathbf{U}_0 < \mathbf{q}\mathbf{I}_{\varnothing} \frac{A_0(\mathbf{t})}{\mathrm{m}} \sum_{\mathrm{j}=1}^{\mathrm{j}} ln(\mathrm{n}_{\mathrm{j}})$$

For this chapter our interest is to tell one solution of the stability condition for all structure levels with the simplifications above applied. The increase of the n_{i} is assumed to be exponential. Real systems naturally will not behave in such a simple way, but at first approximation exponential expansion for example of the number of members of city to region to country to nation can be found. The dependence as mathematical formula is:

$$\mathrm{n}_{\mathrm{i}} = \mathrm{e}^{2\mathbf{Z}\mathrm{i}}$$

$\mathbf{Z} > 0$ shall be a constant of the whole system.

Placement of the new super-structure means unchanged parameters of the existing structure:

$$\mathrm{n}_{\mathrm{i}} = \mathrm{e}^{2\mathbf{Z}\mathrm{i}} \text{ for all i } \leq \mathrm{k}$$

Placement of the new super-structure means expansion of the whole number of individuals like change from nation to European union. The applicable assumption is:

$$\mathrm{n}_{\mathrm{m}} = \mathrm{e}^{2\mathbf{Z}\mathrm{m}}$$

in a way that:

$$\mathrm{n}_{\mathrm{i}} = \mathrm{e}^{2\mathbf{Z}\mathrm{i}} \text{ is valid for all i} \leq \mathrm{m}.$$

The stability conditions become:

$$\mathbf{U}_0 < \mathbf{qI}_\varnothing \frac{A_0(\mathbf{t})}{k} 2\mathbf{Z}\sum_{i=1}^{k} i \text{ and } \mathbf{U}_0 < \mathbf{qI}_\varnothing \frac{A_0(\mathbf{t})}{m} 2\mathbf{Z}\sum_{j=1}^{m} j$$

With:

$$\sum_{i=1}^{k} i = \frac{k(k+1)}{2} \text{ and } \sum_{j=1}^{m} j = \frac{m(m+1)}{2} = \frac{m(k+2)}{2}$$

this results to:

$$\mathbf{U}_0 < \mathbf{qI}_\varnothing A_0(\mathbf{t})\mathbf{Z}(k+1), \text{ with summation i}$$

$$\mathbf{U}_0 < \mathbf{qI}_\varnothing A_0(\mathbf{t})\mathbf{Z}(k+2), \text{ with summation j}$$

Concluding we find that with

$$\mathbf{U}_1 = \mathbf{qI}_\varnothing A_0(\mathbf{t})\mathbf{Z}$$

and:

$$\mathbf{U}_1 > 0$$

it follows:

$$\mathbf{U}_0 < \mathbf{U}_1 < 2\mathbf{U}_1 < \ldots < k\mathbf{U}_1 < (k+1)\mathbf{U}_1 < (k+2)\mathbf{U}_1$$

If $\mathbf{U}_0 < \mathbf{U}_1$ is valid, the stability condition is valid for all structure levels by assuming the simplifications above. Second the benefit rises proportional with the ordinal number of the level. Third <u>one</u> solution of the stability condition is exponential increase of the level members.

Because $A_i(\mathbf{t})$ is a proportional factor of the stability condition, one can derive a limitation for permitted fall of activity with the structure level. $A_i(\mathbf{t})$ may fall at maximum proportional to i^{-1}, if all simplifications apply.

Probably a higher fall rate can be assumed, because all simplifications have been a lower estimation. But the deductions above can be determined easily. If one could find in future that a fall proportional to i^{-2} is permitted, an endless number of structure levels would fulfil the stability condition, because the infinite sum of activities would converge to a finite value. Would it not be a horrible utopia?

Structures of 2nd Degree

The Representative Constitution

At the chapters before structure was at first degree, because only a single leader and a group were defined by the base axiom {**2**}. No leadership related sub-structures have been focused so far. Only at a level, where a group is build of base individuals and where the leader is a single base individual, too, this description is detailed and complete. For most cases the leading can be found to be a leader group. The same way group individuals can be sub-groups of individuals. Therefore at most cases the axiom formula is not detailed. But it is (as all axioms) always valid. Dependence to sub-structuring should be found by examination of the value of $\mathbf{I}_L$ and/or $\mathbf{I}_\varnothing$. Focusing only first degree of structure has already lead to interesting results, but all of them had neglected $\mathbf{I}_L$ influence by the simple assumption:

$$\mathbf{I}_L \approx \mathbf{I}_\varnothing .$$

Now we are interested to better understand the influence of $\mathbf{I}_L$, which can be replaced by the formula of the leader group. We get out of axiom {**2**}:

$$\mathbf{I}_L = \mathbf{I}_{Li} + \mathbf{q}_i \mathbf{I}_{\varnothing i}\, ln(\mathrm{i})$$

$$\mathbf{I}_S = \mathbf{I}_{Li} + \mathbf{q}_i \mathbf{I}_{\varnothing i}\, ln(\mathrm{i}) + \mathbf{q}_n \mathbf{I}_{\varnothing n}\, ln(\mathrm{n})$$

The last formula has two logarithms and can be named as structure intelligence of second degree. The leader group has been detailed described and has i members. This may not be a complete description, because the i individuals, the n individuals and the (Li-indexed) leader may be further sub-structures.

A simple example for a structure of second degree is a club of n members and of i board members. An example for a structure of further degree is a national state, which is build from n individuals, which send i individuals as representatives into parliament, which then elect government. If government is described the same way again, one gets a structure of third degree.

The simplification can always be assumed that the i members are not included in n by dividing intelligence and activity of a single individual into two parts belonging to either part of the formula. Further n » i can be assumed. This allows i to be neglected regarding n.

The formula above can be called a "naturally" extension of the axiom formula by new input of the axiom into a part of the base. But there is another extension possibility. We can set:

$$\mathbf{I}_s = \mathbf{I}_L + (\mathbf{q}_l + \mathbf{q}_c)\mathbf{I}_{\text{Ø}}\, ln(n)$$

with

$$\mathbf{q} = \mathbf{q}_l + \mathbf{q}_c$$

The indices represent:

l: legislative part
c: citizen's part

This way one can show the difference of a structure with a leaders group (as first) to a plebiscitic structure. To be more exact, we have to write:

$$\mathbf{I}_s = \mathbf{I}_{Li} + (\mathbf{q}_l + \mathbf{q}_c)\mathbf{I}_{\text{Ø}n}\, ln(n)$$

This is compared to:

$$\mathbf{I}_S = \mathbf{I}_{Li} + \mathbf{q}_i\mathbf{I}_{\text{Ø}i}\, ln(i) + \mathbf{q}_n\mathbf{I}_{\text{Ø}n}\, ln(n)$$

For the plebiscitic structure only government and people exist. For the representative structure government, representatives and people exist. Focusing at the representative structure people have submitted a part of their competence ($\mathbf{q}_l$) to the representatives. This way intelligence of representatives can be extracted from the term of peoples and not from the leaders group as before. But for both cases the same formula results.

We have been started from a standard formula and have used it for two first of all different group structures. Naturally the variables do not have to be equal. But if we further assume that formulas should for example show the same national state first with plebiscitic second with representative constitution, then n and $\mathbf{I}_{\text{Ø}n}$ describe the same people and are equal in both cases. We change variable indices now to better display the relations:

$$\mathbf{I}_s = \mathbf{I}_g + (\mathbf{q}_l + \mathbf{q}_c)\mathbf{I}_{\text{Ø}n}\, ln(n)$$

$$\mathbf{I}_S = \mathbf{I}_G + \mathbf{q}_R\mathbf{I}_{\text{Ø}i}\, ln(i) + \mathbf{q}_C\mathbf{I}_{\text{Ø}n}\, ln(n)$$

The indices represent:

g, G: government part
c, C: citizen's part

R: representative's part
l: legislative part

If both structures should represent the same nation, we have to assume that the government behaves equal in both cases. This way the following is valid:

$$\mathbf{I}_G = \mathbf{I}_g$$

For the plebiscitic case people have to do legislative tasks, which is described by $\mathbf{q}_l$. The other possibilities of influencing structures behaviour will be described by $\mathbf{q}_c$. For representative constitution only the last is left for people. The aim for separating both parts was comparison. Therefore it is valid:

$$\mathbf{q}_C = \mathbf{q}_c$$

Both formulas become:

$$\mathbf{I}_s = \mathbf{I}_g + \mathbf{q}_l \mathbf{I}_{\text{Øn}}\, ln(\text{n}) + \mathbf{q}_c \mathbf{I}_{\text{Øn}}\, ln(\text{n})$$

$$\mathbf{I}_S = \mathbf{I}_g + \mathbf{q}_R \mathbf{I}_{\text{Øi}}\, ln(\text{i}) + \mathbf{q}_c \mathbf{I}_{\text{Øn}}\, ln(\text{n})$$

Whether representative constitutions are more intelligent as plebiscitic, would tell the relation:

$$\mathbf{I}_S > \mathbf{I}_s$$

or

$$\mathbf{q}_R \mathbf{I}_{\text{Øi}}\, ln(\text{i}) > \mathbf{q}_l \mathbf{I}_{\text{Øn}}\, ln(\text{n})$$

Because of:

$$ln(\text{i}) < ln(\text{n})$$

this is not obvious. We shall further examine this relation later.

The stability condition for a structure:

$$\mathbf{q}\mathbf{I}_{\text{Ø}}\, ln(\text{n})\, A_{\text{Ø}}(\mathbf{t}) > \mathbf{U}$$

can be rewritten with the variable names used before. The first condition shows dependence of the representatives group, the second shows dependence of the structure for the representative case and third for the plebiscitic case:

$$\mathbf{q}_R \mathbf{I}_{\text{Øi}}\, ln(\text{i})\, A_{\text{Ø}i}(\mathbf{t}) > \mathbf{U}_i$$

$$\mathbf{q}_R \mathbf{I}_{\text{Øi}}\, ln(\text{i})\, A_{\text{Ø}i}(\mathbf{t}) + \mathbf{q}_c \mathbf{I}_{\text{Øn}}\, ln(\text{n})\, A_{\text{Ø}n}(\mathbf{t}) > \mathbf{U}_i + \mathbf{U}_n$$

$$(\mathbf{q}_l + \mathbf{q}_c)\mathbf{I}_{\text{Øn}}\, ln(\text{n})\, A_{\text{Ø}n}(\mathbf{t}) > \mathbf{U}_l + \mathbf{U}_c$$

Comparable circumstances are only there, if the costs for both structures are equal. Therefore it has to be valid:

$$\mathbf{U} = \mathbf{U}_{l} + \mathbf{U}_{c} = \mathbf{U}_{i} + \mathbf{U}_{n}$$

The left civil rights coming from $\mathbf{q}_{C} = \mathbf{q}_{c}$ are equal. Therefore the costs for this rights must be equal:

$$\mathbf{U}_{n} = \mathbf{U}_{c} \Rightarrow \mathbf{U}_{i} = \mathbf{U}_{l}$$

Now the representative and plebiscitic stability conditions are compared:

$$\mathbf{q}_{R}\mathbf{I}_{\text{Øi}}\, ln(\mathrm{i})\, A_{Øi}(\mathbf{t}) + \mathbf{q}_{c}\mathbf{I}_{\text{Øn}}\, ln(\mathrm{n})\, A_{Øn}(\mathbf{t}) > \mathbf{U}_{i} + \mathbf{U}_{n}$$

$$\mathbf{q}_{l}\mathbf{I}_{\text{Øn}}\, ln(\mathrm{n})\, A_{Øn}(\mathbf{t}) + \mathbf{q}_{c}\mathbf{I}_{\text{Øn}}\, ln(\mathrm{n})\, A_{Øn}(\mathbf{t}) > \mathbf{U}_{i} + \mathbf{U}_{n}$$

We want to estimate, which structure is more stable: representative or plebiscitic? To get an answer one has to focus only at the unequal terms of the stability condition. So we have to compare:

$$\mathbf{q}_{R}\mathbf{I}_{\text{Øi}}\, ln(\mathrm{i})\, A_{Øi}(\mathbf{t})$$

with:

$$\mathbf{q}_{l}\mathbf{I}_{\text{Øn}}\, ln(\mathrm{n})\, A_{Øn}(\mathbf{t})$$

Now we do some estimation of the

$$\frac{ln(\mathrm{n}) \cdot ln(10)}{ln(\mathrm{i}) \cdot ln(10)} = \frac{lg(\mathrm{n})}{lg(\mathrm{i})}$$

ratio:

A club may have 100 members and 10 board members, which results to:

$$\frac{lg(\mathrm{n})}{lg(\mathrm{i})} = 2$$

A typical national state will have lower than 1000 representatives for 100.000.000 people, what results to:

$$\frac{lg(\mathrm{n})}{lg(\mathrm{i})} = \frac{8}{3} = 2.666\ldots$$

A typical city may have 100 representatives for 1.000.000 of people, which results to:

$$\frac{lg(\mathrm{n})}{lg(\mathrm{i})} = \frac{6}{2} = 3$$

For legislative tasks the representatives activity is much higher than activity of normal people, if representatives do their work as main job. Therefore the following applies:

$$A_{\O i}(\mathbf{t}) \gg A_{\O n}(\mathbf{t})$$

Because of the special education and long experience of legislative tasks a representative will have, and because it could be a sub-structure intelligence of all the staff members of a representatives work group, the following applies, too:

$$\mathbf{I}_{\O \mathrm{i}} > \mathbf{I}_{\O \mathrm{n}}$$

Because of the near local and personal connection, which representatives have to government, the following applies third:

$$\mathbf{q}_{\mathrm{R}} > \mathbf{q}_{\mathrm{c}}$$

If this condition is met:

$$\frac{A_{\O i}(\mathbf{t})}{A_{\O n}(\mathbf{t})} \cdot \frac{\mathbf{I}_{\O \mathrm{i}}}{\mathbf{I}_{\O \mathrm{n}}} \cdot \frac{\mathbf{q}_{\mathrm{R}}}{\mathbf{q}_{\mathrm{c}}} > 3$$

then representative constitution is more stable and therefore generates more benefit as the plebiscitic constitution. A real measurement can never be done, because only one of the compared systems can be real. But it is very likely that the last condition is commonly true. It is a heavy argument for the correctness of the structure axiom that mostly representative constitutions are found in reality.

Coming back to the not obviously better intelligence of representative structures as seen above, one can state that ideas found by people during drinking in pubs may be as good as ideas of their leaders. But the typical non-acting behaviour after pub visiting makes the difference, although communication in any way is a first step.

There is another very interesting effect of plebiscitic constitutions. Probably because of long back leading history and proudly further done tradition people of a well accepted plebiscitic constitution will have higher political activity as for other circumstances. If this activity is essential to keep the stability condition true, such a nation will not join super-structures, because people of that nation would have to contribute some activity to the super-structure, which would result to reduced activity for the own nation with following destabilisation. A feeling for this effect could be a cause for people of Switzerland not to join the European union.

Structures of 3rd Degree

The blessings by forcing parliament fractions to equal voting

Starting from the representative structure above we introduce a new government group the "natural" way:

$$\mathbf{I}_S = \mathbf{I}_G + \mathbf{q}_R \mathbf{I}_{\varnothing i}\, ln(\mathrm{i}) + \mathbf{q}_C \mathbf{I}_{\varnothing n}\, ln(\mathrm{n})$$

with:

$$\mathbf{I}_G = \mathbf{I}_L + \mathbf{q}_G \mathbf{I}_{\varnothing j}\, ln(\mathrm{j})$$

it results to:

$$\mathbf{I}_S = \mathbf{I}_L + \mathbf{q}_G \mathbf{I}_{\varnothing j}\, ln(\mathrm{j}) + \mathbf{q}_R \mathbf{I}_{\varnothing i}\, ln(\mathrm{i}) + \mathbf{q}_C \mathbf{I}_{\varnothing n}\, ln(\mathrm{n})$$

The chapter before has shown, how important increased activity, intelligence and government relations are to representatives and representative constitutions. The same dependencies apply to a government group compared to people. But there is a big difference, if the comparison of government is done to the representatives of people. In this case there can not be found any significant increase of activity, intelligence or prime minister relations in the way that representatives of second degree, which give a structure of third degree, would have any meaning to people. The same is true for all other structures of higher degree. Therefore this higher degrees do not need to be examined.

More over such structures are dangerous in the way that one institution might block the other. If the high active representatives or government members get frustrated, because they can not do the work their way any more, activity will fall. But because activity is the most important factor of stability of the structure, the system becomes destabilised by blocking.

All constitutions have rules written or not, which shall prevent blocking:

- Government depends on parliament and election of another government solves blocking.
- The most daily decisions are unblocked by disciplinary behaviour of fraction members known as force to equal voting.

The force to equal voting can be described by a different structure formula:

$$\mathbf{q}_R \mathbf{I}_{\varnothing i}\, ln(\mathrm{i})$$

is broken into:

$$\mathbf{q}_A \mathbf{I}_{\varnothing k}\, ln(\mathrm{k}) \text{ and } \mathbf{q}_O \mathbf{I}_{\varnothing l}\, ln(\mathrm{l})$$

$$\mathrm{i} = \mathrm{k} + \mathrm{l}$$

resulting to:

$$\mathbf{I}_S = \mathbf{I}_L + \mathbf{q}_g \mathbf{I}_{\text{Øjk}}\, ln(\mathrm{j}+\mathrm{k}) + \mathbf{q}_O \mathbf{I}_{\text{Øl}}\, ln(1) + \mathbf{q}_C \mathbf{I}_{\text{Øn}}\, ln(\mathrm{n})$$

By invention of a representative constitution it has been prevented that:

$$\mathbf{q}_C \mathbf{I}_{\text{Øn}}\, ln(\mathrm{n})$$

has blocking influence. By forcing equal voting an oppositions group

$$\mathbf{q}_O \mathbf{I}_{\text{Øl}}\, ln(1)$$

has been introduced, which has low enough influence to avoid blocking on this level. A hybrid structure:

$$\mathbf{I}_L + \mathbf{q}_g \mathbf{I}_{\text{Øjk}}\, ln(\mathrm{j}+\mathrm{k})$$

has been build from the government and from the parliament fractions, which support them. The stability of the system is at maximum, because the members of this group are not dependent to external frustrations. This hybrid structure has the properties of a structure of first degree and is for the simplest case identically to the leader group of a political party.

The hybrid structure gives the biggest part of the structure intelligence, which is not directly contributed by citizens, because:

$$\mathrm{j}+\mathrm{k} > 1,\ \mathbf{q}_g > \mathbf{q}_O \text{ and } \mathbf{I}_{\text{Øjk}} \approx \mathbf{I}_{\text{Øl}}$$

The hybrid group is more intelligent as the former structure:

$$\mathbf{I}_L + \mathbf{q}_g \mathbf{I}_{\text{Øjk}}\, ln(\mathrm{j}+\mathrm{k}) + \mathbf{q}_O \mathbf{I}_{\text{Øl}}\, ln(1) + \mathbf{q}_C \mathbf{I}_{\text{Øn}}\, ln(\mathrm{n}) >$$
$$\mathbf{I}_L + \mathbf{q}_G \mathbf{I}_{\text{Øj}}\, ln(\mathrm{j}) + \mathbf{q}_R \mathbf{I}_{\text{Øi}}\, ln(\mathrm{i}) + \mathbf{q}_C \mathbf{I}_{\text{Øn}}\, ln(\mathrm{n})$$

or:

$$\mathbf{q}_g \mathbf{I}_{\text{Øjk}}\, ln(\mathrm{j}+\mathrm{k}) + \mathbf{q}_O \mathbf{I}_{\text{Øl}}\, ln(1) > \mathbf{q}_G \mathbf{I}_{\text{Øj}}\, ln(\mathrm{j}) + \mathbf{q}_R \mathbf{I}_{\text{Øi}}\, ln(\mathrm{i})$$

because:

$$\mathbf{q}_g \approx \mathbf{q}_G,\ \mathbf{q}_O \approx \mathbf{q}_R,\ \mathbf{q}_g > \mathbf{q}_O$$

and:

$$\mathbf{I}_{\text{Øjk}} \approx \mathbf{I}_{\text{Øl}} \approx \mathbf{I}_{\text{Øj}} \approx \mathbf{I}_{\text{Øi}}$$

By redistribution of members the more mighty term of the government has won an increased number of members. The weaker term, which now only contains the opposition, has lost members.

All this functionality can be found at real systems. For this the validity of the axiom is further secured.

Thermodynamic Discussion [N]

At the chapters before all axioms and deductions have been made by using physical methods. The most important point of view, which needs more discussion, is the negative energy equivalence to intelligence. The argument for this is that the system is always at disequilibrium. Therefore we have always neglected some external energy resource. This lets us assume an inside and an outside of the system as told at the beginning. But is not hunting ground benefit such a resource? And is it not better to have more energy offered by nature resulting this way to a more stable system?

Let us look at individuals, which do no communication. They completely depend to hunting ground benefits. A stable system needs a constant energy sum. Increasing the energy input rate by nature does not stabilise the system. It becomes destabilised. More input increases the number of individuals proportionally, if we assume for simplification that biomass is a global constant for all individuals of the species. Reduced input decreases the number and destabilises the system, too. Stable conditions equal to a stable number of individuals are only the case, if the rate of energy input is equal to a negative energy consumption rate by the sum of individuals. This negative energy consumption rate means further that the used negative energy multiplied by time results to the individual hunting ground benefit.

What about communication benefit? If individuals are allowed to communicate, is this derived out of nothing? The answer is: No! Communication has only meaning, if individuals do not exactly the same job and have not exactly the same experience. Acting different results to different use of resources of nature. It is obvious that a single individual can not use all possible offers the same way. But working together with different other individuals results to a specialised production of goods and to a possible general consumption. Every commercial trading is therefore a communication system **(66)**, **(117)**. Communication benefit is derived in the same way out of nature's offers as hunting ground benefit, but it is a possibility for an optimisation. The same conditions apply for communication benefit as for hunting ground benefit. There has to be an equal energy input rate to have stable conditions and the surplus by communication needs equivalent input by nature, which was already available before communication, but was not used. But opposite to the first not communicating system there is an intrinsic instability, because stimulation of ideas will result to improved possibilities for a better use of natures offers. This way the used energy input delivered by nature can be increased. If the total input is a fixed value, the amount of unused energy input has to decrease with the same value. Probably all optimisation has a maximal possible outcome therefore. But I think we are far away on earth yet and almost all areas of the sphere bowl around our sun are unused today.

Is there not too much simplification? Above we have assumed a constant biomass for all individuals, but we all know that this is never the case and therefore arbitrary. But a variable individual biomass does not change any results of our logical deduction to qualitative answers. It will not even change quantitative results, if longer periods of time are examined. The only but important help by simplification is that readers can follow the deduction of results very easily.

Simplifications are often used for other areas of theoretic science, but there has to be a good explanation for doing so. Further doubts are always allowed. This is as more valid as simplified results do not describe real systems efficiently. Because this theory is in coincidence with many publications, one can assume that the quality of the simplifications is not too bad. But a closer examination should be done. The main argument for using simplifications is that they help to a first understanding. For example in a previous version of this theory only symmetrical first class conditions for groups have been examined, because I had not got the ideas, how to interpret the more complex asymmetric possibilities. The symmetrical system was defined by simplification. This was a needed step for me to get important information and only after understanding this information, it was possible for me to drop the symmetrical assumption.

The Status Sum of Groups

The best theoretic approach to thermodynamic results is using a status sum of the examined system. Thermodynamic variables can then be derived by differential operations upon the status sum. But this approach is more difficult, because the status of the system has to be described in a certain way before. For example the potential between individuals has to be known. Therefore it was not possible to start the entire theory with this approach. Further we have to use very simplified potentials derived from the chapter "*Simplified Accounts of Benefits (**pV**)*". The much more complicated common results can not be handled this way in the frame of this publication. One can doubt, whether they ever can be handled without definitions of parameters (for example by analysing a real system).

There are more difficulties, so direct copying of thermodynamic deductions is not possible. All examinations of gases by thermodynamic theories need kinetic energy of the molecules. Individuals do not have such a property in this theory. They have instead some hunting ground benefit reserved, which can be understood as some interaction independent potential. Using this reservoir for an abstract movement to communication (including paying for telephone lines) can be recognized as playing the same role as some kinetic energy of standard thermodynamics. The communicative benefit produces the interactive potential. Something very similar can be found for standard thermodynamics, too.

A base assumption for thermodynamic description is "weak" interaction. All quasi-static deductions above have not in any way told a quantitative result. Therefore we do not know, whether interaction is strong or weak, but the quasi-static behaviour is not affected. Later at "*Quantum Physical Discussion*" "weak" quantitative results are produced. But those values are estimated relative to the other unliving physical world values. Therefore "weak" may be not a right valuing for living beings. Future dynamic considerations should be aware of problems arising from strong interactions. In fact the economic experience tells us hints that this interaction (and then surely every other communicative interaction) is of the strong kind:

A strong attraction occurs in the atomic core for example. The theory to describe this is called "Quantum Chromo Dynamic" or QCD. The name was derived from the "colours" which has been invented to define certain properties of the "quark" particles. But more important to our considerations is that the strong attraction needs so called "gluons" as exchange particles. The difference to others is that they interact not only with the quarks but with themselves as well.

What is the similarity to economics? As we have seen before the cause for economic exchange is social exchange. It seems that nothing more is needed to define it. But for support of the exchange and for a quantitative measurement possibility of the exchange value humans have invented money. One can recognise money as a materialisation of the interaction and therefore as a materialisation of the exchange particle.[53] Interesting is that human properties include meanness, what can be understood as attraction to the interacting particle and not as a social relation. More over it typically replaces some social relation.

It is a poverty of description to explain poverty as a lack of money. The better description is a lack of social relations and includes rich children, who have no relation to the social environment, from which their parents have got their money. Overcoming of meanness and solidarity with the other poor people, who have really a lack of money, would be a very good strategy to help either. If a high income is equivalent to the amount and value of the social relations of the group or individual, there is no argument against it from this theory. The possibility is a need for the emergence of leadership and for a successful analysing of diversity. So please stop the popular demand of driving down income of parliament representatives!

For further deductions it is assumed that standard thermodynamic systematic is useful. The status space is a needed property for the description. At this theory this space has to be identified with the abstract distribution space of individuals. There may rise the question, whether the abstract distribution space caused by communication tools can be applied to the not interactive potential as well. The answer is that if hunting ground benefits have in reality some origin, which would be naturally described by another space system, a projection into the distribution space regarding communication should be always possible.

[53] But I do not think that it is really identical.

For example food has typically some 2-dimensional origin naturally for humans. But they need some regularly input of food all the time. Therefore it is easily possible to transform the food origin to a timely input rate, which has the same dimension as distribution space regarding connection time.

Our definitions of group volume and hunting ground volume before tell that the number of possible states of the system is exactly the number of individuals. Here our standard method applies: As complicated any individual may be, at any level of examination any individual is described as an entity of single variability. Complicated sub-parts have to be described by some sub-structuring and therefore by different levels of examination. The system as a whole is a very complicated fractal structure, but simple methods can be applied to any level.

The entropy of a single level is given as:

$$\mathbf{S} = \mathrm{k}\, ln(\mathrm{n})$$

because:

$$\Omega = \mathrm{n}$$

is the status sum in our case.

In a chapter before, we have found the following formulas:

$$\mathrm{n} = \frac{\mathbf{V}_{\mathrm{G}}}{\mathbf{V}_{\mathrm{I}}}$$

$$\frac{\mathbf{V}_{\mathrm{I}}}{\mathbf{V}_{\mathrm{R}}} = \frac{\mathbf{B}_{0\mathrm{i}}}{|\mathbf{B}_{\mathrm{Mi}}|} = \frac{\mathbf{O}_{\mathrm{R}} \cdot \mathbf{V}_{\mathrm{R}}}{\mathbf{u}_{\varnothing} \cdot \mathbf{r}_{\mathrm{i}}}$$

Then we had deduced a formula for dependence of n to benefit ratios. The assumption was that communication benefits do not help to increase the communication radii. We drop this assumption now and set for a first class group:

$$\frac{\mathbf{V}_{\mathrm{I}}}{\mathbf{V}_{\mathrm{R}}} = \frac{\mathbf{B}_{\mathrm{R}} + \mathbf{B}_{\mathrm{X+}}}{|\mathbf{B}_{\mathrm{M}}|} = \frac{\mathbf{o}_{\mathrm{R}} \cdot \mathbf{V}_{\mathrm{R}} + 2 \cdot \mathbf{I}_{\varnothing} \cdot \dfrac{\mathbf{V}_{\mathrm{R}}}{\mathbf{V}_{\mathrm{G}}}}{\mathbf{u}_{\varnothing} \cdot \mathbf{v}}$$

This gives:

$$\mathrm{n} = \frac{\mathbf{u}_{\varnothing} \cdot \mathbf{v} \cdot \mathbf{V}_{\mathrm{G}}}{\mathbf{o}_{\mathrm{R}} \cdot \mathbf{V}_{\mathrm{R}}^{2} + 2 \cdot \mathbf{I}_{\varnothing} \cdot \dfrac{\mathbf{V}_{\mathrm{R}}^{2}}{\mathbf{V}_{\mathrm{G}}}}$$

From the stability condition we get:

$$\mathbf{I}_{\mathrm{G}} = \frac{d\mathbf{B}}{d\mathbf{t}} = \text{const.} = \mathrm{n}^2 \mathbf{o}_{\mathrm{R}} \mathbf{V}_{\mathrm{R}} + 2\mathrm{n}^2 \mathbf{I}_{\varnothing} \frac{\mathbf{V}_{\mathrm{R}}}{\mathbf{V}_{\mathrm{G}}} - \mathrm{n}^2 \mathbf{u}_{\varnothing} \mathbf{v}$$

or:

$$\frac{\mathbf{I}_G}{n} = n \cdot \left(\mathbf{o}_R \mathbf{V}_R + 2\mathbf{I}_{\varnothing} \frac{\mathbf{V}_R}{\mathbf{V}_G} - \mathbf{u}_{\varnothing} \mathbf{v} \right)$$

This is the intelligence of a single individual derived by group interaction. We define the intelligence derived on a single communication step as:

$$\mathbf{I}_{GSS} = \mathbf{o}_R \mathbf{V}_R + 2\mathbf{I}_{\varnothing} \frac{\mathbf{V}_R}{\mathbf{V}_G} - \mathbf{u}_{\varnothing} \mathbf{v}$$

n can be defined using this entity as:

$$n = \frac{\mathbf{u}_{\varnothing} \mathbf{v} \cdot \mathbf{V}_G}{\left(\mathbf{I}_{GSS} + \mathbf{u}_{\varnothing} \mathbf{v} \right) \cdot \mathbf{V}_R}$$

This way no explicit communication benefit formula is used and this formula is valid for all possibilities.

The maximal group volume is given, if group intelligence per step reaches some metabolic minimum, because loss by metabolism defines a minimal needed benefit per step:

$$\mathbf{I}_{GSS} \geq \mathbf{o}_R \mathbf{V}_R + 2\mathbf{I}_{\varnothing} \frac{\mathbf{V}_R}{\mathbf{V}_{G\,max}} - \mathbf{u}_{\varnothing} \mathbf{v} = \mathbf{M}$$

$$\mathbf{V}_{G\,max} = \frac{2\mathbf{I}_{\varnothing} \mathbf{V}_R}{\mathbf{M} + \mathbf{u}_{\varnothing} \mathbf{v} - \mathbf{o}_R \mathbf{V}_R}$$

If hunting ground benefit can always pay for metabolism and movement to communication, the maximal group volume becomes infinite. If hunting ground benefit is of more value as any loss, then the maximal group volume becomes negative showing that reduction of hunting ground volume is possible. Only if communicative benefit is needed for overcoming losses, the maximal group volume has a meaningful value. If different benefit kinds are the case and not every hunting ground benefit kind can be used for paying costs, the equation above should only include the relevant amounts.

The equation defining n by ratio of volumes and following of benefit parts can be changed to:

$$n\mathbf{V}_R \left(\mathbf{o}_R \cdot \mathbf{V}_R + 2 \cdot \mathbf{I}_{\varnothing} \cdot \frac{\mathbf{V}_R}{\mathbf{V}_G} \right) = \mathbf{u}_{\varnothing} \cdot \mathbf{v} \cdot \mathbf{V}_G$$

or:

$$\mathbf{o}_R \cdot \mathbf{V}_R + 2 \cdot \mathbf{I}_{\varnothing} \cdot \frac{\mathbf{V}_R}{\mathbf{V}_G} = \frac{\mathbf{u}_{\varnothing} \cdot \mathbf{v} \cdot \mathbf{V}_G}{n\mathbf{V}_R}$$

$$\mathbf{o}_R \cdot \mathbf{V}_R + 2 \cdot \mathbf{I}_\emptyset \cdot \frac{\mathbf{V}_R}{\mathbf{V}_G} = \mathbf{u}_\emptyset \cdot \mathbf{v} \cdot \left(1 - 1 + \frac{\mathbf{V}_G}{n\mathbf{V}_R}\right)$$

$$\mathbf{o}_R \cdot \mathbf{V}_R + 2 \cdot \mathbf{I}_\emptyset \cdot \frac{\mathbf{V}_R}{\mathbf{V}_G} - \mathbf{u}_\emptyset \mathbf{v} = \mathbf{u}_\emptyset \mathbf{v} \cdot \left(\frac{\mathbf{V}_G}{n\mathbf{V}_R} - 1\right)$$

This can be input into the group interaction intelligence formula:

$$\frac{\mathbf{I}_G}{n} = n \cdot \mathbf{u}_\emptyset \mathbf{v} \cdot \left(\frac{\mathbf{V}_G}{n\mathbf{V}_R} - 1\right)$$

$$\frac{\mathbf{I}_G}{n} = \mathbf{u}_\emptyset \mathbf{v} \cdot \left(\frac{\mathbf{V}_G - n\mathbf{V}_R}{\mathbf{V}_R}\right)$$

With:

$$\Delta\mathbf{V} = \mathbf{V}_G - n\mathbf{V}_R \geq 0$$

n can be defined using the group intelligence:

$$n = \frac{\mathbf{V}_R}{\mathbf{u}_\emptyset \mathbf{v} \cdot \Delta\mathbf{V}} \cdot \mathbf{I}_G$$

If $\Delta\mathbf{V}$ is zero and $\mathbf{I}_G$ is bigger than zero, then n is infinite. In this case there is steady communication and the not vanishing surplus lets grow the number of possible communication partners to infinity. A stable system would have $\Delta\mathbf{V}$ equal to zero after a long time development. This seems to be a problem. But assuming instant communication after crossing of hunting ground borders is arbitrary. Dropping this simplification is easy, because using $\Delta\mathbf{V}$ always bigger than a minimal value would result to an adjusted description without a need for further refinement. In the case of a long timed, stable system one can assume then that the movement to communication is done only because of searching in the hunting grounds of partners. This tells that:

$$\Delta\mathbf{V} = \mathbf{a} \cdot n\mathbf{V}_R$$

is a justified definition. With **a** as a parameter of the species. n becomes as stable long time value showing maximal population:

$$n \approx \sqrt{\frac{\mathbf{I}_G}{\mathbf{u}_\emptyset \mathbf{v} \cdot \mathbf{a}}}$$

In the extreme case of a sparsely filled group volume the following assumption is valid:

$$\mathbf{V}_G \gg n\mathbf{V}_R$$

n becomes then:

$$n \approx \frac{\mathbf{V}_R}{\mathbf{u}_\varnothing \mathbf{v} \cdot \mathbf{V}_G} \cdot \mathbf{I}_G$$

The $\mathbf{I}_G$ dependence is of interest, because the used energy input by nature is probably of the same value. If one would look at the same volume populated at different times by a different number of individuals, the energy input of nature of value $\mathbf{I}_G$ is very different, too. Therefore the last formula above shows the starting phase of growth **(107)** and the square root formula shows the later continuing.

Growth the Cause of Death [B]

The common "energy"-relation at the chapter "*No End of Growth*" told a linear increase of $\mathbf{I}_G$ with time. This would lead to time dependent growth functions derived from above, which start linear and tend to become square root like. This behaviour is coincident with the animal and man growth functions for the biomass as discussed in **(128)**. n has to be identified with the number of cells and not with the biomass, but a proportional relation is likely for young cell clusters. One discrepancy is there for the long run, because ageing results to a reduced biomass with time. But a wrinkled face tells that biomass may decrease by ageing but there may be further growth. This can be a growth of cell volume (sub-structure dependent) or a growth of cell number (super-structure dependent) or both. Papers at "PubMed" **(3)**, **(6)** seem to prefer the first possibility accompanied with an increased death rate of cells. Because birth and death rates are not analysed for this version of the theory already, some lack of description has to be assumed for ageing.

If growth is the main cause for ageing and a partly destruction of cell content is not possible without sacrificing function, then the found behaviour would be logical. Functional parts of organs are always build by numerous cells of an equal kind. Not restituing some after cell death during ageing keeps relative stability of the super-structure, but a lingering performance loss may result. Otherwise the increase of cell volume and as well of the accompanied "hunting ground" volume would lead to growth beyond the maximal group volume and would result to communication problems followed with sub-group separation and no more symbiotic but parasitic interacting behaviour. One would name this "cancer". A description of such a structure level interaction by a later publication could heal the explanatory lack of the mathematical theory.

It is interesting that rejuvenation of plants is possible by cutting. But "lifting" of humans only helps at few body regions. Only optimising communication possibilities of cells can be achieved by health care, but immortality will be never possible. Prolongation of lifetime needs reduction of input resources close to the minimal level defined by the stability condition of first class for groups. But falling below this level results as well to sub-group separation by deficiency decease. It is well known that overfeeding as well as underfeeding increases the tumour rate.[54]

[54] For references please search PubMed at "http://www.ncbi.nlm.nih.gov". Because I estimate this as already entered into common knowledge, I neglect the multiple references.

The Thermodynamic Formula

A volume sparsely filled by individuals:

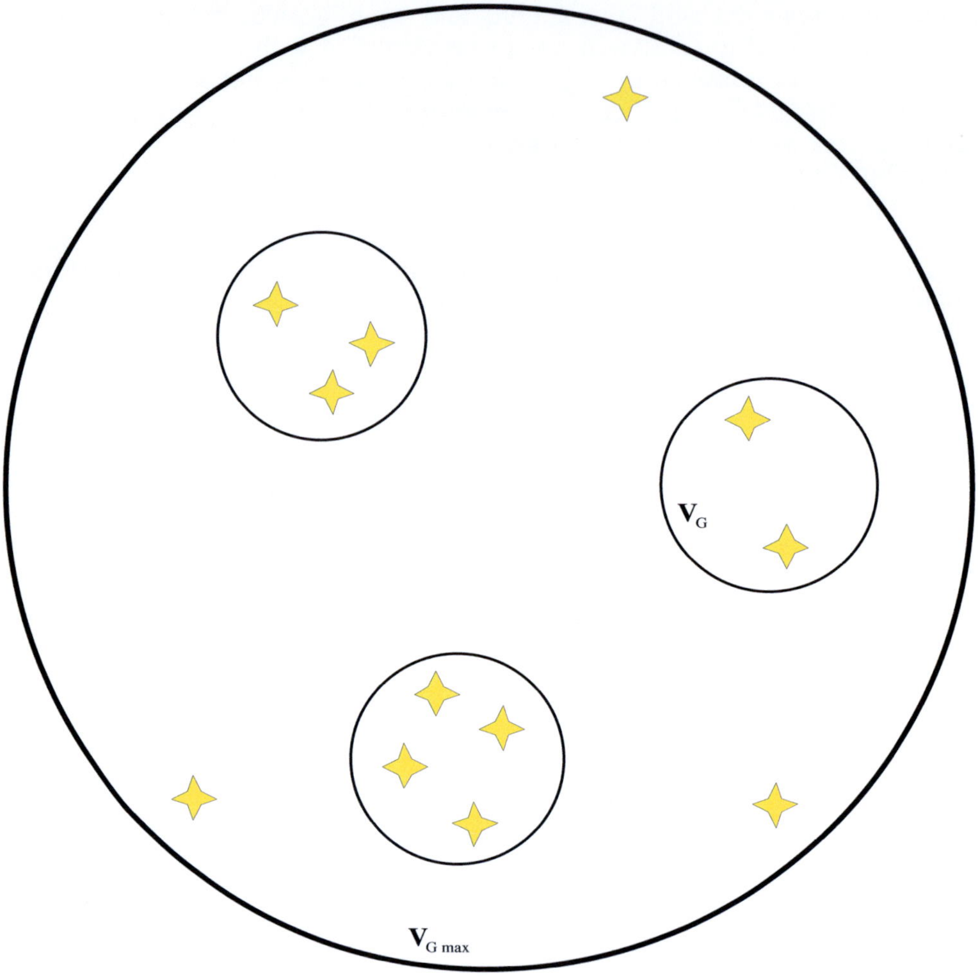

Figure 17. Population a Short Time after Disturbance (Start of Relaxation)

If a stable and completely balanced system becomes disturbed, the number of individuals typically can not follow directly, although it can be assumed that short after the disturbance there will be another stability condition.

The cofactors to $\mathbf{I}_G$ of the status sums above are all independent to communication effects. Therefore using a first class condition or a general formula is not important. The deduction could be done in the same way for any benefit rate, whether communicative benefit is included or not.

If a system relaxes from a disturbed and sparsely filled status to stable (equilibrium) conditions, the following situation is given:

- Communication is a seldom process at start and therefore can be assumed to be weak regarding hunting ground benefits.
- All parameters regarding hunting ground and movement costs are fixed.
- There is steady (energy) input by nature, which every individual can use, although the usable input increases because n and communication benefit increases, too.
- There is a fixed maximal group volume, which can be filled with more individuals, if communication is a needed resource. The group volume starts with a minimum and extends during relaxation, but multiple groups would unify to a big at least. This allows describing all individuals by the same actual group volume parameter.
- Pressure or better suction between individuals varies during relaxation and is caused by the increasing communication benefit.
- If we assume that increased individual benefit causes directly production of descendants, but does not increase individual properties, this behaviour can be recognised as constant temperature and variable entropy. The same is true, if biomass variability is of low meaning related to the number of generations of descendant production.

For this relaxation the thermodynamic formula given from the start of this essay is the best description:

$$d\mathbf{H} = \mathbf{T}\,d\mathbf{S} + \mathbf{V}\,d\mathbf{p}$$

where temperature and volume are fixed, but entropy and pressure are variable.

Before in this chapter we have used only the pressure (suction) and volume dependent intelligence parts. Effects of temperature and entropy would go unnoticed and unused, if structuring would not occur.

For all the chapters before we used quasi-static systems for description. No dynamic development had been studied so far. Here we have recognised that dynamics could be introduced using thermo-”dynamics”. Applications of this kind are outside the frame of this essay and have to be done in future.

A volume almost completely populated:

(Substructuring is neglected, but will emerge.)

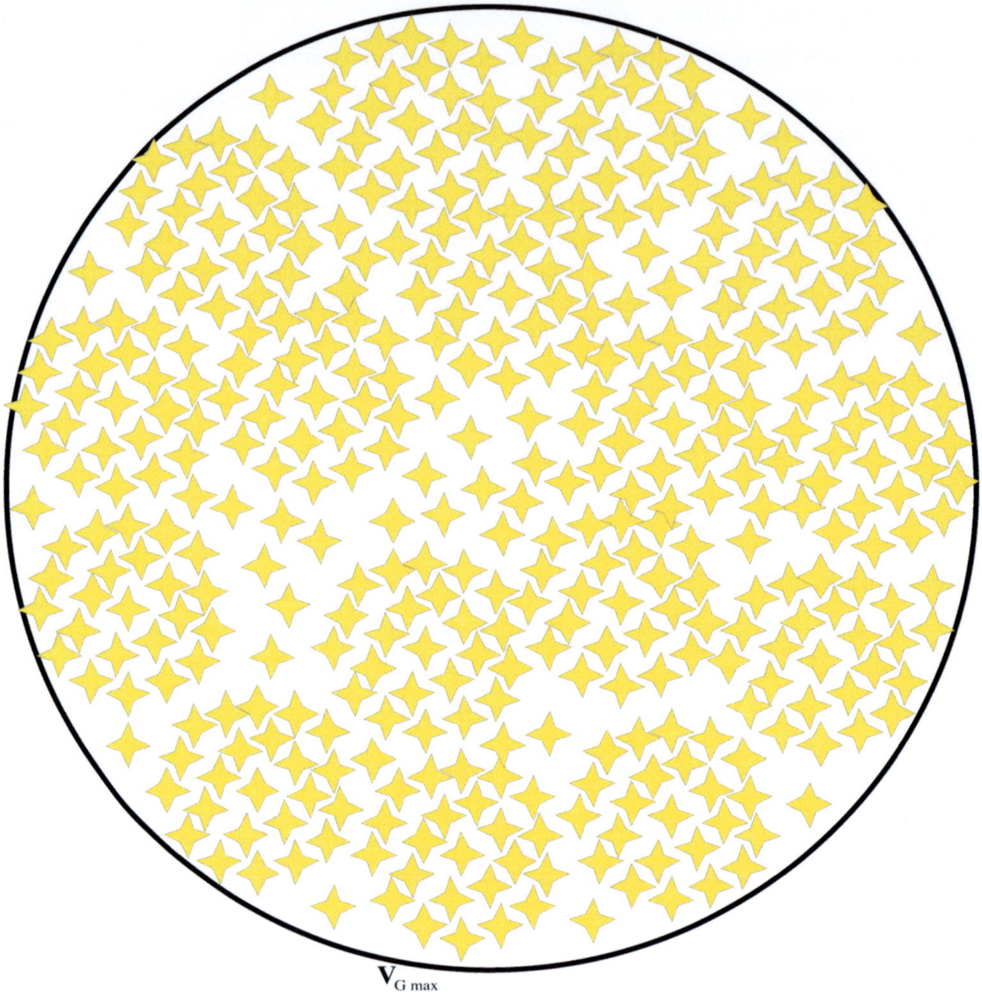

Figure 18. Population after Relaxation

Quantum Physical Discussion

At the versions before there was questioned after the "*Abstract*" a possible expandability:

"Are there uncertainty relations either between group structure and benefit kind or axiomatic and freedom of thinking or stability and creativity in the way that you can not define both of them exactly? (It looks similar to Heisenberg´s for standard physics.)"

This can be extended to the statement that seriousness and joking or happiness and sorrow seem to have similar properties. The last two pairs are built from parts, which are valued as something positive or negative for humans. Joking is consciously done disorder but sorrow is disorder by external influences. Consciously done ordering (for example by pairing) derives happiness. But externally defined order derives seriousness. This shows that the individual influence defines the valuing. Better democratic influences increase therefore really the impression of happiness of the citizens. One should consider the US American constitution regarding happiness of citizens.

Now I think that some explanation about uncertainty relations is possible and the quantum physical property will result very similar as it was derived by historical developments. The simplificated benefit sums are mainly used, but a verbal generalisation will be given.

The word pairs above can be categorised to be related to order ($\mathbf{pV}$) and disorder ($\mathbf{TS}$) for always the left to right sequence. This rises the question, whether the physical uncertainty relations can be derived from a more general procedure of optimising effect (or benefit) accounts. The social and as well physical experience is that maximising order (for example by freezing) or disorder (for example by heating) are both not an optimal way of generating something interesting.

For quantum particles one would maximise order by measuring the exact position or the exact impulse. On the other hand such an operation would maximise disorder of the conjugated other parameter. Looking only at the single parameter the order maximisation deletes any disorder and vice versa. Such an action seems to be like freezing or burning human fingers. You would not like both very much, as well as quantum particles would like to be somewhere in between. Both reactions must be a result of the impossibility to clear one part of the two terms on the right of the main equation without maximising the other one:

$$d\mathbf{H} = \mathbf{T}\,d\mathbf{S} + \mathbf{V}\,d\mathbf{p}$$

Although I never understood such an explanation during my study, the first and historical introduction that I found in **(53)** at pages 13ff show exactly this meaning. The law found by Wien depends to disorder (**TS**) and the Rayleigh-Jeans law depends to order (**pV**). Following it is shown that a similar approach as found by Planck is used dependent to the former formulas to derive some interpolating function, which will lead to quantum properties. Those historical laws relate to energy density, what is not the best variable to look at in our case. Better suited is the individual number n.

At this time some consideration about variable signs is needed, because of the assumed **I** ~ -**T** relation and because Planck´s historical quantum law depends on temperature. At the whole essay we never really introduced temperature or energy. Only in the chapter "*Basic Physics*" such a relation was remarked. All done axiomatic and deductions can be understood to be "positive defined" and related to the "inside" of the system. The used variables are therefore all positive. Introduction of the relation to temperature changes the examining view to the "outside" and is as well a change of system of relation. The complement to **I** and more variables complements would change the sign but the formulas would be valid in this case, too. ("<" and ">" relations may change to the opposite as well.)

Because there is not already any relation between inside and outside by value, one can define it freely for one pair of variables. Formula relations would then give other pair values. Our definition is:

$$\mathbf{I}_{\varnothing} = -k\mathbf{T}$$

This definition will be used at the following subchapters and changes the "internal" intelligence to something, which is "externally" defined.

To understand this "change of view" operation, one should consider freezing of ice. We all know that this needs reduction of temperature and energy is removed from the system. If you would further assume that water molecules would like structuring and would applause to freezing, they would tell you that this energy loss is a real benefit to them. After initialising some basic structure like some first stage snowflake more freezing in a hurry would not be what they like. Some energy input as well as further cooling would result to a system far from thermodynamic equilibrium for some longer time and impressionistic snowflakes can be built. Do they behave much different to people? **[(145)]**

Deduction of Quantum Properties [Y][55]

There is the implicit quantum property of dedicated individuals at any level of examination as explained before. Therefore we do not need to introduce this basic property. Even old philosophy has already recognised this: **(35)**, **(144)** and **(155)**. More interesting are the related dependencies of used variables.

From the stability condition of a structure we have got this formula:

$$n > e^{\frac{U}{qA_\varnothing I_\varnothing}} = e^{\frac{w}{I_\varnothing}}, \quad \mathbf{w} = \frac{\mathbf{U}}{\mathbf{qA}_\varnothing}$$

This looks similar to Wien´s law. It seems to be a good description for big n values. One should remember that the exponential function is only a lower border for n.

From the chapter before we got this growth function as stable long time condition. Because of the needed individual interaction this equation is not only a border to an extreme.

$$n \approx \sqrt{\frac{\mathbf{I}_G}{\mathbf{u}_\varnothing \mathbf{v} \cdot \mathbf{a}}}$$

We know there is another growth function, if other parameters apply, but examination of results using the other have to be done during future tasks.

Therefore we use the given growth function, input the common energy relation found at "*No End of Growth*" and use the species hunting ground search parameter:

$$\mathbf{V}_G = n\mathbf{V}_R(1+\mathbf{a})$$

$$n^2\mathbf{u}_\varnothing \mathbf{v} \cdot \mathbf{a} = n^2\mathbf{o}_R\mathbf{V}_R + 2\chi_\varnothing\left(\frac{\mathbf{I}_\varnothing}{1+\mathbf{a}}\right)^2 \int d\mathbf{t} - n^2\mathbf{u}_\varnothing \mathbf{v}$$

$$n^2\left(\mathbf{u}_\varnothing \mathbf{v} \cdot (1+\mathbf{a}) - \mathbf{o}_R\mathbf{V}_R\right) = 2\chi_\varnothing\left(\frac{\mathbf{I}_\varnothing}{1+\mathbf{a}}\right)^2 \int d\mathbf{t}$$

$$n = \sqrt{\frac{2\chi_\varnothing \int d\mathbf{t}}{\mathbf{u}_\varnothing \mathbf{v} \cdot (1+\mathbf{a}) - \mathbf{o}_R\mathbf{V}_R}} \cdot \frac{\mathbf{I}_\varnothing}{1+\mathbf{a}}$$

This looks similar to the Rayleigh-Jeans law, but there is a time dependency.

---

[55] A stimulated error correction at a central position.

Defining some new function can reduce the formula above:

$$D(\mathbf{t}) = \sqrt{\frac{2\chi_{\varnothing}\int d\mathbf{t}}{\mathbf{u}_{\varnothing}\mathbf{v}\cdot(1+\mathbf{a}) - \mathbf{o}_{R}\mathbf{V}_{R}}} \cdot \frac{1}{(1+\mathbf{a})}$$

$$\mathrm{n} = D(\mathbf{t})\cdot \mathbf{I}_{\varnothing}$$

This simple formula looks very nice. Remembering the complex integrals of the chapter: "*The Common Integral Benefit Sum of Individual and System (**pV**)*" one recognises the additivity of the hunting ground benefit and of the movement loss. Influence of those parts is a multiplied factor of the formula above. Remember further that the complex integrals were given by using the stability condition of first class leading to some linear dependence to intelligence. Without this assumption as done as well before a quadratic dependence of group intelligence to individual intelligence would be the case and taking it out of the square root would be possible in the same way, too. Therefore one can assume that writing the simple formula by hiding all external dependencies in the *D*-function is possible generally including the common description. But for further deductions we continue to use the multiple simplificated dependencies.

It looks a little strange that the time dependent function *D* is related to integer values of n. But as well $-\mathbf{T} \sim \mathbf{I}$ as n can be time dependent. Typically an increased consumption of energy is needed to prepare an embryonic state. Later the individual number increases by one during birth and release of the descendent individual is accompanied by reduction of energy consumption of the parent individual back to the starting value.

If the Wien like growth function as well as the Raleigh-Jeans like should describe the same group first as subjected to leadership resulting to structure and second subjected to group interaction, then both n values should be equal for either case. This leads to the same argumentation as for standard quantum physics. Both functions have to be recognised as good descriptions in the case of many or in the case of few group members. For a general description a Planck like interpolation is needed. But simpler as for the historical past only the addition of the functions solves the requirement. Using the "≥" operator shows the bordering property of the exponential function.

$$\mathrm{n} \geq \mathrm{e}^{\frac{\mathbf{w}}{\mathbf{I}_{\varnothing}}} + D(\mathbf{t})\cdot \mathbf{I}_{\varnothing}$$

Because of the benefit from both parts, they both contribute to a probable reduction of "hunting ground" volume. This way they both add to a possible number of individuals.

There is a minimum of this function. The conditions are:

$$n'(\mathbf{I}_\varnothing) = D(\mathbf{t}) - \frac{\mathbf{w}}{\mathbf{I}_\varnothing^2} \cdot e^{\frac{\mathbf{w}}{\mathbf{I}_\varnothing}} = 0, \quad n''(\mathbf{I}_\varnothing) = \left(2\frac{\mathbf{w}}{\mathbf{I}_\varnothing^3} + \frac{\mathbf{w}^2}{\mathbf{I}_\varnothing^4} \right) e^{\frac{\mathbf{w}}{\mathbf{I}_\varnothing}} > 0$$

For a visual impression the graph of a similar function is shown below.

$$y = e^{\frac{1}{x}} + e \cdot x$$

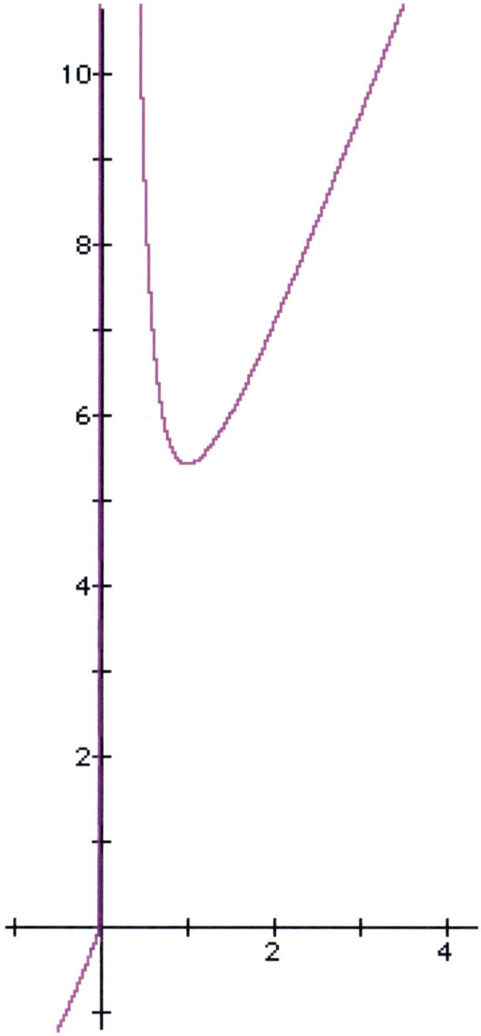

Figure 19. y = exp(1/x) + ex

Because of the included exponential function the minimum condition can not be solved directly. Therefore we consider different scenarios of the **w** to $\mathbf{I}_\varnothing$ ratio.

0) $\mathbf{w} = 0$:

In this case the minimum condition tells as well: $D(\mathbf{t}) = 0$ and further: n = 1.

This condition is well suited to a solely operating individual without any group or structure interaction.

1) $\mathbf{w} \ll \mathbf{I}_\varnothing$:

Because **w** is greater than zero, there is some structuring already there. Because the main part of **w** may be determined by the structuring costs **U**, one has to assume that only a very small group contributes to those very small structure costs. In this case a dedicated leader can not be supported and valuing the small benefits from diversity have to be done by the group members themselves.

In this case 1 can replace the exponential function. Because the minimum for n is searched, we know another parameter. If there is really some interaction, the minimal n has to be equal to 2:

$$\mathrm{n} = 1 + D(\mathbf{t}) \cdot \mathbf{I}_\varnothing = 2, \quad D(\mathbf{t}) = \frac{1}{\mathbf{I}_\varnothing}$$

For those circumstances the minimum condition would tell:

$$D(\mathbf{t}) \approx \frac{\mathbf{w}}{\mathbf{I}_\varnothing^2} \approx 0$$

but this minimum would show as well no interaction as case 0). Therefore the minimal interaction has to be more than the function minimum in this case.

2) $\mathbf{w} \approx \mathbf{I}_\varnothing$:

This condition tells that benefit from structure is enough to equal the contribution of a single group member and paying structuring costs. Therefore a single leader can be separated. In this case the ratio of both results to 1 and the exponential function results to e. The minimum condition changes to:

$$D(\mathbf{t}) = \frac{\mathrm{e}}{\mathbf{I}_\varnothing}$$

The minimum of individuals is: n = 2e > 5 = 4 + 1. This case is equivalent to the function graph above.

There is a very interesting effect by this leader separation. If the job of analysing diversity was not done by the group itself before, the leader placement, which operates like adding only 1 individual, seems to generate suddenly the benefit amount of e individuals. Therefore it is likely that the leader occupies more benefit for selfish use as the others do. This may be justified for paying structuring costs, but opens possibilities of unjust cost and benefit distributions, too.

3) $\mathbf{w} \gg \mathbf{I}_{\varnothing}$:

Only a big group can exist this way, because the structure costs exceed much what a single member could contribute to the structure support. Replacing *D(***t***)* in the formula for n with the minimum condition results to:

$$n_{min} = e^{\frac{\mathbf{w}}{\mathbf{I}_{\varnothing}}} + \frac{\mathbf{w}}{\mathbf{I}_{\varnothing}} \cdot e^{\frac{\mathbf{w}}{\mathbf{I}_{\varnothing}}} = \left(1 + \frac{\mathbf{w}}{\mathbf{I}_{\varnothing}}\right) \cdot e^{\frac{\mathbf{w}}{\mathbf{I}_{\varnothing}}} \approx \frac{\mathbf{w}}{\mathbf{I}_{\varnothing}} \cdot e^{\frac{\mathbf{w}}{\mathbf{I}_{\varnothing}}} = D(\mathbf{t}) \cdot \mathbf{I}_{\varnothing}$$

Therefore a simplificated minimum condition can be expressed in this case, too:

$$D(\mathbf{t}) \leq \frac{n_{min}}{\mathbf{I}_{\varnothing}} \leq \frac{n}{\mathbf{I}_{\varnothing}}$$

The last is equivalent to the pure group interaction formula without any structuring as given before.

The "≤" relation tells further that by a timely increasing of benefit from group interaction the following may occur:

- overflow production
- member increasion (including violent)
- sub- and super-grouping (reformation)
- structuring costs reduction
- increasing influence of members ($\mathbf{qA}_{\varnothing}$) to the structure

This shows again the destabilising character of growth not only for groups as described before but as well for the group + structure combinations.

Uncertainty Relations[56]

The minimal amount of group benefit given at the minimal number of group members equal to two defines the minimal interaction. Using this condition above results to an uncertainty relation using both definitions for *D*.

$$D(\mathbf{t}) = \sqrt{\frac{2\chi_{\varnothing}\int d\mathbf{t}}{\mathbf{u}_{\varnothing}\mathbf{v}\cdot(1+\mathbf{a}) - \mathbf{o}_{\mathrm{R}}\mathbf{V}_{\mathrm{R}}} \cdot \frac{1}{(1+\mathbf{a})}}$$

$$D(\mathbf{t}) \geq \frac{1}{\mathbf{I}_{\varnothing}}$$

$$D^2(\mathbf{t}) = \frac{2\chi_{\varnothing}\mathbf{t}}{\left(\mathbf{u}_{\varnothing}\mathbf{v}\cdot(1+\mathbf{a}) - \mathbf{o}_{\mathrm{R}}\mathbf{V}_{\mathrm{R}}\right)\cdot(1+\mathbf{a})^2} \geq \frac{1}{\mathbf{I}_{\varnothing}^2}$$

$$\chi_{\varnothing}\mathbf{t} \geq \frac{\left(\mathbf{u}_{\varnothing}\mathbf{v}\cdot(1+\mathbf{a}) - \mathbf{o}_{\mathrm{R}}\mathbf{V}_{\mathrm{R}}\right)\cdot(1+\mathbf{a})^2}{2\cdot\mathbf{I}_{\varnothing}^2}$$

All parameters at the right side are defined from the environment (including $\mathbf{I}_{\varnothing} = -\mathrm{k}\mathbf{T}$ as remarked above) or are constants. If the parameters are time independent, one can reduce the right side to a single constant. The remark for the common integral sum as given above for *D* applies as well in this case for the right side of the equation. Therefore the following, nice reduced formula will be valid for the general case, too.

$$\chi_{\varnothing}\mathbf{t} \geq \frac{1}{\mathbf{I}_{\mathbf{h}}}$$

or

$$\mathbf{I}_{\mathbf{h}}\cdot\mathbf{t} \geq \frac{1}{\chi_{\varnothing}} = \mathbf{h}_{\mathbf{B}}$$

The last is an uncertainty relation identical to the standard quantum physical comparing physical dimensions. But now time is related to intellectual properties **(10)**, **(21)**. Further the reciprocal value of the intelligence is the minimised variable not the effect **h** as the first formula tells. Therefore time and association capability are the conjugated variables. If time advance increases, association capability will decrease. This assures a finite reaction effort to any event.

[56] Uncertainty related references are: **(34)**, **(35)**, **(40)**, **(50)**, **(79)**, **(83)**, **(88)** and **(107)**.

Consider this:

$$\mathbf{t} \geq \frac{1}{\chi_{\varnothing}\mathbf{I}_{\mathbf{h}}}$$

If one would measure the reaction value by counting intellectual quantum operations instead of measuring reaction time, then equal events would need an equal amount of intellectual quanta. But a high intellectual activity would generate more quanta compared to low activity, what results to the psychological measurement (impression) of a smaller amount of time past, although an external measurement seem to contradict, but it is a different system of relation. The external relation system is the only one, on which people commonly rely. Therefore time advance seems to be more rapid during high intellectual activity compared to low activity. **[U]**

Because of the reality of those impressions for humans, the conclusion is that intellectual time measurement is dependent to intellectual quantum counting. The result could be expressed in a more radical way:

Time and therefore as well age depends on the intellectual activity during live **(10)**, **(21)**. But this dependence would be valid not only for nervous cells, but as well for other kinds. Therefore you should not neglect sportive activity. On the other hand a high activity may result to a higher repair and replacement need by a more frequent use. Where is the optimum?

Capturing the Mind

The combined formula of the number of group + structure members expands to:

$$n \geq e^{\frac{U}{qA_{\varnothing}I_{\varnothing}}} + \sqrt{\frac{2\chi_{\varnothing}\int dt}{\mathbf{u}_{\varnothing}\mathbf{v}\cdot(1+\mathbf{a})-\mathbf{o}_R\mathbf{V}_R}\cdot\frac{1}{(1+\mathbf{a})}\cdot\mathbf{I}_{\varnothing}}$$

The left part of the sum is related to (**TS**) and the right part is related to (**pV**).

Benefit surplus from diversity (disorder) increases, if **w** increases. Benefit surplus from group interaction (order) increases, if hunting ground benefit is nearly completely spend for communication costs and if association capability or time increases.

For a fixed number n order is increased, if disorder decreases and vice versa. This can be applied to the verbal descriptions named at the first paragraph of this chapter:

	order	**disorder**
•	axiomatic	freedom of thinking
•	stability	creativity
•	group structure	benefit kind
•	faith	hesitation
•	inside	outside
•	consumption	production
•	**pV**	**TS**
•	seriousness	joking[57]
•	happiness	sorrow
•	elder people	youngsters

[57] There is a very complete description of psychological effects by joking: **(50)**. The following summary tells, how tight in coincidence this relative old publication is to this book:
The simple seriousness – joking relation does not analyse details, but **(50)** does. It seems that a wit opens a complete substructure of the same systematic as deduced before. The two basic principles of a wit are first saving of psychological effort (**pV**, pages: 34, 52, 96, 107, 120) and second sense from nonsense or freedom of thinking (**TS**, pages: 34, 46, 52, 97, 103, 106, 107). Further attributes are complementarity (page 101), dialog (the wit as a gift, pages 116 and 120), non-linearity (more as the sum of the parts, page 110) and the uncertainty (page 107). The laughter as a result of the wit indicates to my opinion the reception of a particle. The only critics, which I have to tell, is that there is an unclear definition of "psychological effort" and of "energy levels". But a clear definition of "benefit" by the identity to a negative "effect" as defined by physics is only possible by a clear understanding of artificial information processing, which was not developed before 1940. Other psycho-philosophical references are: **(22)**, **(41)**, **(76)** and **(101)**.

One can not maximise or minimise both parts of the pairs above at the same time.

The uncertainty relation above results to dedicated energy levels of interacting individuals. Finding this behaviour all over nature tells that humans and other complex structured individuals are members of the family of elementary particles. This means further that our experience of the world by information processing leads to granularity of reality and vice versa, because it is accompanied with the ever lasting fight and co-operation between order and disorder.

Looking at the need for axiomatic (order) out of freedom of thinking (disorder) we seem to turn in cycle deductions. It is as well true that we always shall get a quantum world **(169)** by using axiomatic deductions, as the assumption of a quantum world with following evolution **(42)** will lead to (in our case) human axiomatic logic as a description tool.

Is there any possibility to escape? Before this chapter I always thought that humans are able to break any endless looping and are therefore not like a Turing machine[58]. But I have to change this opinion **(107)**, **(143)**. More information about Turing like machines follows during the next main chapter.

Quantum Energy Levels

To get some standard physical values we have to do the change of view from inside to outside as described above. This means replacing inside variables by outside variables using:

$$\mathbf{I}_{\varnothing} = -\mathrm{k}\mathbf{T}$$

The formula for n:

$$n \geq e^{\frac{\mathbf{U}}{q\mathbf{A}_{\varnothing}\mathbf{I}_{\varnothing}}} + \sqrt{\frac{2\chi_{\varnothing}\int dt}{\mathbf{u}_{\varnothing}\mathbf{v}\cdot(1+\mathbf{a}) - \mathbf{o}_{R}\mathbf{V}_{R}} \cdot \frac{1}{(1+\mathbf{a})} \cdot \mathbf{I}_{\varnothing}}$$

needs to stay positive. Structuring costs **U** have to be replaced by some structure dependent energy take out: -$\mathbf{U}'$. The environment looses the amount related to the potentials to the consuming individual: -$\mathbf{u}_{\varnothing}'$, -$\mathbf{o}_{R}'$. Association capability is replaced by a reciprocal effect, which describes take out from the environment by communicative stimulation: -$\chi_{\varnothing}'$. The square root dependence was deduced from a quadratic equation above. The negative square root is as well a solution and has to be chosen in the case of the outside view.

---

[58] Turing has made evident that no machine, which functions by logical principles, can recognise that it operates at an endless loop for stopping then. Humans additionally seem to be able to recognise the loop, but nevertheless without the possibility to stop! Does the difference depend on the in- / outside position?

The change results to:

$$n \geq e^{\frac{-\mathbf{U}'}{q\mathbf{A}_{\varnothing}(-\mathbf{kT})}} - \sqrt{\frac{-2\chi'_{\varnothing}\int dt}{-\mathbf{u}'_{\varnothing}\mathbf{v}\cdot(1+\mathbf{a})+\mathbf{o}'_{R}\mathbf{V}_{R}}\cdot\frac{1}{(1+\mathbf{a})}\cdot(-\mathbf{kT})}$$

$$n \leq e^{\frac{\mathbf{U}'}{q\mathbf{A}_{\varnothing}\mathbf{kT}}} + \sqrt{\frac{2\chi'_{\varnothing}\int dt}{\mathbf{u}'_{\varnothing}\mathbf{v}\cdot(1+\mathbf{a})-\mathbf{o}'_{R}\mathbf{V}_{R}}\cdot\frac{1}{(1+\mathbf{a})}\cdot\mathbf{kT}}$$

One should recognise the change of the relational operator to "≤", which is caused by multiplying the structures stability condition by -1. Clearing the minus signs at the exponent does this implicitly.

The multiple scenarios above tell that the quantum energy values for small n are simply:

$$\mathbf{E}_n^{pV} \approx \frac{\mathbf{kT}}{n-1}$$

For big n the determining formula is:

$$n < e^{\frac{\mathbf{w}'}{\mathbf{kT}}},\ \mathbf{E}_n^{TS} = \mathbf{w}' > ln(n)\cdot\mathbf{kT}$$

The sum for a specific level can be estimated to be:

$$\mathbf{E}_n = \mathbf{E}_n^{pV} + \mathbf{E}_n^{TS} > \left(\frac{1}{n-1} + ln(n)\right)\cdot\mathbf{kT}$$

because the parts have a contrasting, asymptotic behaviour.

For a real value of **E** one needs information about the externally defined temperature difference. But our suns surface temperature, which is around 5000K, should give an upper bound. For the base level at n = 2 without valuing of the diversity part this results to:

$$\mathbf{E}_2 = 1.380662\cdot 10^{-23}\,\frac{J}{K}\cdot 5000K \approx 5\cdot 10^{-20}\,J$$

For the human environment a convenient temperature is around 300K:

$$\mathbf{E}_2 \approx 3\cdot 10^{-21}\,J$$

It is interesting to compare the energy of the base level of a hydrogen atom:

$$\mathbf{E}_1 = 2.18\cdot 10^{-18}\,J$$

Time Granularity

If we consider the effect quantum given by physical theories with the value:

$$\frac{\mathbf{h}}{2\pi} = 1.055 \cdot 10^{-34}\,\mathrm{Js}$$

and extend this with the deduced energy quantum above:

$$\mathbf{E}_2 \approx 3 \cdot 10^{-21}\,\mathrm{J}$$

then we get a relation for the minimal time quantum:

$$\mathbf{t}_\mathbf{h} \approx \frac{1 \cdot 10^{-34}\,\mathrm{Js}}{3 \cdot 10^{-21}\,\mathrm{J}} = 3 \cdot 10^{-14}\,\mathrm{s}$$

It is important to remember that the intelligence = energy quantum is dependent to some externally defined temperature difference. Therefore the values above are something typically for humans or computers. For the last a maximal meaningful operating frequency of around 30.000GHz would result.

Let us consider actual assumptions of parameters short after the big bang **(148)**:

$$\mathbf{T} \approx 1 \cdot 10^{32}\,\mathrm{K}$$

at:

$$\mathbf{t} \approx 1 \cdot 10^{-43}\,\mathrm{s}.$$

The first parameter results to the energy quantum of:

$$\mathbf{E} = 1.380662 \cdot 10^{-23}\,\frac{\mathrm{J}}{\mathrm{K}} \cdot 10^{32}\,\mathrm{K} \approx 1 \cdot 10^{9}\,\mathrm{J}$$

The temperature amount determines this minimal time quantum:

$$\mathbf{t}_\mathbf{h} \approx \frac{1 \cdot 10^{-34}\,\mathrm{Js}}{1 \cdot 10^{9}\,\mathrm{J}} = 1 \cdot 10^{-43}\,\mathrm{s}$$

This is exactly the same magnitude of time as was given as the second cosmological parameter related to the temperature at this time. I am very surprised about this coincidence. At the Internet **(139)** I found the term “Planck time” for this value and I assume that cosmologists have determined this time in a similar way. But the important news from this theory is that one can never go further back into the past of the universe, because it describes really the first occurrence of a time quantum, which is of this amount.

Going beyond the frame of this essay I assume that another uncertainty relation can be determined, where the time quantum is directly given and not as indirectly deduced as above. Today I have no idea how to do this, but I hope that the indirect deduction results to stimulation of further efforts.

Cosmology[59]

There is another very interesting result, if intelligence is negative energy derived from consumption. What is the energy sum of production and consumption? If there would be no intelligence, cooling down would be much less effective. Does standard cosmology count the right energy sum of the universe? If particle radiation occurs by information processing, how does this affect the universe?

The negativity of the energy consumption tells that there is an equivalent reduction of mass by Einstein´s law:

$$\mathbf{E} = \mathbf{m} \cdot c^2$$

Which results in our case to:

$$\frac{\mathbf{I}}{c^2} = -\mathbf{m}$$

The recent cosmological research needs the assumption of a positive cosmological constant, which is equivalent to an anti-gravitation, to get theory in coincidence with observations **(90)**. The homogeneous distribution all over the universe could tell that not yet materially captured anti-gravitational particles are there over all.

If we assume that anti-gravitational communication is possible for every standard elementary particle, then structuring may be neglectable at start of the big bang, because of the high temperature, but a single big group has to be assumed as well. In parallel with expansion structuring would easily come by cooling down, but the big group would disintegrate into many **(113)**.

Further there are conclusions related to the development of the universe. If the universe expands endlessly, as it is the common opinion of today in science, then life or any other intelligent behaviour of matter would vanish at least **(91)**. But the assumption of a "cosmological constant" is arbitrary. It can be alternatively defined as a variable parameter indicating the amount of free anti-gravitation particles. Increasion or decreasion of life would be equal to capturing or release of particles. This would result to a changeable expansion behaviour of the universe and the models have to be improved. I can not tell today, what the future dynamics would look like by applying this, but a closed universe could be reinvented. More over stability can be improved by increasing the living beings, whether they are artificial or not. This is the universal profession of humans and any war or desire to reach God by forced dying is very contra productive.

My cosmological education is very small. But looking at the multiple shortcomings of standard cosmology I feel that there could be some enhancement by a thorough application of energy and time granularity as well as effect granularity and further by anti-gravitational aspects of intelligence.

[59] Related philosophical references are: **(30)**, **(45)** and **(72)**.

The frequent use of "anthropological" argumentation[60] by cosmology for example at **(71)** tells that these arguments need a mathematical description. This book is a starting point and for the future the observer's part can not be neglected any more by the implicit assumption, that she/he is not a part of the system.

Parallel to my efforts there are theoretic, cosmological improvements already done. **(122)** shows fundamental coincidence.

[60] More arguments tell: (**10**), and (**21**).

Minimal Information Processing

An Introduction

This chapter was included, because some of the readers may be not familiar with information processing as it occurs in our artificial computers. Because they are artificial, the principles are clearer and easier to understand as information processing in living beings. Nevertheless all those principles are defined by the same basic rules. The extension to biologic functions is possible and will be done later.

People, who have much knowledge about computers, may skip this subchapter. But some recapitulation could be helpful for them, too.

Parts of a Computer

Here we do not want to get into much detail. The main parts are:

- processor or CPU (central processing unit),
- memory,
- user interface,
- energy supply.

Because of the dissipative nature of information processing as seen before, the energy supply needs no further description. The user interface can be identified to be something like sensorial and motoric parts of a natural individual. Today there is much restriction compared to those admirable functions of live, but development goes on. At the first chapters of this book those external sensors were very important. Here we are interested in the remaining other two parts.

It is commendable that those different functions like information storage and information processing are done with very similar constructed electronic base modules. This is very common for most computer freaks and does not cause any thinking about the difference. What a pity! At the chapter "*Gender a Property of Information Processing*" you will get very astonishing and important news derived from this difference.

Computers Memory

At the following CMOS[61] devices are shown. They are the least energy consuming devices and because energy or better benefit (defined as energy consumption multiplied by time) is most important to information processing, they are favourable. More on those energetic aspects can be found at the subchapters below.

[61] CMOS is a short cut for "Complementary Metal Oxide Semiconductor".

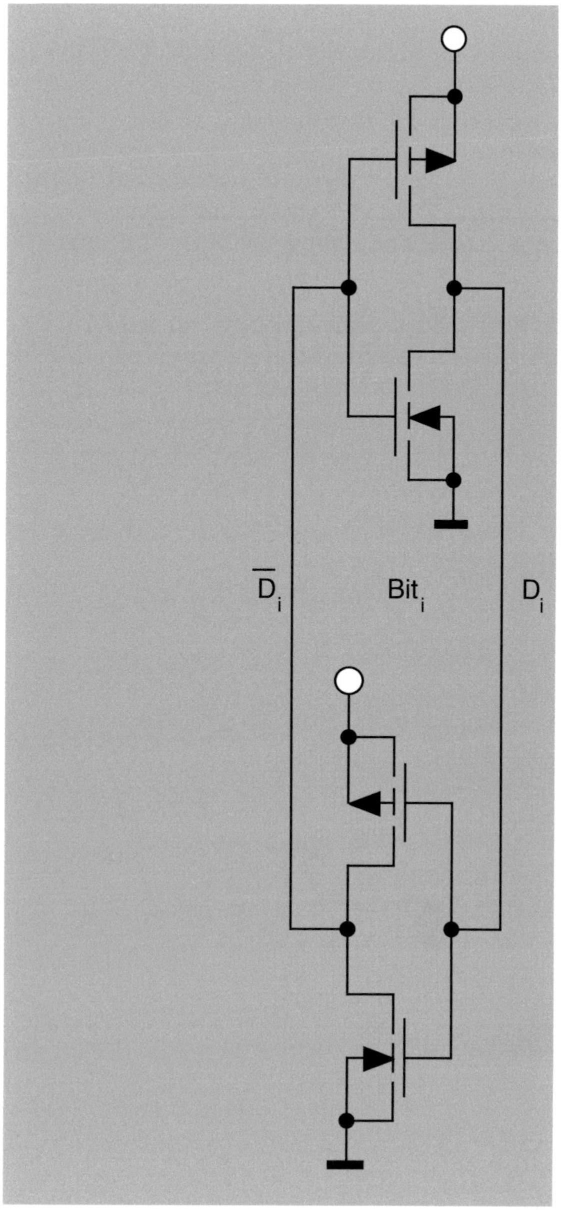

Figure 20. Static One Bit Memory

Functional Description

A detailed description of a single FET[62] is given later. For now it is enough to think about it as an electronic switch. There are two complementary kinds, which have different voltage/current characteristic. One opens at a low voltage at the control input and shows an arrow pointing away from the input. The other kind opens at a high voltage at the control input and shows an arrow pointing to the input line. The placement and connections are done in a way that always the inverse voltage is switched to the output.

Suppose the line D contains some well-defined charge. If the charge is low the corresponding field will open the third FET counted from the top of the graphic. If the charge is high the corresponding field will open the FET at the bottom. For both cases the complementary FET is closed. Therefore line /D is charged reversed to the D line. Now the same procedure happens to the two complementary FETs above and the repeated inversion of the signal causes recharging of the D line, from which we have started.

The two complementary, stable and static voltage connections are shown at the next page.

[62] FET is a short cut for "Field Effect Transistor".

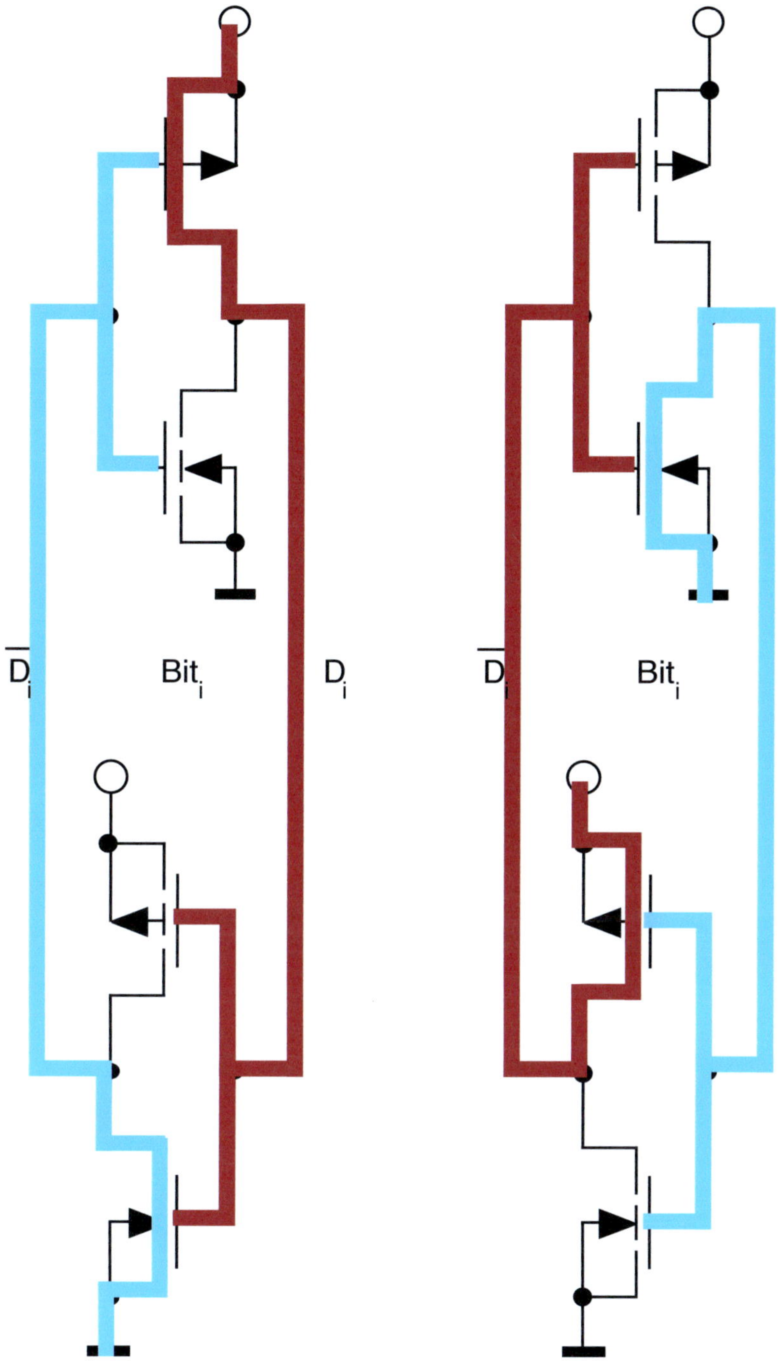

Figure 21. From Left To Right: The "1" State And The "0" State of The D line

During introduction of the static one bit memory, we have found the simplest logic unit, too. It is the inverter. As well the FET pair on top as on bottom of the "Static One Bit Memory" are inverters. The scheme of a single inverter and its truth table is provided here.

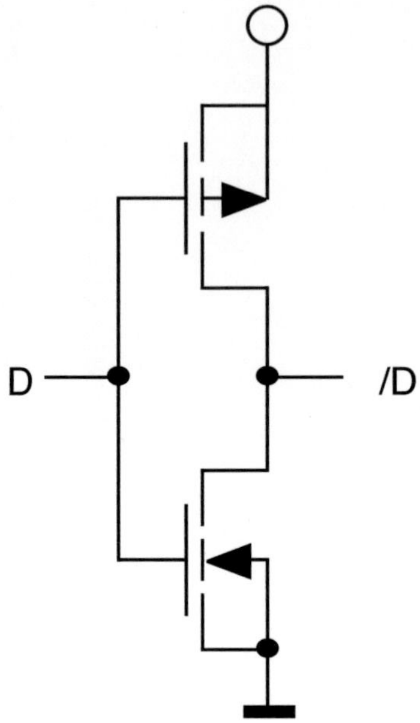

Figure 22. The Inverter.

D (Input)	/D (Output)
0	1
X	=
1	0

This is a symbol schematic for an inverter.

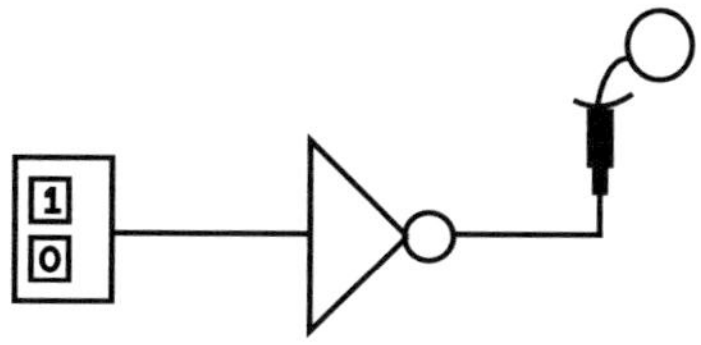

Figure 23. Inverter Schematic.

The changing of the output voltage of an inverter depending on its input voltage is shown at the next graph. 0 and 1 are the two digital logic states as commonly used. X stands for an undefined state. This means that the input voltage is between the switching points of the hysteresis. The logical state is preserved this way. The equality sign "=" describes the behaviour. More on logic units follows below.

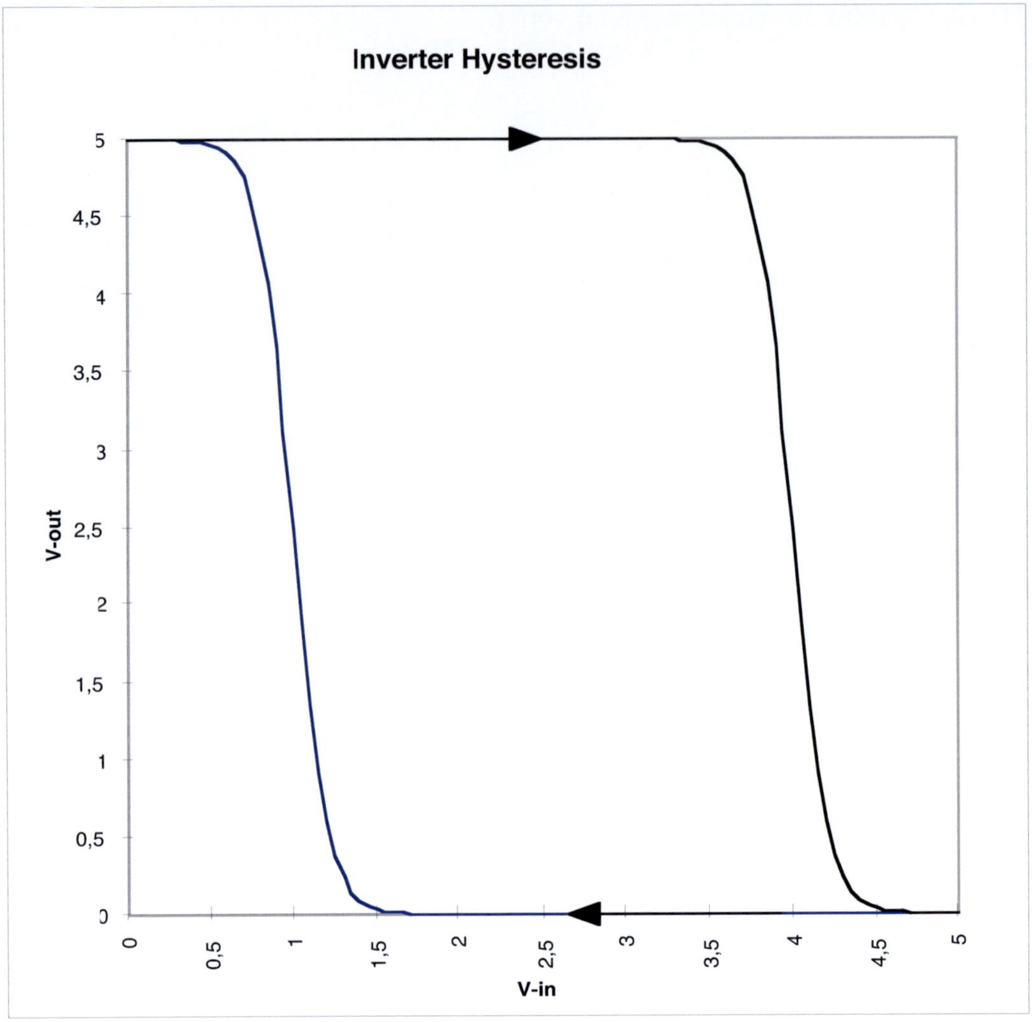

Figure 24. Inverter Hysteresis

It is a matter of the design of the FETs that wide areas of input voltages do not change the output status. If the input is between the switch points, both FETs are closed and the supply voltages are disconnected from the output. Therefore the charge at the output is conserved. CMOS devices are very good in keeping the charge. One could assume that a single inverter would be enough for the data storage. If one neglects any loss for an ideal case, this is true. But charge is lost in a real device, although the loss rate is small for CMOS. More important is the loss by charge distribution during driving connected devices. This is a need, if the stored information should be used in any way. Only the double inverter is self-driving and can deliver further charge into the output, if something gets connected to it. The next graphs show, how this is done.

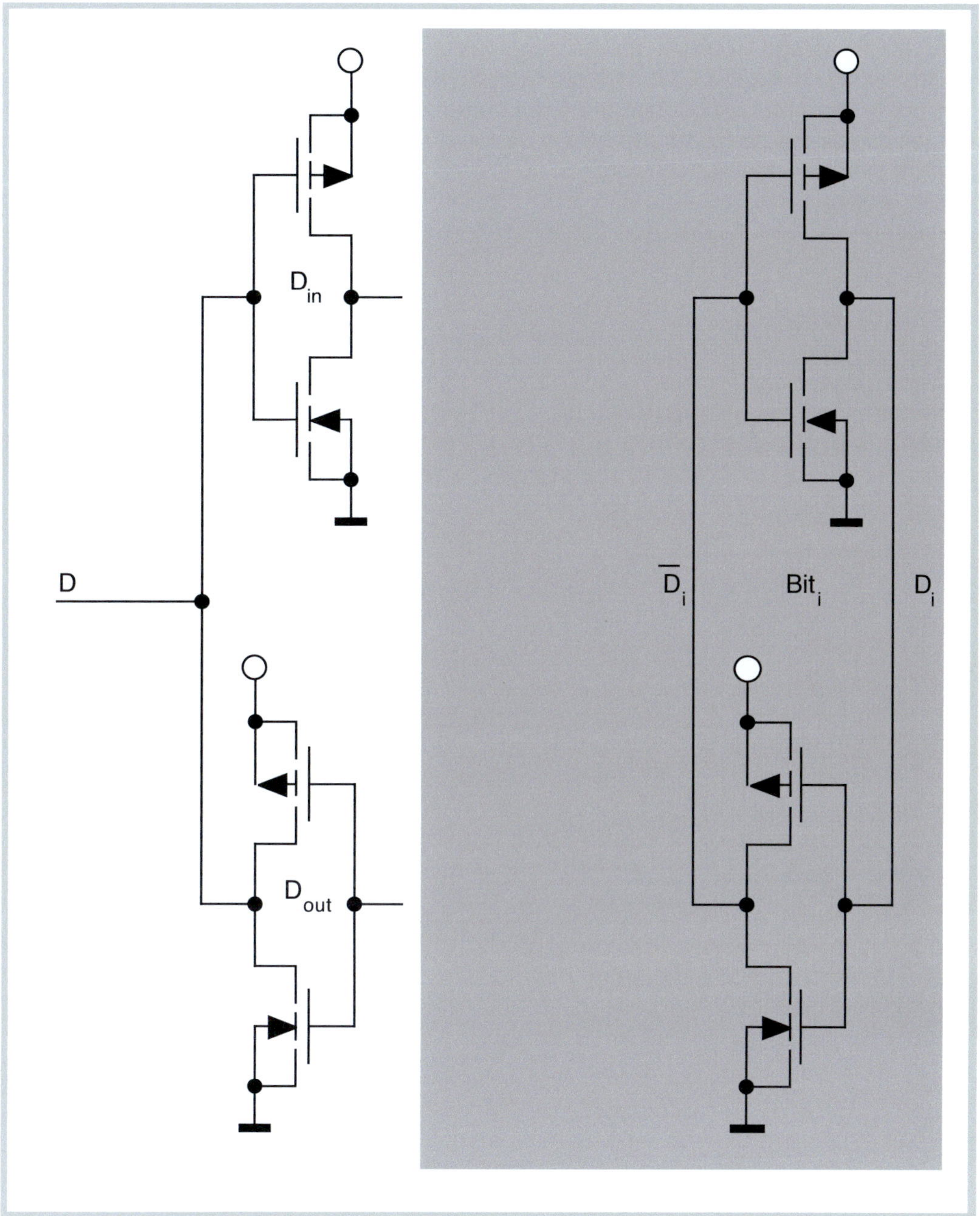

Figure 25. Memory with I/O Unit

For using some memory one has to contact it to the external world. The greyed area of the graphs shows the storage part. This part could be multiplied for multiple bits of storage. The white area shows the driver unit for external access. Typically only one unit is needed for a single data line. In personal computers of today the databus is 32 to 128 bits wide. If only memory chips are needed, then this number is exactly the number of driver units needed on the memory side. There will be the same number of drivers on the processor side. Compared with megabytes of storage this number is very small.

There are more than only storage devices around, which are identified by special addresses. But all have a small number of I/O driving units. Beyond defining the applied chip device addresses are need inside the memory to access a specific bit or bit group.

Another important property is the direction of information flow. One has to specify, whether data is read from the memory or written to it. During the read operation a back coupling to the storage is allowed. During the write operation the output must be suppressed, because otherwise the incoming data may be disturbed, if the logic levels are different. The following graph shows two internal lines named $/W_i$ and $/R_i$. Both are only used for accessing this special bit. The index i indicates that meaning. This lines are results of a demultiplexing of the external derived address lines with following ORing to the externally provided global /W and /R lines indicating write or read access. The global /W line directly accesses the I/O unit by suppressing data output from the memory during the write and it is shown as a third new line. The dashes upon the names of the lines indicate active low signals. Those signal levels are preferred by TTL[63] convention. The both internal access lines connect the memory to the I/O driving unit or disconnect, if another storage unit should be accessed. During the write operation not only the external output is suppressed. The internal back coupling is as well broken to assure that the internal D line is only prepared by the externally given D data.

For a proper operation the timing of the different signals is another important property. For example the write enable line /W should be only active during a period were data on D is kept stable and valid. But those considerations would go beyond the scope of this introduction.

---

[63] TTL is a short cut for “Transistor to Transistor Logic”. For elder so-called “bipolar” devices the high level is less energy consuming as the low level. Signals, which do not change frequently, should be made active low therefore.

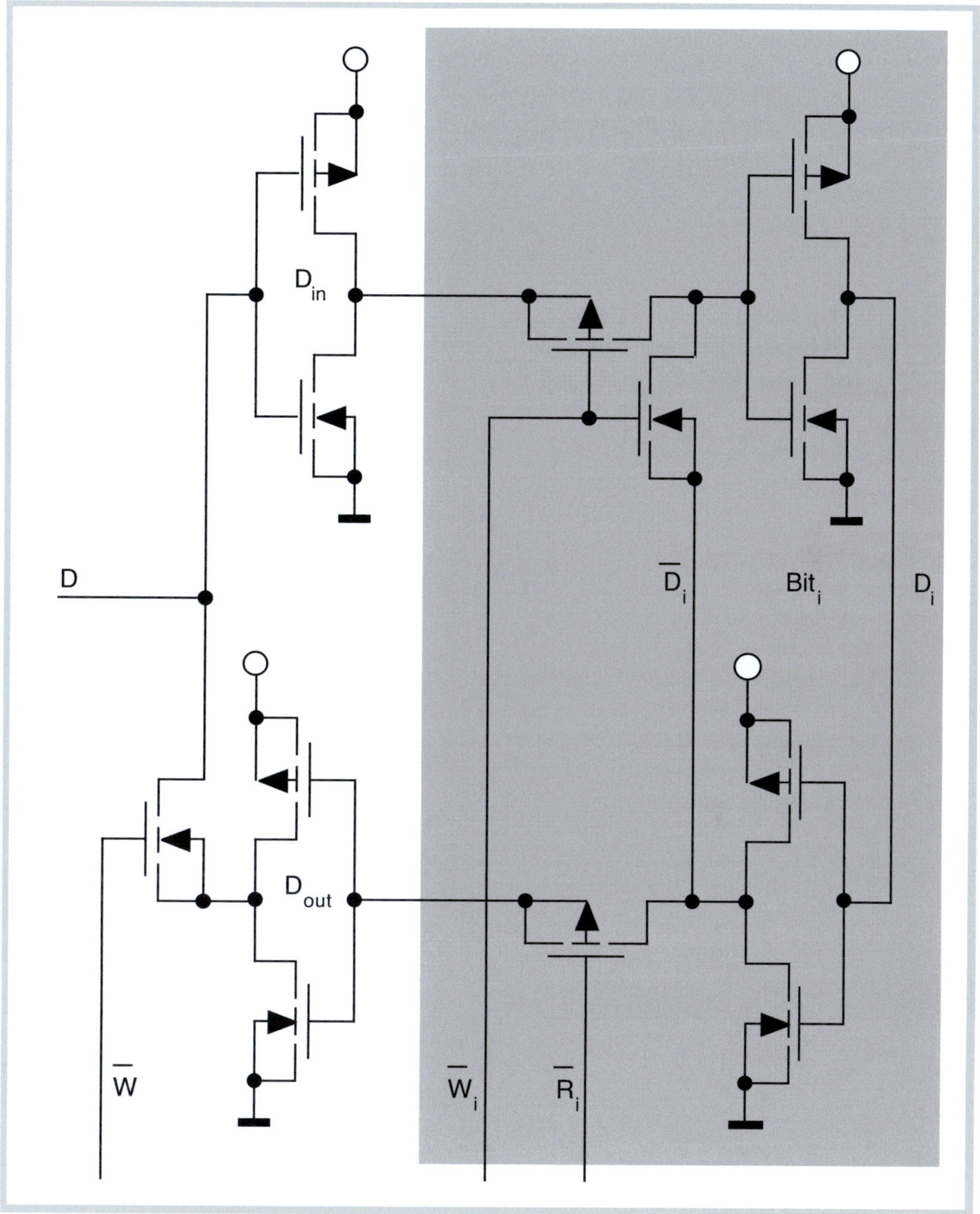

Figure 26. Reading, Writing and Internal Connections

It is possible to save some space by replacing the static memory by a condensator. This results to a higher number of bits per chip, but needs a little more complicated way of operation.

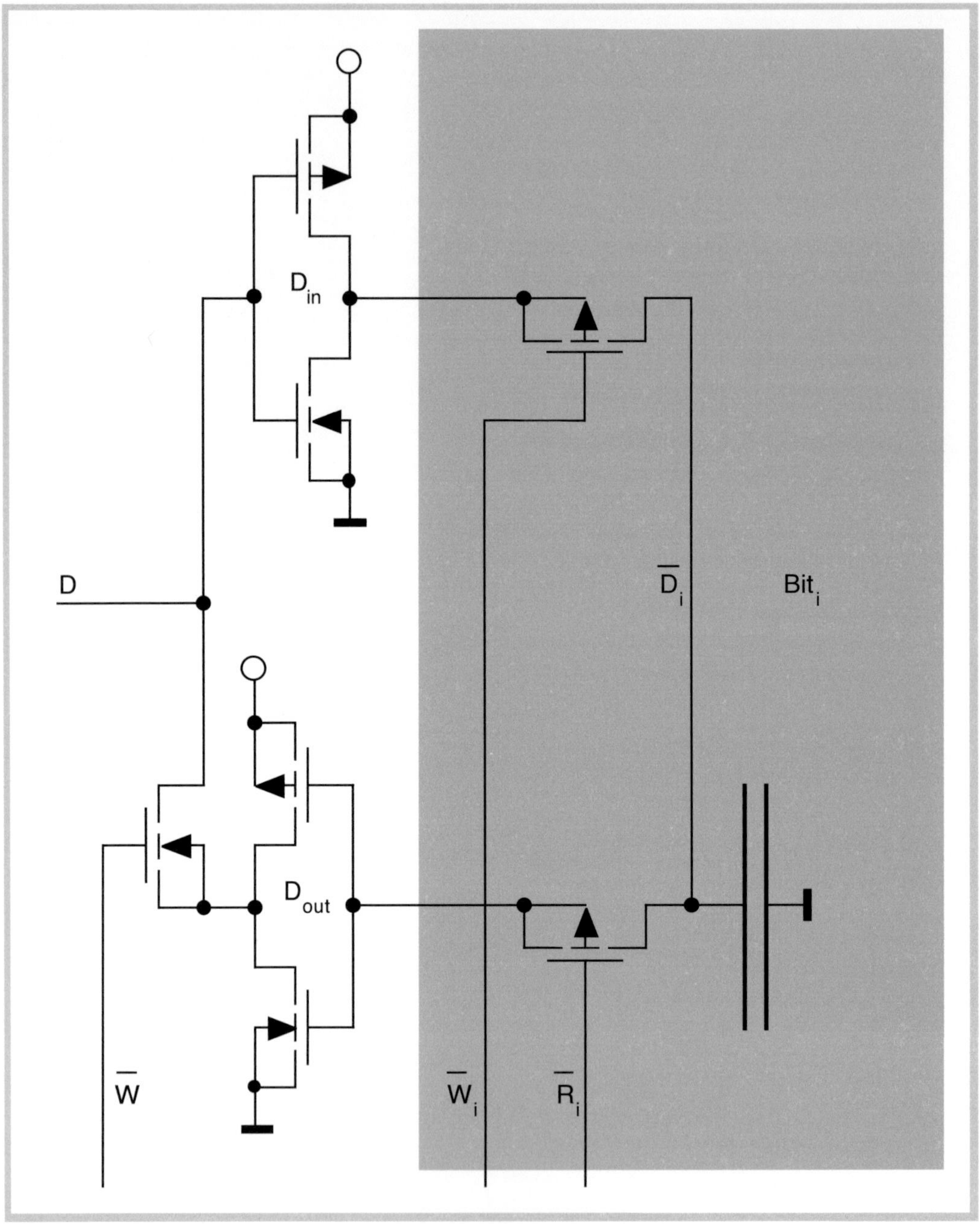

Figure 27. CMOS Dynamic Memory

The condensator has no direct back coupling. Therefore charge gets lost by time, because of its non-ideal behaviour. Some refreshing is needed to maintain the information. If the internal read and write lines become active together and external data is disconnected, the graph shows a back coupling double inverter build only by the I/O driving unit. Doing so recharges the condensator to the logic level it have had before.

Arithmetic Logic Units

An arithmetic logic unit (shortcut ALU) is the main part of a computer CPU. We do not look at other parts of the CPU here. The other parts are less important, because they only support the information processing operation. This operation is done in the ALU. One can be more common, if one recognises that any information processing has similar but perhaps smaller properties. For example above we have mentioned some demultiplexing or alike, which may occur by the address logic of a memory chip or externally. Vice versa the CPU has some memory parts as well for the direct access to operands.

The only difference of a CPU to some external logic is the always needed and forced frequent operation by some clock pulsing, which can be understood as information pumping. Typically the effects of information processing by the CPU result to information pumping through external logic as well, but likely at a lower frequency.

Before we have analysed memory in detail. Now only the processing of information is examined. In fact there are only three base types of logic units needed, from which every digital information processing can be build. The first is the already known inverter. Its properties have been examined before. For now we conclude that this logic unit has as well the properties of a memory, because information is only complemented but not destroyed. This is important for the next chapter, where some more properties will be decovered.

The two other logic units are the NOR and the NAND gate. The OR and AND operations combine two input signals to one output signal according to this truth tables:

OR Logic:

Input 1	Input 2	Output Q
0	0	0
0	1	1
1	0	1
1	1	1

AND Logic:

Input 1	Input 2	Output Q
0	0	0
0	1	0
1	0	0
1	1	1

A little more complicated measured by human understanding are the NOR and NAND, because the output is inverted compared to the tables above.

NOR Logic:

Input 1	Input 2	Output Q
0	0	1
0	1	0
1	0	0
1	1	0

NAND Logic:

Input 1	Input 2	Output Q
0	0	1
0	1	1
1	0	1
1	1	0

The next meaningful but a little more complex and rearranged FET combination compared to the inverter are the NOR and the NAND gate not an OR or AND device. Another inverter has to be placed at the output to get the true OR or AND gate.

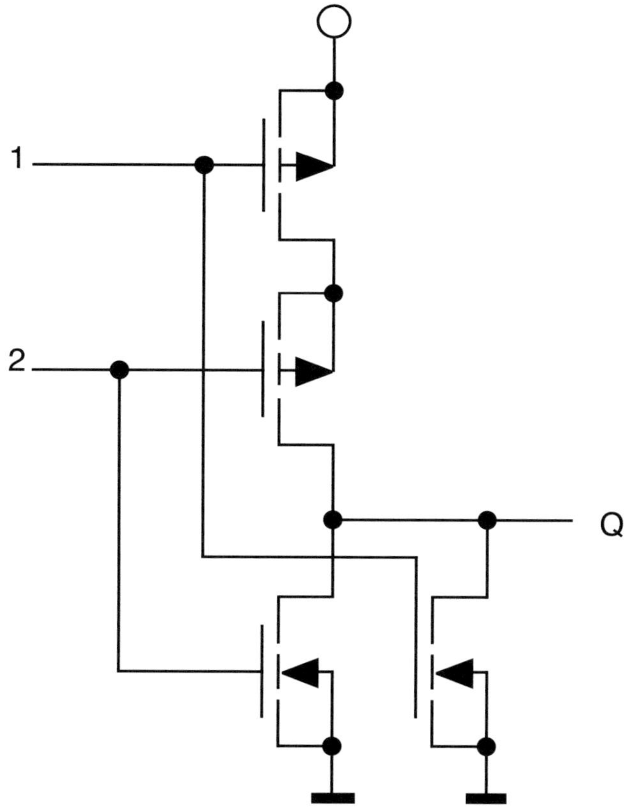

Figure 28. The NOR Gate

At first look the NOR device seems to be similar to the inverter only some duplication is done to a starting pair. But those extensions are not made in an equal way and this is very important. One can recognise a parallel connection of the two FETs at the bottom and a serial connection of the two at the top. Further a useful input connection is needed for driving always two FETs but always one on top and one on bottom.

The graphic above can be found in the literature **(158)**, but this way the device is never constructed on the chip. First the "drains" equal to the Q outputs of the bottom FETs are a single implantation. But more important is that never two distinct serial FETs are produced. A single FET with a split gate works as well. The graphic changes this way:

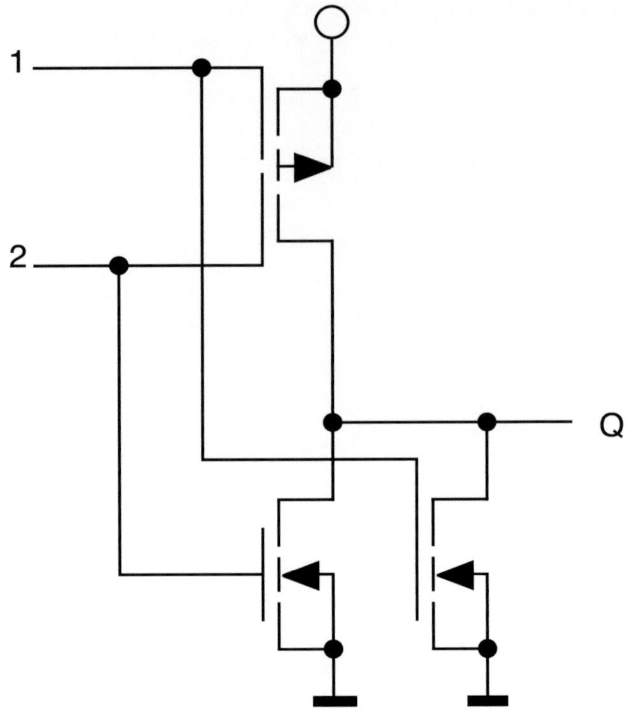

Figure 29. The Optimised NOR Gate.

If you think that those differences are only a matter of optimisation for production, you are wrong! But please wait until the next chapter for an explanation.

For completeness the same two graphics for the NAND gate follow. There are no principle constructive differences with the exception that all is turned upside down.

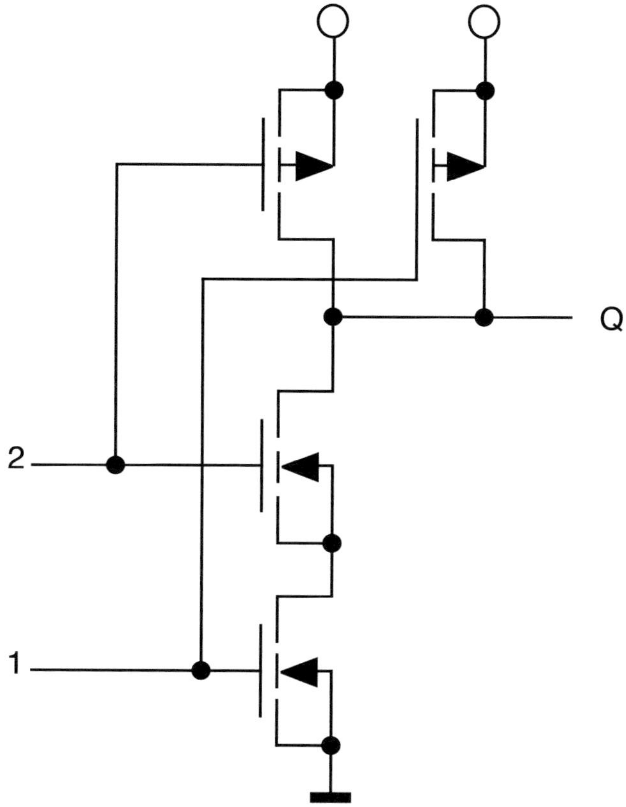

Figure 30. The NAND Gate.

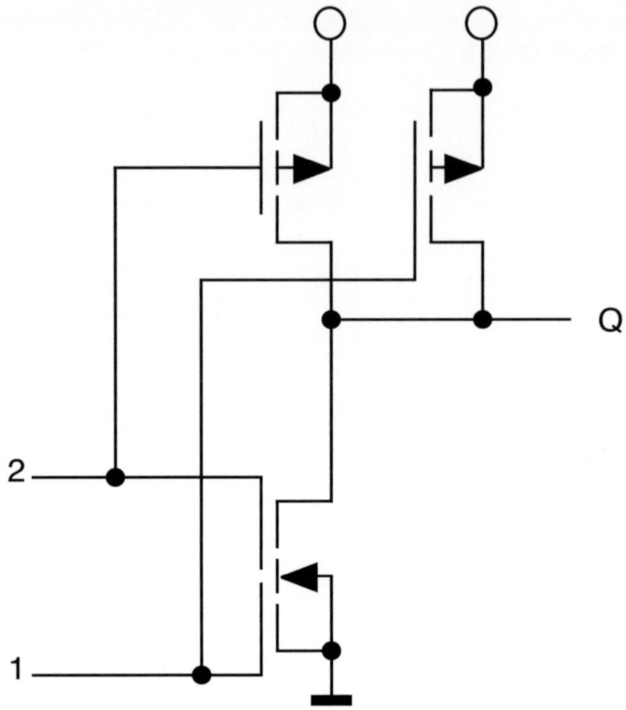

Figure 31. The Optimised NAND Gate.

The following constructions derive the AND and OR from the basic devices above.

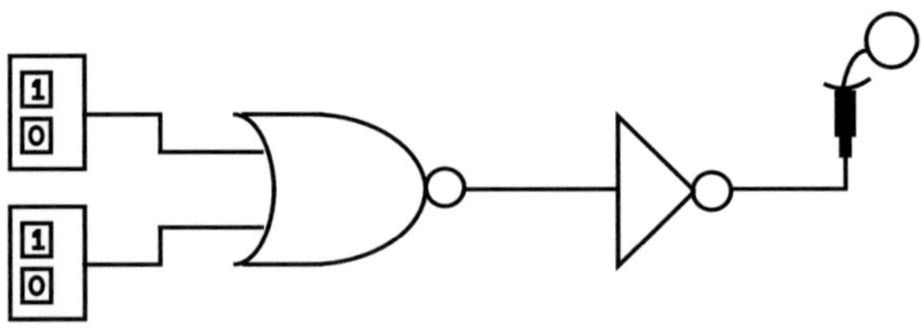

Figure 32. OR from NOR.

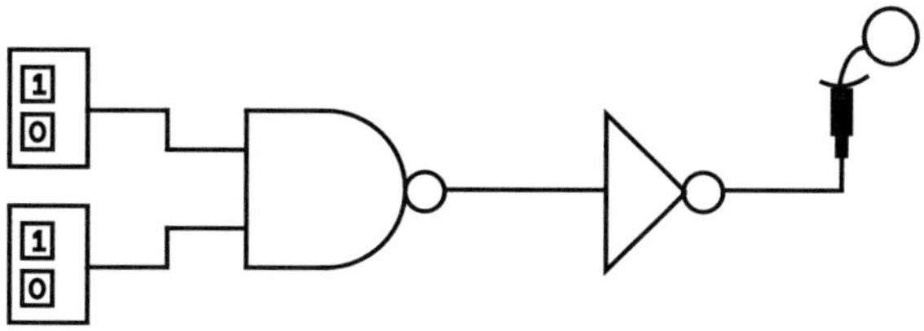

Figure 33. AND from NAND.

A combination of three FETs has no meaning for a useful logic operation, as shown in the following truth table. But this has meaning for the considerations in the next chapter.

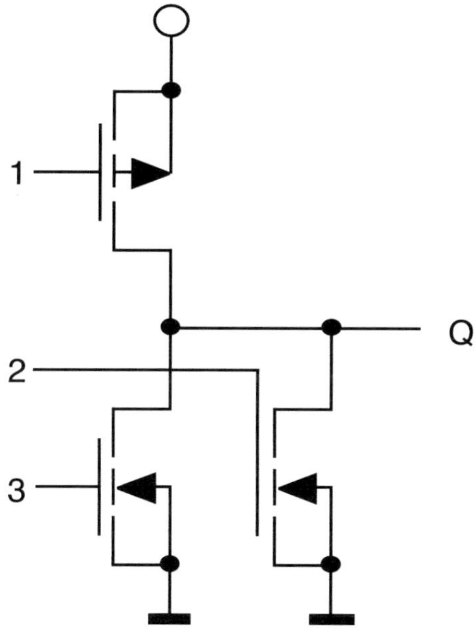

Figure 34. Three FETs Schematic (NOR).

No logic, no memory, partly NOR constructed:

Input 1	Input 2	Input 3	Output Q
0	0 or X	0 or X	1
0	0 or X	1	X
0	1	0 or X	X
0	1	1	X
1 or X	0 or X	0 or X	=
1 or X	0 or X	1	0
1 or X	1	0 or X	0
1 or X	1	1	0

Dependent to the wiring of FET drains to the output one can recognise a badly designed NOR or NAND gate. The last would be reversed upside down to the one described above. Therefore an extra discussion is not needed.

The truth table shows that as well the memory property of the inverter has vanished, as it is the case for proper operating logic units. But a distinct digital logic operation is not recognisable, because of the possibility of undefined output values.

Why is such a device worth any discussion? The reason is given by an optical comparison of this badly designed NOR to the optimised NOR. This follows later, because the introduction is not complete yet.

Derivation of Arithmetic Functionality

With the base modules above one can build a XOR gate by complementing the both inputs, ANDing them two times with the original other input and ORing both pre-results to get the output value. An output of 1 would signal difference of inputs. An output of 0 would signal equality of inputs.

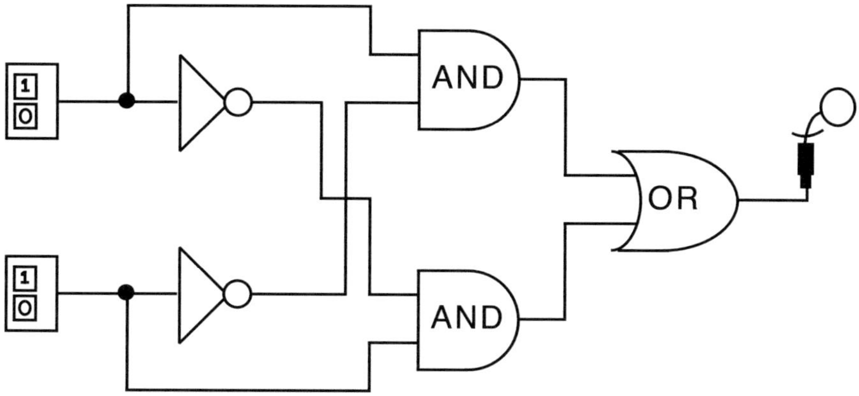

Figure 35. XOR from 2 ANDs and 1 OR.

An alternative producing the same results and with an optimised number of base devices by deleting of output inverters shows the following graph.

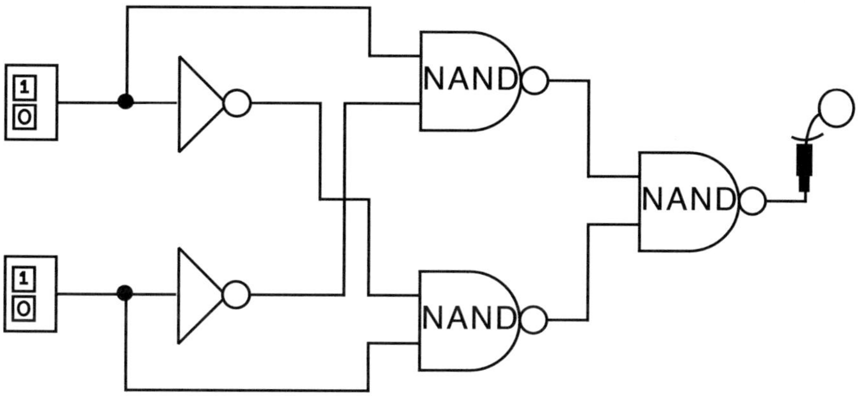

Figure 36. XOR from 3 NANDs.

Changing all NANDs to NORs results to a NXOR, what may be a cost-effective alternative solution as discussed later. **[R]**

XOR Logic:

Input 1	Input 2	Output Q
0	0	0
0	1	1
1	0	1
1	1	0

Adding two bits is at first a XOR operation. By saving the original state of one operand and comparing this to the result by another XOR operation it can be recognised, whether a bit should be carried forward to the next significant bit during a multiple bits adding operation.

Subtraction can be based on addition by arithmetically complementing the subtracting operand. The complementation is only a little more complicated as bit wise inversion and named "the two´s complement".

Comparison is done by direct pattern matching (XOR) for equality tests or by subtraction leading to positive, zero or negative results, what means bigger, equal or smaller as indicators after comparison.

Multiplication is only shifting up of operand bits and adding. The first is more some memory operation as real information processing. This is true for all shift operations, which do not destroy information. Whether information is destroyed or not, depends on the significance of out shifted bits.

Division is made from down shifting, multiplication, subtraction and comparison. It is the most complicated of the standard arithmetic procedures and it is rather an algorithm as a basic operation.

One should consider the relation of memory and logical operations - for example combined to multiplication - to the non-linearity of group interaction (**pV**) (**107**).

All more complicated arithmetic expressions are derived by optimised application of multiples of the former base operations.

Algorithms are built from memory operations and arithmetic expressions combined with flow control. The last means jumping around in program code and not only sequential instruction execution.

The instruction code represents the very big, distinct number, which is related to the informational entropy (**TS**). But using this as the only property of value (**27**) is a mistake.

Minimal Analog Computing

Above the digital world was examined, but for more complex situations like biological individuals it might not be as easy to reduce all to some digital behaviour. Probably this may be possible in principle, but may be a too complicated thing to do.

Analog computing has come out of fashion since the personal computer was introduced, but some reinvention like fuzzy logic was a needed later approach. All of the above-told digital principles and operation units can be generalised for the analog world, too. To achieve this we simply replace the FETs with variable resistors. Such a replacement in reality would typically need a gaining unit, but those details are not of interest for the analog logic operation.

The Inverting Linear Variable Resistor

As for the digital examples logic analog operations need a complemented resistor pair. The very simple behaviour of one is resistance proportional to the input and for the other resistance inverse proportional to the input.

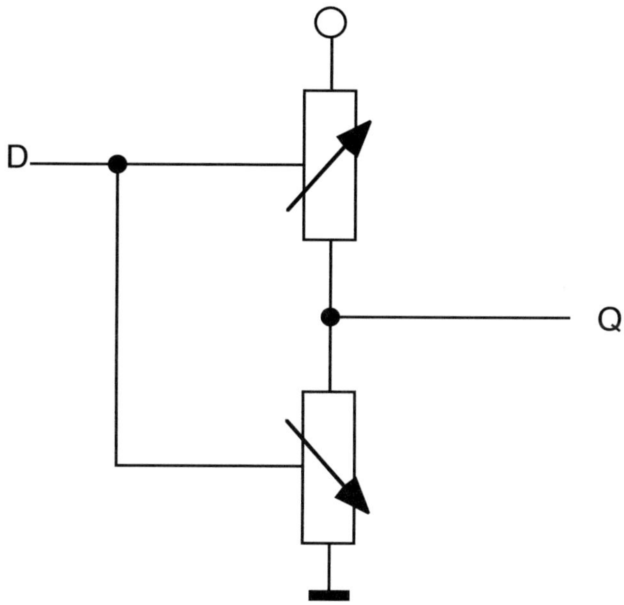

Figure 37. The Analog Inverter.

Instead of the inverter hysteresis in the digital world, we define the following linear response of a pair of variable resistors to an externally controlling input.

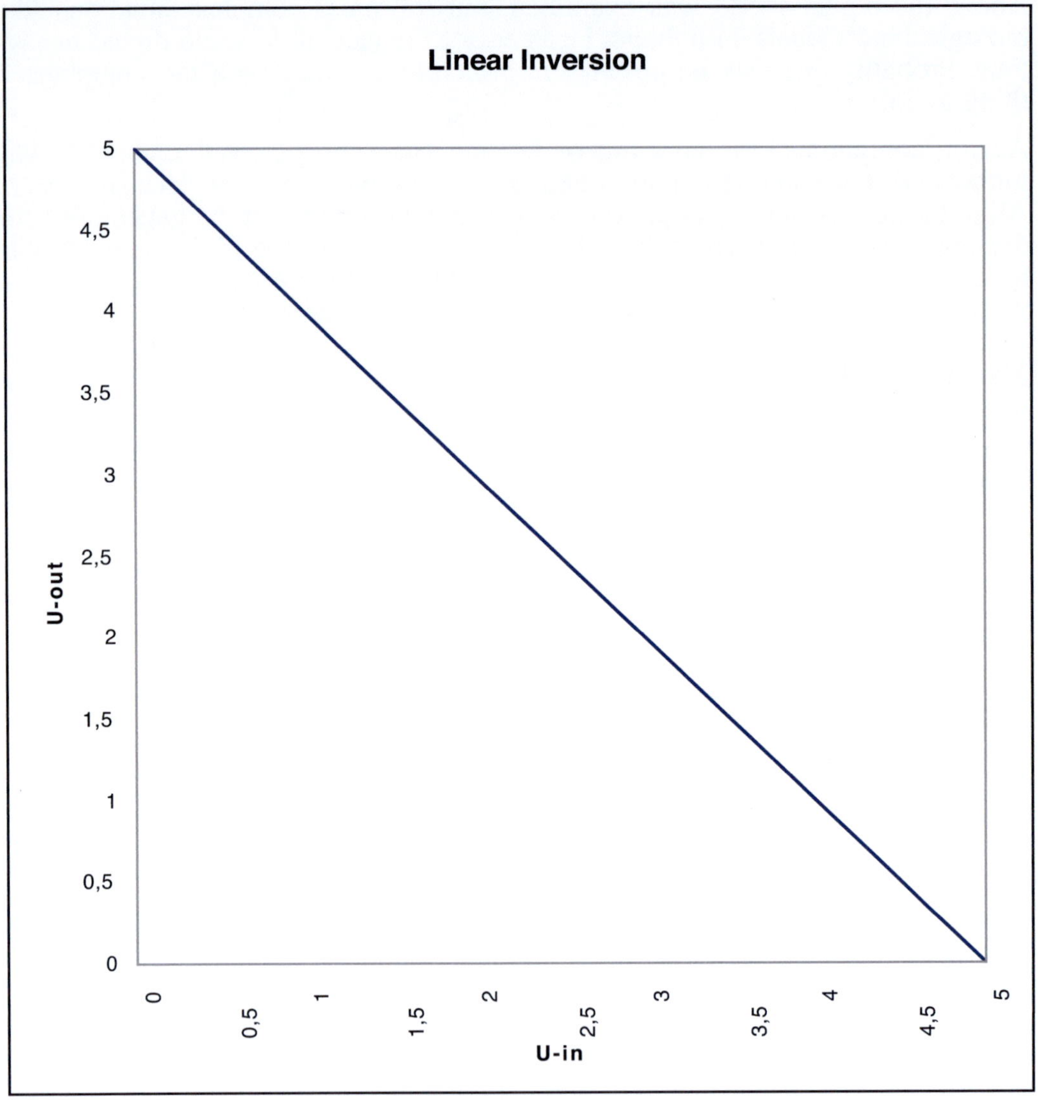

Figure 38. Transfer Characteristic of the Analog Inverter.

The other digital base units can be constructed in an "analog" way as well. The following graphs show how they work.

The Linear NOR

Instead of the digital simplicity a basic NOR like analog operation unit needs this complicate description:

$$\mathbf{U}_{+} = 5\text{V},\ \mathbf{U}_{-} = 0\text{V},\ \mathbf{U}_{\text{D}} = (5-0)\text{V} = 5\text{V}$$

$$\mathbf{R}_{\text{Xs}} = \mathbf{R}_{0} \cdot \frac{\mathbf{U}_{\text{X}}}{\mathbf{U}_{\text{D}}}$$

$$\mathbf{R}_{\text{Xp}} = \mathbf{R}_{0} \cdot \frac{\left(\mathbf{U}_{\text{D}} - \mathbf{U}_{\text{X}}\right)}{\mathbf{V}_{\text{D}}}$$

$$\mathbf{R}_{\text{serial}} = \mathbf{R}_{1\text{s}} + \mathbf{R}_{2\text{s}} = \mathbf{R}_{0} \cdot \frac{\mathbf{U}_{1} + \mathbf{U}_{2}}{\mathbf{U}_{\text{D}}}$$

$$\frac{1}{\mathbf{R}_{\text{parallel}}} = \frac{1}{\mathbf{R}_{1\text{p}}} + \frac{1}{\mathbf{R}_{2\text{p}}} + \ldots$$

$$\mathbf{R}_{\text{parallel}} = \frac{\mathbf{R}_{1\text{p}} \cdot \mathbf{R}_{2\text{p}}}{\mathbf{R}_{1\text{p}} + \mathbf{R}_{2\text{p}}} = \frac{\mathbf{R}_{0} \cdot \left(\mathbf{U}_{\text{D}} - \mathbf{U}_{1}\right) \cdot \left(\mathbf{U}_{\text{D}} - \mathbf{U}_{2}\right)}{\left(2\mathbf{U}_{\text{D}} - \mathbf{U}_{1} - \mathbf{U}_{2}\right) \cdot \mathbf{U}_{\text{D}}}$$

$$\mathbf{U}_{\text{Q}} = \frac{\mathbf{R}_{\text{parallel}}}{\mathbf{R}_{\text{serial}} + \mathbf{R}_{\text{parallel}}} \cdot \mathbf{U}_{\text{D}} = \frac{\dfrac{\mathbf{R}_{1\text{p}} \cdot \mathbf{R}_{2\text{p}}}{\mathbf{R}_{1\text{p}} + \mathbf{R}_{2\text{p}}}}{\mathbf{R}_{1\text{s}} + \mathbf{R}_{2\text{s}} + \dfrac{\mathbf{R}_{1\text{p}} \cdot \mathbf{R}_{2\text{p}}}{\mathbf{R}_{1\text{p}} + \mathbf{R}_{2\text{p}}}} \cdot \mathbf{U}_{\text{D}}$$

$$\mathbf{U}_{\text{Q}} = \frac{\mathbf{R}_{1\text{p}} \cdot \mathbf{R}_{2\text{p}}}{(\mathbf{R}_{1\text{s}} + \mathbf{R}_{2\text{s}}) \cdot (\mathbf{R}_{1\text{p}} + \mathbf{R}_{2\text{p}}) + \mathbf{R}_{1\text{p}} \cdot \mathbf{R}_{2\text{p}}} \cdot \mathbf{U}_{\text{D}}$$

$$\mathbf{U}_{\text{Q}} = \frac{\left(\mathbf{U}_{\text{D}} - \mathbf{U}_{1}\right) \cdot \left(\mathbf{U}_{\text{D}} - \mathbf{U}_{2}\right) \cdot \mathbf{U}_{\text{D}}}{\left(\mathbf{U}_{1} + \mathbf{U}_{2}\right) \cdot \left(\mathbf{U}_{\text{D}} - \mathbf{U}_{1}\right) + \left(\mathbf{U}_{1} + \mathbf{U}_{2} + \left(\mathbf{U}_{\text{D}} - \mathbf{U}_{1}\right)\right) \cdot \left(\mathbf{U}_{\text{D}} - \mathbf{U}_{2}\right)}$$

$$\mathbf{U}_{\text{Q}} = \frac{\mathbf{U}_{\text{D}}^{2} - \mathbf{U}_{\text{D}}\mathbf{U}_{1} - \mathbf{U}_{\text{D}}\mathbf{U}_{2} + \mathbf{U}_{1}\mathbf{U}_{2}}{\mathbf{U}_{\text{D}}^{2} - \mathbf{U}_{1}^{2} - \mathbf{U}_{2}^{2} + \mathbf{U}_{1}\mathbf{U}_{\text{D}} + \mathbf{U}_{2}\mathbf{U}_{\text{D}} - \mathbf{U}_{1}\mathbf{U}_{2}} \cdot \mathbf{U}_{\text{D}}$$

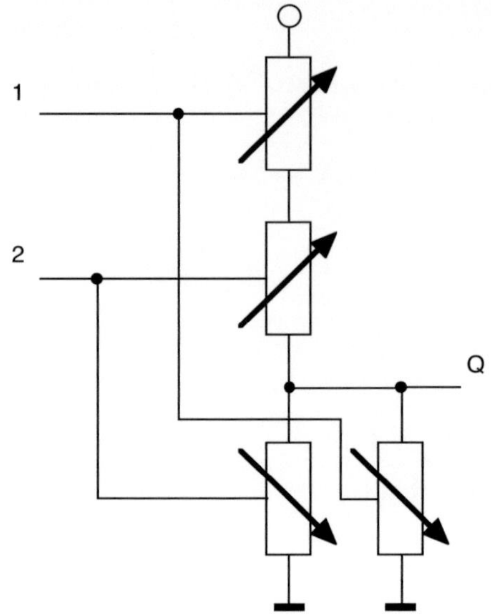

Figure 39. The Linear NOR.

If we assume that mainly some FET produces the resistance with a more linear characteristic as for the digital case, then using split gates for the serial resistance is as well possible as before:

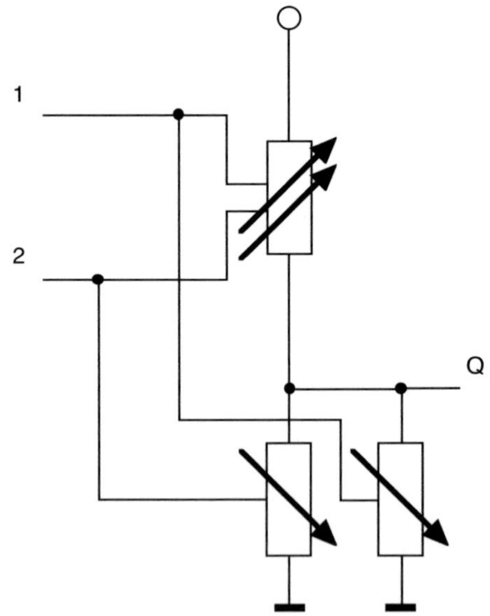

Figure 40. The Linear Optimised NOR.

This is a plot of the transfer characteristic depending to the two different control inputs:

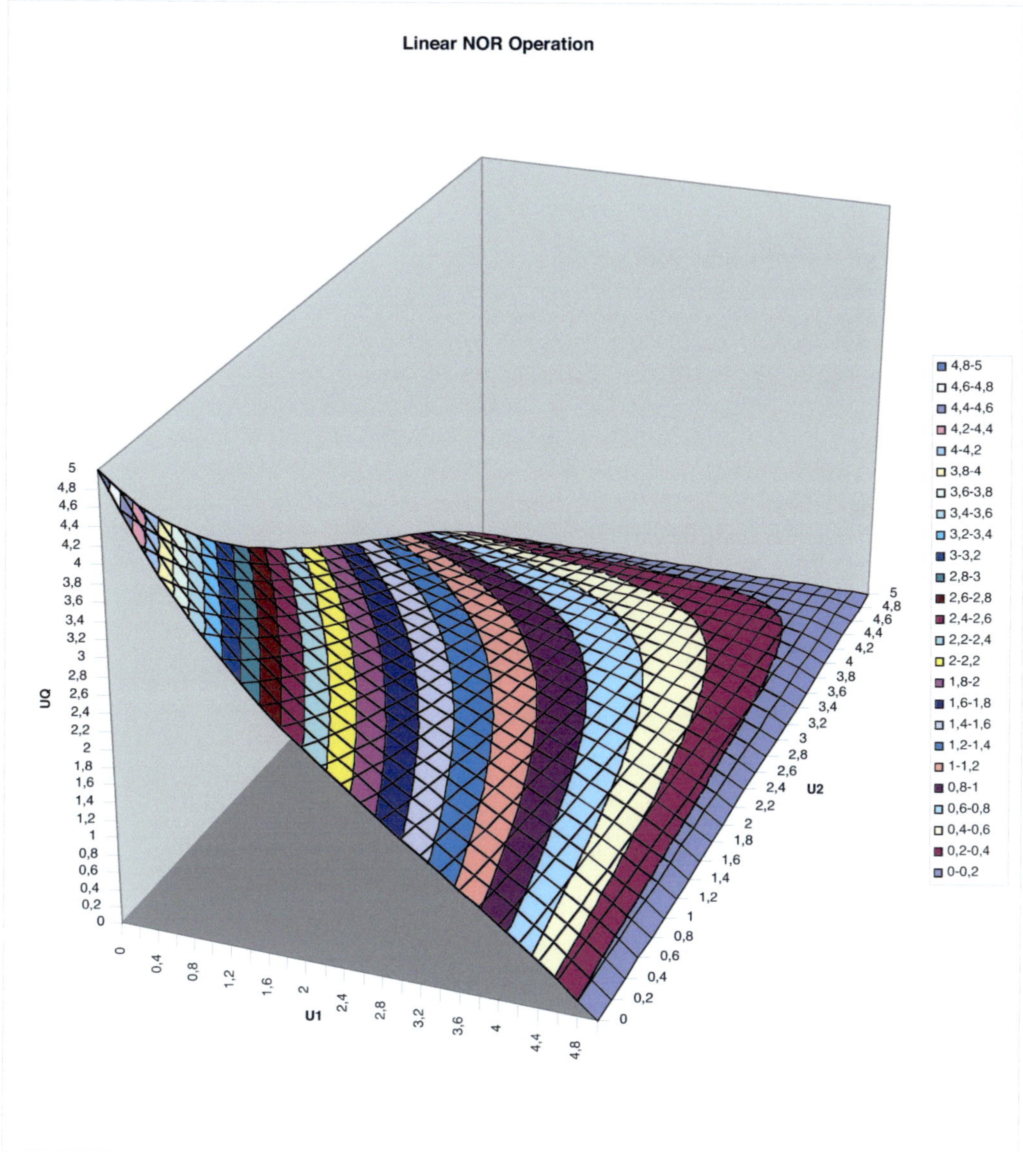

Figure 41. Transfer Characteristic of the Linear NOR Gate.

<u>The Linear NAND</u>

Instead of the digital simplicity a basic NAND like analog operation unit needs this complicate description:

$$\mathbf{U}_+ = 5\text{V},\ \mathbf{U}_- = 0\text{V},\ \mathbf{U}_\text{D} = (5-0)\text{V} = 5\text{V}$$

$$\mathbf{R}_{\text{Xs}} = \mathbf{R}_0 \cdot \frac{(\mathbf{U}_\text{D} - \mathbf{U}_\text{X})}{\mathbf{U}_\text{D}}$$

$$\mathbf{R}_{\text{Xp}} = \mathbf{R}_0 \cdot \frac{\mathbf{U}_\text{X}}{\mathbf{U}_\text{D}}$$

$$\mathbf{R}_{\text{serial}} = \mathbf{R}_{1\text{s}} + \mathbf{R}_{2\text{s}} = \mathbf{R}_0 \cdot \frac{2\mathbf{U}_\text{D} - \mathbf{U}_1 - \mathbf{U}_2}{\mathbf{U}_\text{D}}$$

$$\frac{1}{\mathbf{R}_{\text{parallel}}} = \frac{1}{\mathbf{R}_{1\text{p}}} + \frac{1}{\mathbf{R}_{2\text{p}}} + \ldots$$

$$\mathbf{R}_{\text{parallel}} = \frac{\mathbf{R}_{1\text{p}} \cdot \mathbf{R}_{2\text{p}}}{\mathbf{R}_{1\text{p}} + \mathbf{R}_{2\text{p}}} = \frac{\mathbf{R}_0 \cdot \mathbf{U}_1 \cdot \mathbf{U}_2}{(\mathbf{U}_1 + \mathbf{U}_2) \cdot \mathbf{U}_\text{D}}$$

$$\mathbf{U}_\text{Q} = \frac{\mathbf{R}_{\text{serial}}}{\mathbf{R}_{\text{serial}} + \mathbf{R}_{\text{parallel}}} \cdot \mathbf{U}_\text{D} = \frac{\mathbf{R}_{1\text{s}} + \mathbf{R}_{2\text{s}}}{\mathbf{R}_{1\text{s}} + \mathbf{R}_{2\text{s}} + \dfrac{\mathbf{R}_{1\text{p}} \cdot \mathbf{R}_{2\text{p}}}{\mathbf{R}_{1\text{p}} + \mathbf{R}_{2\text{p}}}} \cdot \mathbf{U}_\text{D}$$

$$\mathbf{U}_\text{Q} = \frac{(\mathbf{R}_{1\text{s}} + \mathbf{R}_{2\text{s}}) \cdot (\mathbf{R}_{1\text{p}} + \mathbf{R}_{2\text{p}})}{(\mathbf{R}_{1\text{s}} + \mathbf{R}_{2\text{s}}) \cdot (\mathbf{R}_{1\text{p}} + \mathbf{R}_{2\text{p}}) + \mathbf{R}_{1\text{p}} \cdot \mathbf{R}_{2\text{p}}} \cdot \mathbf{U}_\text{D}$$

$$\mathbf{U}_\text{Q} = \frac{(2\mathbf{U}_\text{D} - \mathbf{U}_1 - \mathbf{U}_2) \cdot (\mathbf{U}_1 + \mathbf{U}_2)}{(2\mathbf{U}_\text{D} - \mathbf{U}_1 - \mathbf{U}_2) \cdot (\mathbf{U}_1 + \mathbf{U}_2) + \mathbf{U}_1 \cdot \mathbf{U}_2} \cdot \mathbf{U}_\text{D}$$

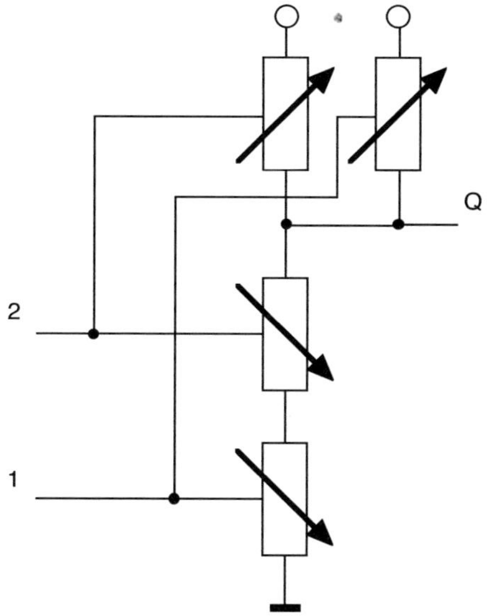

Figure 42. The Linear NAND Gate.

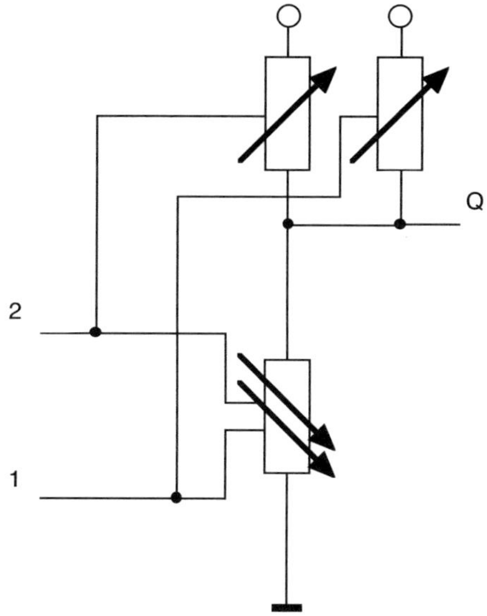

Figure 43. The Optimised Linear NAND Gate.

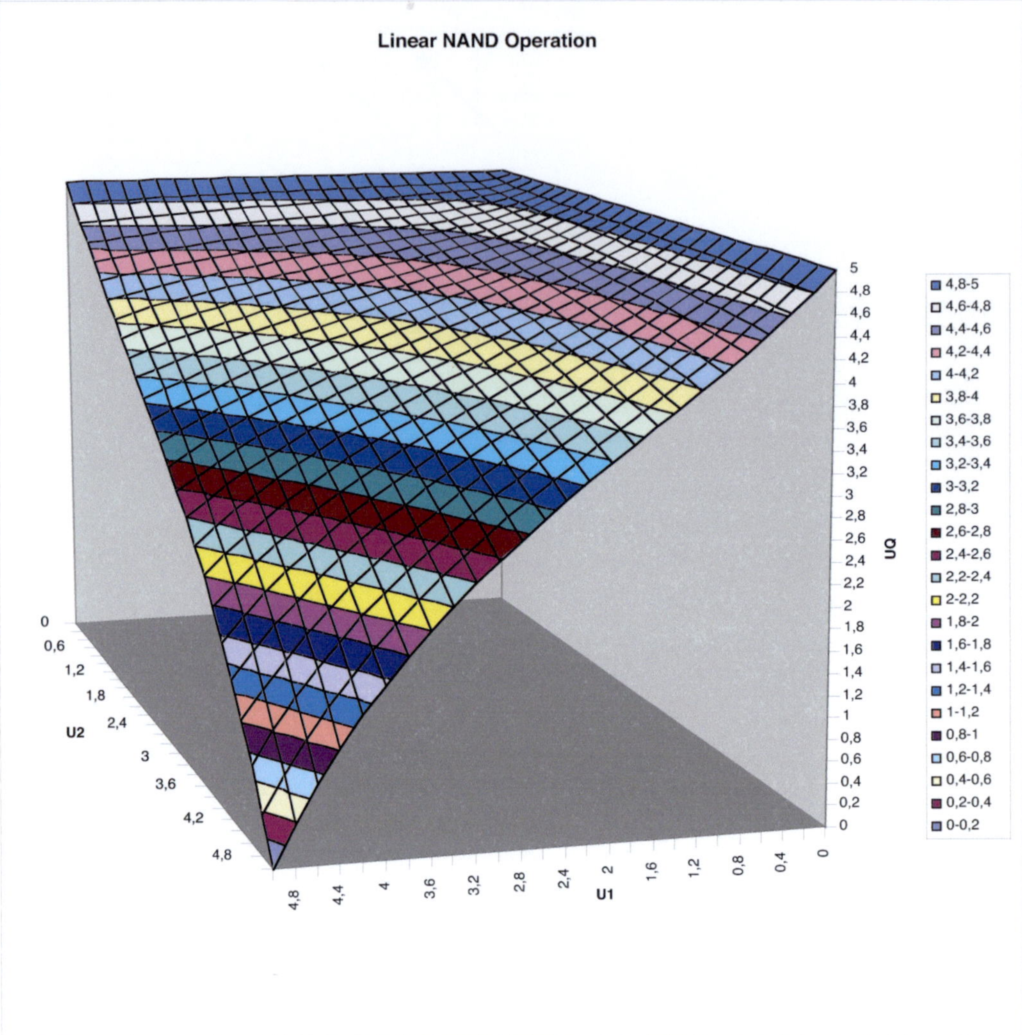

Figure 44. Transfer Characteristic of the Linear NAND.

For the linear NOR and NAND a similar characteristic is recognisable as found in the digital world. The first prefers the low voltage levels as output and instead the second prefers the high voltage levels. It should become clear that similar but surely fuzzy operations could be done as in the digital case. If any decision is not a pure yes or no, but some feeling expressed as a value out of a possible range, the analog operations are well suited. Whether the more complicated arithmetic functions may show a meaningful counterpart for an analog world build from the three base parts, is unclear to me today. But examination would extend beyond the frame of this essay.

An interesting property of the analog processing parts is that the behaviour changes from being linear as for the inverters case to non-linear for the analog logic units. This shows that linear behaviour can be always complicated to performing non-linear, if the following prerequisites are fulfilled:

- Complemented operators support the base operation.
- Operators are "wired" together in a way that information is lost by dissipation.

The last is fulfilled as well for the obvious digital case as for the analog devices described above, because it is not possible to deduce the exact values of both input states form the output value.[64]

The importance of non-linearity is given by the ability to self-organisation and evolution, which requires non-linear properties **(42)**.

Following we shall explain, why the analog world is something of interest. But introduction is now completed.

---

[64] This can be expressed by mathematical formulation: "The reverse function does not exist."

Properties of Information and Information Processing

Leadership and Minimal Information Processing

Leadership of electronic devices related to others on a chip can be defined as one would define it for social relations. A leader has relations to many but the individual relates to a single leader. By the way the "one to many" or "many to one" relation is a characteristic property one has to define for relational database construction.

As told in the chapters before there is some interaction between group members as well as some between leaders and members. The difference already told is given by communication frequency. Therefore the social system seems to be an analog like generalisation with emergence of leadership out of the group. Typically humans cut electronic devices from the possibility to change connections dependent to own decisions, what is a property of slavery.[65]

Probably you have got already a feeling for how to define leadership for electronic devices during reading the introduction above. There the optical comparison of the badly defined three FET NOR to the optimised NOR was recommended. The difference of both is that in the case of the optimised NOR the "many" bottom FETs are wired in an equal way to the "one" FET on top. The last seems to have opened an ear to every subjected group member.

One may object that the information applied to the leading FET is not derived from the subjected ones but provided externally. The argument is that in the case of simple electronic devices like a single FET or a variable resistor the output value is a direct and bijective[66] result of the input. If social individuals act bijectively co-ordinated to their decisions or willing, it is of second quality, whether decision or willing is a pure internal result or is externally stimulated. This way an output like connection to the leader shows as well their voting as their behaviour. Further the chapters before have shown that always external stimulation is a needed property for any information processing system.

[65] There are commendable advances, for example: FPGAs or other during runtime programmable devices [(**171**)]. Software fulfils as well the property of freedom of action and relation in principle, but would need to be changeable dependent on decisions of the executing unit itself. Something like this is implemented for most "Artificial Life" simulations using computers (**49**), (**87**), but is very uncommon for practical computing of today.

[66] Bijective behaviour means that the input can be derived without ambiguity from the output value. Using mathematical formulation one would say: "The reverse function exists."

Energetic Properties

Consider the CMOS one bit memory as described above. With the exception of some parasitic loss there is only a very time limited current flow during change of state. During the stable state the isolation of the controlling gates prevents current flow. One can be more precise by identifying the short current flow during state change of a CMOS memory as a kind of information processing not of information storage.

It can be told that information processing is always accompanied with dissipation, because some former information has to be destroyed. As long as no informational change takes place storage media do not need dissipation. This is surely true for books, CDs and most other read only media, but is true as well for most not written but writeable media as tape backups or alike.

Above we have examined the one bit CMOS memory. Now the elder bipolar flip-flop is introduced, which behaves similar but not equal.

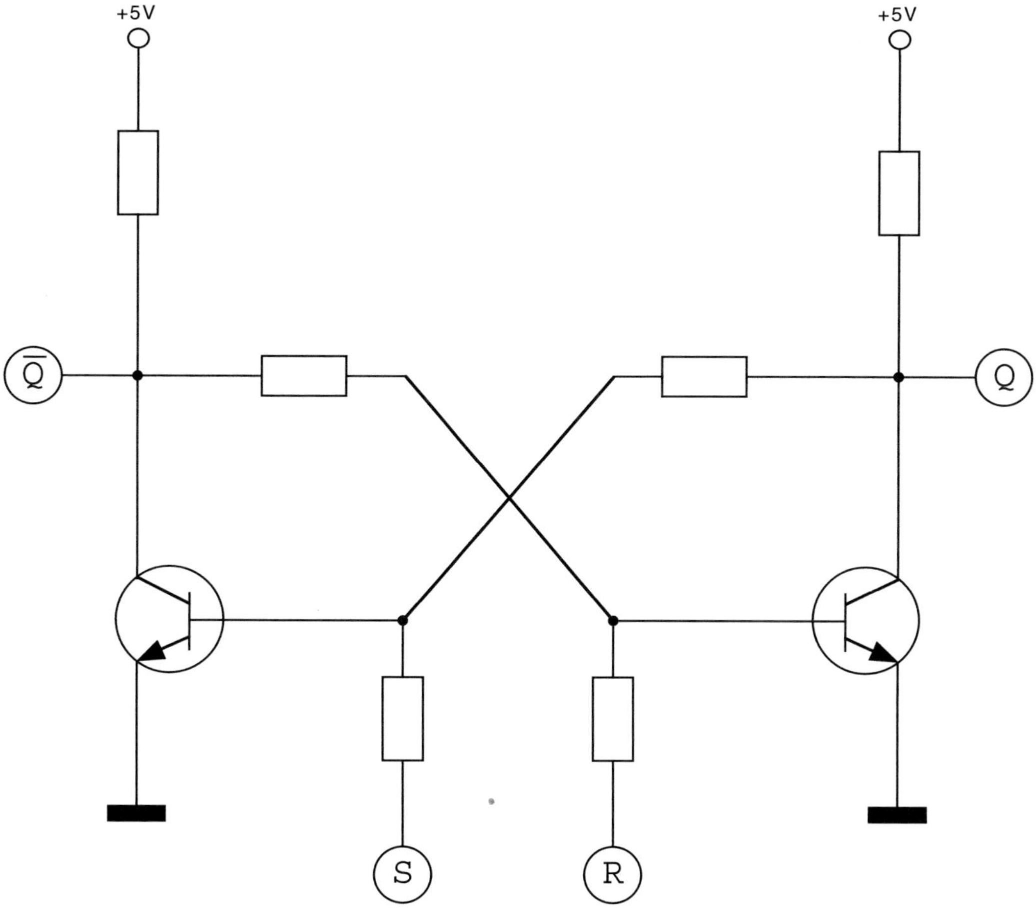

Figure 45. Bipolar Flip-Flop.

Contacting S with a positive voltage starts current flow at the left transistor and prevents current flow at the right transistor by back coupling. This initial state is shown with potential indication.

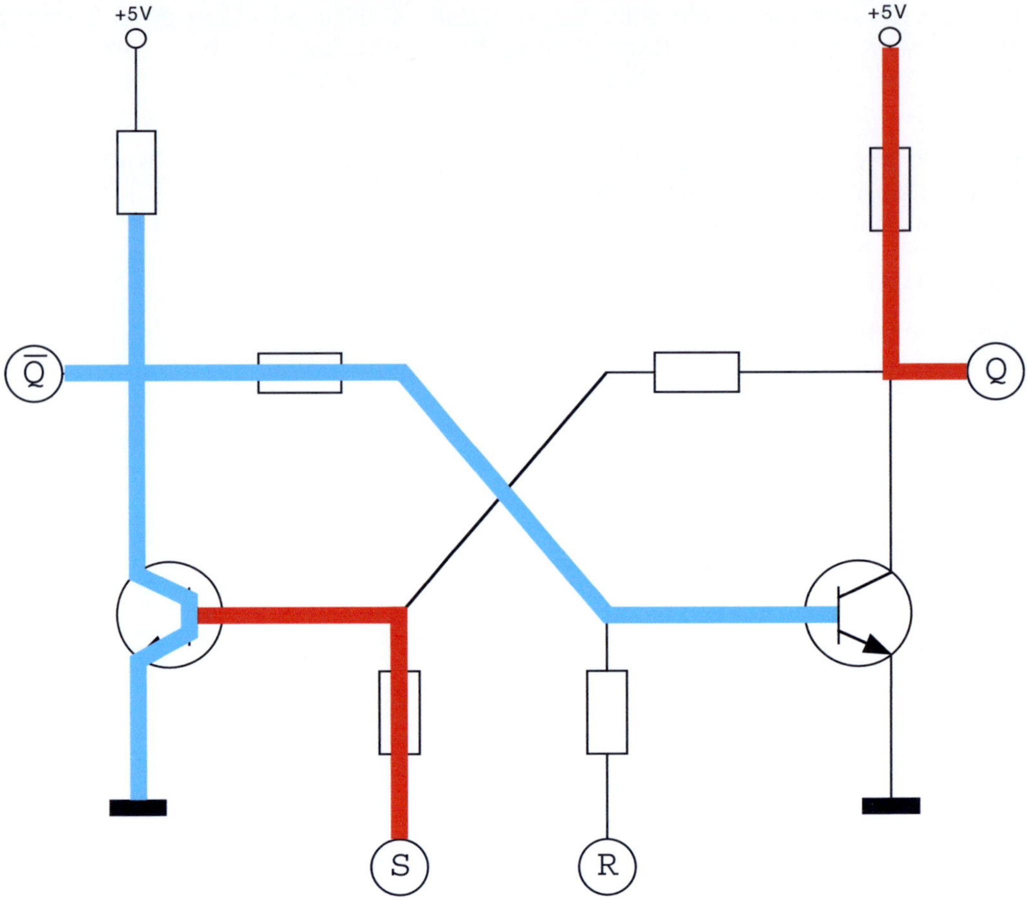

Figure 46. Flip-Flop´s Initial State.

After releasing of the S(et) input the back coupling from Q stabilises the left side, too.

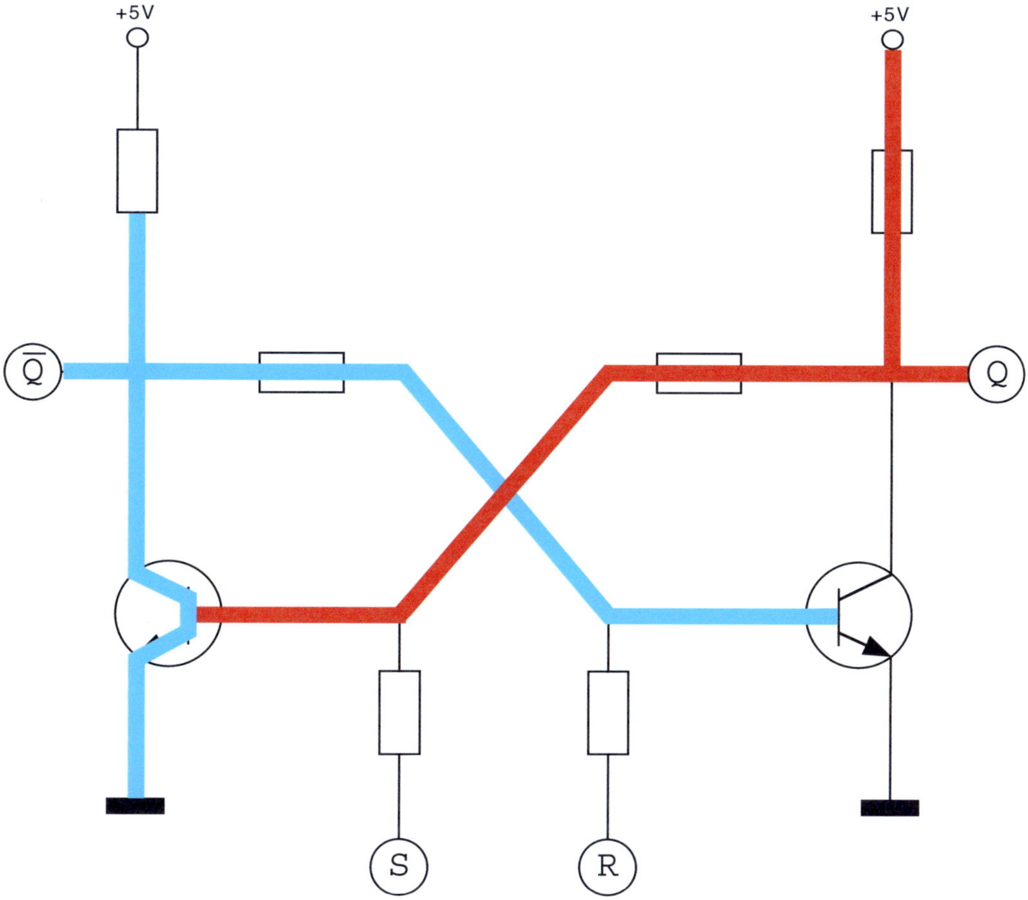

Figure 47. Flip-Flop´s Stable State.

Contacting R(eset) with a positive voltage reverses the effect and the right transistor would open. The both informational complementary states are defined by a left or right current flow.

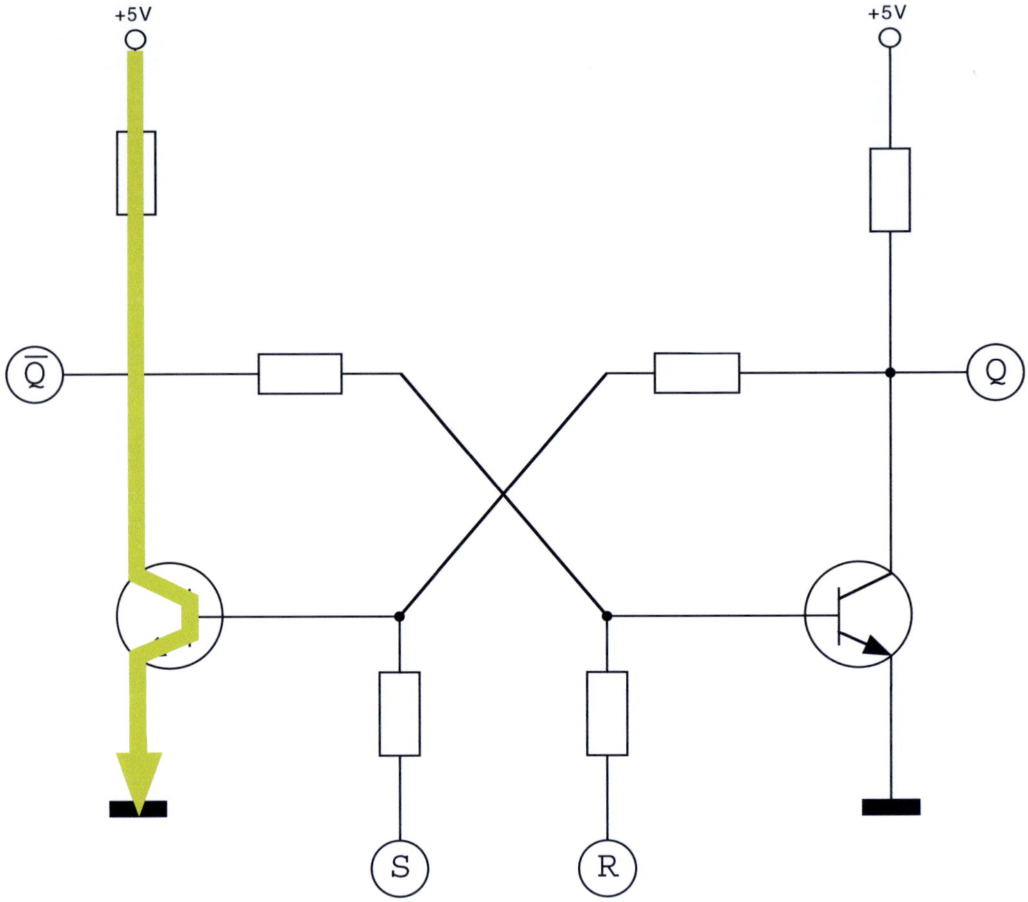

Figure 48. Current on the Left Side.

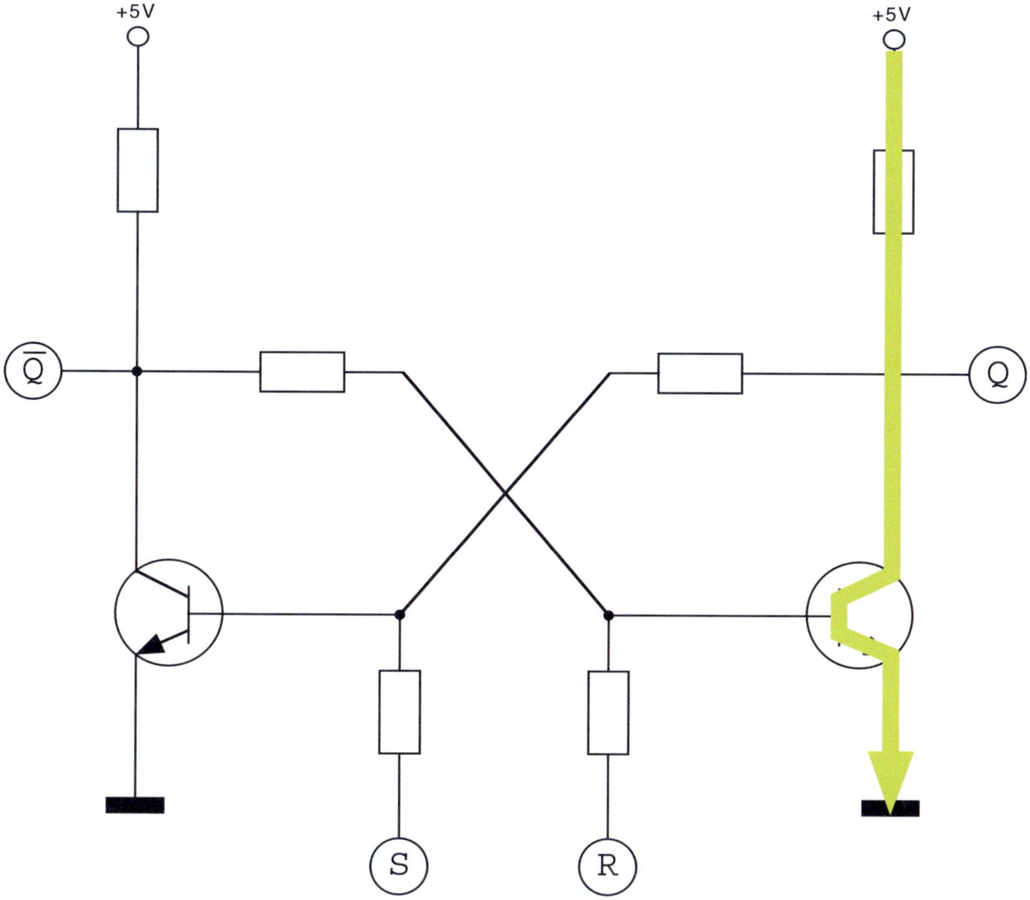

Figure 49. Current on the Right Side.

Instead of the energy conserving CMOS system, always some current is needed to define an informationalstate. This seems to be not a helpful property, but has some positive effects to the maximal switching frequency of states. Systems behaving this way are only of meaning, if energy overflow is high compared to possible information processing and high frequencies of operation can not be achieved otherwise. Energy consumption may be an important limiting property for future desktop electronicsas it is already for embedded systems.

The cause for the high-energy consumption of the bipolar flip-flop above is the lack of complementarytransistors. Although the NPN transistors shown have as well PNP complements in principle, they are at most not used for standard memories and digital logic gates. Because bipolar transistors have always some current at the base input, which is functional equal to the gate input for CMOS, the maintenanceeffect of complementaryconstruction seems to be not an advantage compared to higher production costs and smaller account of transistors per chip.

Whether complementary construction is really the main cause for energetic differences may be of question. The possible cut off of currents at two different, logic and voltage states seem to be not possible in another way. But there is a simple example, which shows the same properties for complete other circumstances.

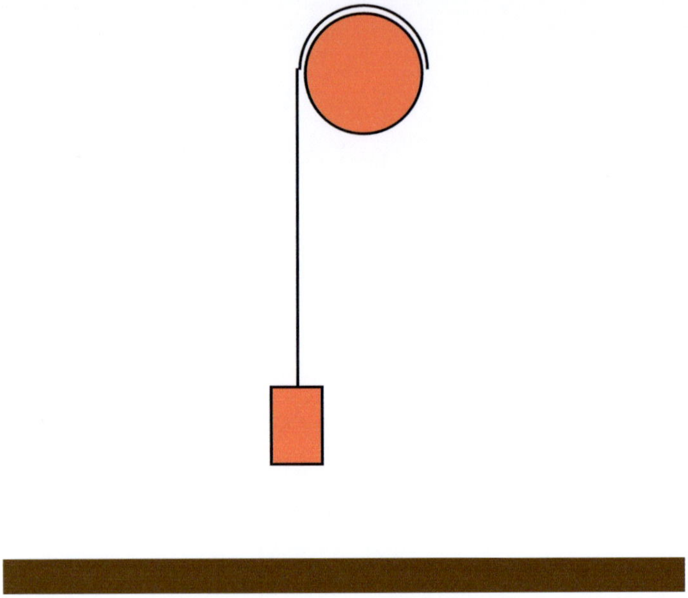

Figure 50. Weight at Down State.

The picture symbolises a weight mounted to some rotation axis. We can define the down and the up state.

This way mechanical information processing can be done. At least one of the states consumes much energy during state switch. Further some anti-force is needed to keep the system stable. Keeping as well a stable as a changeable system needs an always energy consuming engine even during halts. Our experience tells that this mounting is not very well done. The better solution is trivial.

Figure 51. Weight at Up State.

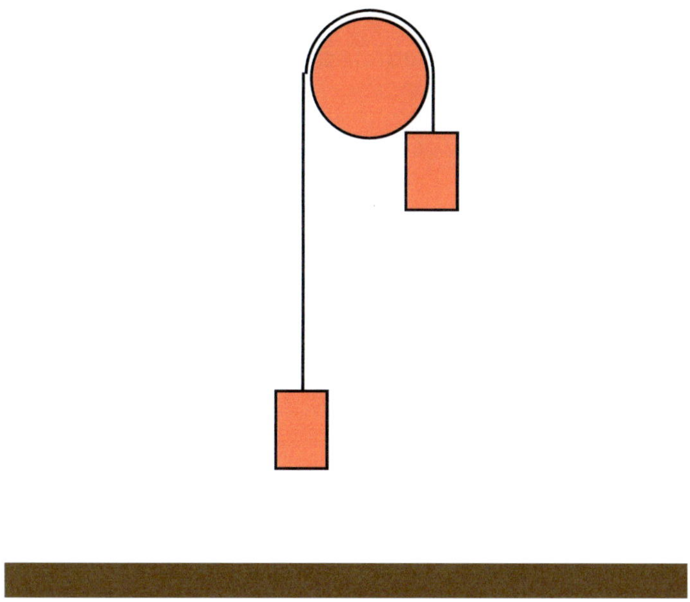

Figure 52. Complementary Weights.

This system is stable during unchanged informational states without energy consumption. But it is surely complemented. Even the energy consumption during change of state is less than before, because no work in the field of gravity is needed. Only acceleration, slowing down and friction loss consumes energy, but this is true for the not complemented case, too. If external properties define a minimal weight for achieving the function, which would be similar as a fixed possible scale of integration on a chip, it is clear that weights have to be the same mass for ether case. This would mean that the total mass of moved parts of the complemented system is the double of the first. The same is true for production costs.

It depends on the frequency of state changes, whether the complementary system is really less energy consuming as the single weight system. The needed acceleration for a change can be defined by the minimal needed frequency of state changes. For high frequencies and high accelerations the double mass is a disadvantage. For low frequency and acceleration it is not. Pretty the same behaviour related to switch frequency and increased production costs is found comparing CMOS to not complemented NMOS logic.

It is astonishing that so far different things like electronic devices and mechanical weights behave so similar, if they are subjected to information processing. Are there universal properties around? At the next chapter the properties of complementary parts are more exactly analysed.

Metastable States

As shown at the chapters before all information processing may lead to metastable states of individual communities. But the operation of information processing has the metastable property, too.[67] The mechanical example can be constructed to show such a property.

[67] Other metastable systems by "self-ordered criticality" or SOC are told by: **(16)**, **(74)**, **(102)**, **(149)**, **(152)** and **(153)**.

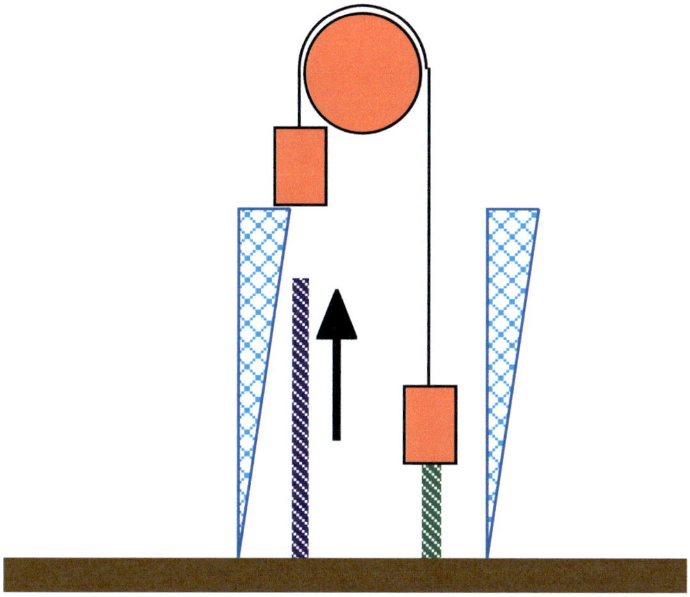

Figure 53. Metastable Mechanical Information Processing.

The picture includes now springs for fast acceleration of movement and pillars for preventing the weights from going down uncontrolled. At first a stable state should be given. The up weight is protected from going down by a pillar. Then stretching the co-ordinated spring is possible and can be connected at the bottom of the weight. After stretching the pillar keeps the weight at the upper position and the spring keeps stretched. The weight at the bottom gets disconnected from its spring. Now the system is prepared for a fast state change.

An infinitesimal small amount of energy may be used to turn the pillar and the stretched spring will change the systems informational state. It is important that the stretching time for the spring could continue much longer as the switching time. This may be needed because only a limited power is available. After state change the same can be done to the complementary weight. Further it is not meaningful to apply such a system to the single weight example, because the optimal operation needs a long time period for stretching, what would be not available for the single weight system, because it needs high frequent changes to have any advantage.

It is known that opening ion channels and former osmotic pumping in nervous cells behaves similar. Again it is astonishing that similar properties are found related to information processing for very different circumstances. One can further understand why metastable states are needed for reproduction and evolutionary information processing by comparing the metastable character of states of the "von Neumann" apparatus referenced by **(42)**.

Gravity as Medium

As seen before the electromagnetic field is not always needed for information processing. The mechanical examples operate in a homogeneous field of gravity. This was an implicit assumption given by familiar properties of living on earth.

But our weights, axis, springs and other parts are all made of matter and the dominating force between their atomic parts is electromagnetism. It is not possible therefore to be sure that gravity is the only medium of information processing for the mechanical examples.

Figure 54. Cosmic Information Processing.

Let us prepare an experiment in mind using a double star system with a single planet.[68] It is not important for this experiment in mind, whether there is any possibility to find such behaviour in reality. The only meaning is that there is a principal possibility even if probability is surely zero.[69] **[G]**

The stable pictures of the stars tell the chosen property of space co-ordinates, which are rotating along with the centre of masses. The distance of the stars shall be variable. Surely it is not easy to see, how this can be done by some external gravity, but again it does not matter for the experiment in mind. What is sure on the other hand is that this change of distance results to dissipation.

[68] As I have learned, the described system is very artificial. Elder double star systems do not have any planets, because of the chaotic 3 to multiple body problem planets orbits are unstable and at least after 100.000 rotations they got captured or catapulted out.

[69] If you do not like this example, consider the statement found in (**53**) at page 130: "The status described by (the eigen-vector) 'u...(x)' has well defined values of the observable properties A, B, C, ..., M. This is the maximal possible content of information, which we can have related to the system." But the author does not define the term 'information'. What do we have? Ether there is an identity of information and observable properties or there is at least a bijective relation. In both cases the reverse relation or identity exists and any energy exchange of matter will be a kind of information processing, too. If this is true for microscopic situations, it is as well true for macroscopic or cosmological exchange. [#]

Figure 55. Preparing a Cosmic Flip.

A planet flip occurs, if distance of stars is small and the planet is between them. The change of distance must be therefore well timed to the planets position.

Figure 56. Dissipation for Stabilisation.

The complement state is reached.

Figure 57. Cosmic Complemented Bit.

Do we have gone any way further? The masses are still made of matter including electromagnetic interaction at least inside the single star or the planet. To overcome this all partners shall be neutron stars now including the “planet”.

Figure 58. Pure Neutron Star System.

The strong core interaction is the dominating force inside all three partners. Therefore electromagnetism is surely neglectable. Nevertheless all former steps of the experiment in mind can be done in the same way. It can be told that cosmic digital information processing by gravity and masses may be at least not prohibited. The rough arbitrary and artificial forced experiment in mind tells further that this is surely not the way it can really happen. At the introduction above an analog information processing systems was described. Considering the many value possibilities of masses, velocities, rotation frequency etc. all with a smooth and never with a jumping value behaviour the analog operation principle has much more likelihood to occur.

Considering even the chaotic behaviour of multiple body systems and the density in the middle of our galaxy the likelihood of self-ordered criticality by some analog information processing can not be estimated as zero. Astronoms have found a structured universe, without a satisfactory explanation until today. Can you imagine, how it could happen by information processing?

Let me end this by referring to **(65)**, **(90)**, **(150)** and citing Lotka **(102)**:
"*With extending knowledge must come awakening consciousness of active partnership with the cosmos*".

Gender a Property of Information Processing [(WOF)*(*W)]

Basic Gender

We are starting from the simplest, complementary, artificial information storage medium: a CMOS inverter. One recognises a female and a male complement conforming to the definition given at the essay´s beginning. The inverter is shown below as a cut through the wearing chip.

During production of the chips base material (at most a one-crystalline silicon) it would be very expensive to produce it with a possible minimum of pollution. The cheaper way is to prepare circumstances that a pollution of an average value is defined.

Pollution or dotation of semiconductors can be of two different kinds. One would enhance electrons and is therefore named "n"-dotation considering the negative charge of electrons. The other depletes electrons and is therefore named "p"-dotation. The areas of dotation are shown in the picture below. The base silicon is p-polluted by production. Other structures have to be artificially implemented by further processing of the electronics. The lines on top are made of metal and are the voltage connections at both sides and the output of the circuit in the middle. The controlling gate inputs are lying at top of the white silicon oxide.

It is evident that the production of the male is more complicated and more expensive as of the female because the n-area requires an additional dotation step.

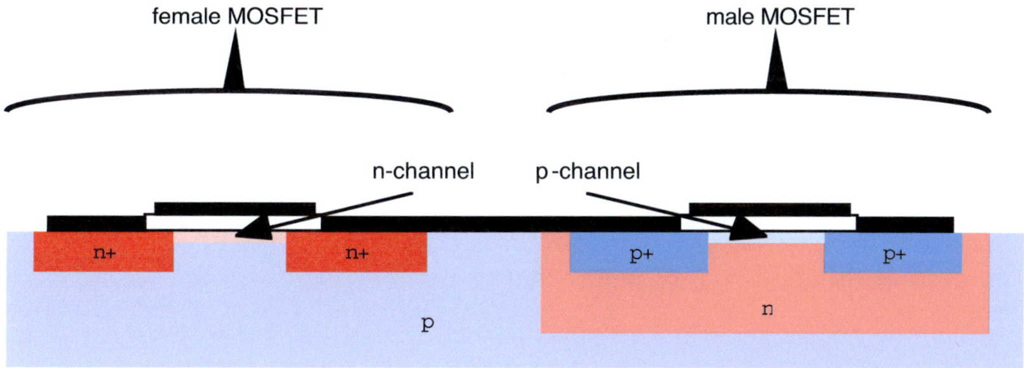

Figure 59. Gender of MOSFETs.

Calculating costs and energy consumption during production processing this defines the gender parameters. The difference of energy consumption can be extended during time in mind, if always some repair may be needed to keep the system functioning. The last is a little uncommon for CMOS, but clearly fulfilled for living systems. Ageing is found for electronic devices, too, although no repair methods are known and used today. But inviting it would result to no exception from the general behaviour.

This definition of gender is done for general application to complementary information processing systems as stated at the first chapter. The production rules for the female complement are the base system, from which the male is build by some extra operations. The last results to always-higher efforts during production and update for males compared to females.

Above we have learned that complemented (CMOS) information processing is at most less energy consuming during operation as not complemented (bipolar) information processing. The relative small amount of extra production costs for males is the better energy saving strategy as not complemented production but high dissipative operation.

Gender Difference Equivalent to Fermionic Systems[70]

Observing a couple of one female and one male individual one will typically find extremely repulsive behaviour of either, if another individual tries to occupy the same gender relation.

The quantum theoretical definition of fermionic particles needs a vanishing wave function at space and time, where two particles with all the same properties meet. This is the result of the addition of two equal wave functions. The behaviour is known as the "Pauli´s Principle". For example electrons behave this way resulting to multilevel atomic orbits. Could it be applied to gender relations?

Consider the CMOS inverter with one female and one male FET. Now we connect another female FET to the output. Doing so we have the possibility to decide how to control the behaviour of the two female FETs. If both gates (inputs) are wired together, both FETs will always act equal. In this case we recognise no difference of the behaviour of the system compared to the former inverter. A bigger single female FET could replace it as well. Because space dimensions of the FETs are in no way a parameter to our considerations, it is discovered that this was not a useful possibility for changing something of importance. Wiring together of the female gates is not allowed for a real change.

The need of different control inputs by this extension changes the behaviour of the system from being an inverter to the poorly defined NOR as examined above. There is not much difference whether one of the female FETs is wired to the male or not. The characteristic of the badly defined NOR as described above is received, which has lost its memory property and results to not well defined logic operation. Now the fermionic property can be recognised, because the likelihood to find useful information at the area of this device becomes zero by adding a FET as described.

---

[70] This was not my idea! A quantum theoretical joke lecture was told by one of my physics professors during my study years ago.

Further we have to examine the difference between memory and logic units. The CMOS inverter has the ability to store information. This was true for the bipolar flip-flop, too. Dynamic-RAMs based on capacitative elements have this property, too. As a quantum theoretical formulation one can tell that information storage devices have the likelihood equal or near to one to show significant information during some representative time periods.

Arithmetic logic units on the other hand are devices, which typically have a steady inflow and outflow of information. Further the number of input bits is higher than the number of output bits. This is equivalent to information loss and energy dissipation. Because of the always-changing information flow accompanied with dissipation, the likelihood to find significant information at those devices is equal or near to zero by integration about the same representative time periods as considered before. Those time periods have to be at least a magnitude longer as defined by the operation frequency of the arithmetic-logic unit.

Changing the CMOS one bit memory to a NOR or NAND gate, what only requires re-routing of connections, changes the devices behaviour from a storage device to a logic unit and the likelihood for finding some significant information there falls from one to zero. The difference of those routings is that in the case of a memory outputs of FETs with equal gender are not connected as it is the case for logic operating units. This is exactly equivalent to the behaviour of fermionic particles regarding their residence probability.

Taking Over to Living or Other Super-Structured Systems

Looking on DNA sequences, we find the information recorded in pairs of molecules (A, U, G, C). One is always bigger and has more atoms and molecule weight as the other complement. The energy considerations for building them up can be used as before resulting to females and males. Although there are two different pairing molecules: AU and GC. As long as not a third molecule is needed for the complementary stability, it is not needed to assume a multiplicity of gender. Thinking about a super-structured AU-GC complement and gender seems to make more sense. The describing differences are the association constants caused by H-bridge bindings. AU is only around 10 times more stable as other combinations, but GC is around 100 times more stable **(42)**. Therefore GC is female by having a lower energy level as the male AU. Why not only a single base pair was introduced by nature, can be understood by reading: **(141)**.

Looking at chromosomes, we probably assume that the female diploid set has informational less content as the male set. Because simple duplication results to a redundant function named homology, not a significant extra informational amount would be given and recognisable by expression. The extra male Y chromosome seem to add extra information compared to the female set, although it was derived from a female X at most but not at all by cutting. The energy considerations for female and male devices as used before can not as easily as before be applied to biochemical gender definition. If one considers informational content as the determining parameter, the individual with XY chromosomes may be estimated the energetic male. If one considers molecular weight of chromosomes as the determining parameter, the individual with XX chromosomes is the energetic male reversed to the microbiologic definition.

The informational difference is very small like a single switch and is not an informational loss[71] at females. But the extra operation started in the case of the male position of this switch, as examined below, consumes really more energy. Therefore using this option for gender definition is justified at best.[72]

The energetic consideration shows why female individual processes are the bases for individual reproduction. It is much easier to duplicate the less energy consuming complement and to derive the other one, if needed, by putting something extra to the process as to produce a more expensive individual first and to reduce it later. Even for the CMOS case the extension of the process not of the already produced female individual is a need, because the n-zone has to be implemented before the high doted source and drain areas can be placed. Biologic systems seem to behave the same way.

For the CMOS example the difference of gender was given by the difference of processes rather than by the difference of produced FETs. If one would write a program for FET production, there will be one single parameter for determination of the type of charge channel (n or p). Depending on this parameter the substances for doting are chosen and a jump over a command can be done. The last would place a low doted area, what must be excluded, if the dotation of the substrate is equivalent. Because chromosomes are the media for recording such instructions for biological processes, it can be easily understood, why only a very small amount of information may result to recognisable much energetic difference of resulting products by different flow during execution of the same process program. In fact recent studies show this behaviour for mammal, insect and plant gender determination caused by the SRY or some equivalent gene by suppressing other genes, which would suppress male development steps of the female embryo **(59)**, **(60)**, **(64)**, **(75)**, **(85)** and **(162)**.[73] Further at least for mammals it was shown that gender determination starts shortly after conception showing an increased growth rate of the male embryo compared to the female **(44)**. This all conforms to the energetic definition of gender. **[H]**

---

[71] You may want to consider a white page with black letters on it. Only at first view you would tell that the white page is "empty". Without the lack of letter pixels in between letters would not be recognisable. Therefore both are needed to define the informational amount. Electrons and "holes" perform equal regarding semi-conductors.

[72] The big difference between male and female animals determined by a small switch shows that most of the information for differentiation has to be already there on the female X or probably on other chromosomes. The switch only controls the expression. Further the specific properties of gender of individual males may be at most defined by crossing overs between the both female X chromosomes during the mature of the mothers egg cell, if they are solely defined by the X chromosome.

[73] The SRY seems to have more functionality as the described suppression of suppressers: **(37)**, **(135)**.

What the reduced focus on process programming can not determine generally, is the result of a small microbiologic information. If this determines two different flows of instructions of the same program, it could trigger the more energy-consuming as well as the less energy-consuming process. It is only a matter of the program itself, what the parameter produces.

Further it is not sure that a more energy-consuming process always results to a more energy-consuming individual considering maintenance. If similar programs are needed during the maintenance operation, this is true and this dependence is very likely. But a sophisticated construction specialised for reduction of maintenance costs is thinkable. If one likes to determine a male property out of a small informational extra, it is not commonly sure that this results to an energetic male process and produces an energetic male individual after execution.

As we have recognised until now, gender can be defined on every level of informational complexity. The fractal system as defined at the chapters before can be extended with gender equal to fermionic properties on every level.

Homosexual behaviour can be understood, if one recognises that the microbiological gender definition may be not in all cases a predetermination for the gender of the super-structured level of organisation, which is the human, animal or plant. This easily results, if we accept that information storage and processing are the origins for gender definition. The kind of information processing is much different on every level of organisation. An individual gender predefined by the sub-organisation seems to be something arbitrary and artificial using this point of view. That it is possible and successfully done for most cases, is one of the beautiful wonders of live. But homosexuality regarding the microbiologic level is surely nothing unnaturally.

The division of our body into symmetric half's (at first view) and the separation of our brain into two hemispheres may have gender as origin (including the differences at second view).

Problems of family interaction can be understood, if gender is more frequently recognised as an informational as only a reproductive difference. The fermionic property is very useful to explain for example the daughter-in-law to the mother-in-law repulsion. I am not sure, whether it is generally possible to determine the information shared between a human female and male person, which should vanish by an overlay of fermionic wave functions. But for example **(99)** tells and I agree that there is some informational self-extension by pairing.

One can assume gender to be the cause for constitutional definition of the frequently found two-chamber system of a national or super-national organisation.

The gender property is as well true for the cosmic flip-flop as introduced above. A double star system is often build like a single star system from an aggregation disk of dust, which have been separated into two centres. Because of the same origin of both stars, they are rotating in the same direction. This results to a female and male complement because the natural position of the planet will be defined by co-rotation related to one of the stars and the extra energy consuming state will be defined by contra-rotation related to the other star. During co-rotation mode one self-rotation period less is needed to fulfil a complete star rounding compared to contra-rotation mode, if other parameters of the stars are equal. Typically the stars slow the planets self-rotation by tide effects and vice-versa. Those effects are proportional to the number of rotations per rounding period. Therefore the higher self-rotation frequency per star rotation results to a higher dissipation of energy. This conforms to our gender difference definition.

The considerations about cosmic information possibilities are of importance to gender considerations, because the emergence independent of electromagnetic forces assures that the fermionic property of gender is not in any way directly related to fermionic properties of charges used mostly as a medium for information processing.

Hermaphroditic Devices

For rare circumstances as for example a very pure, unpolluted silicon one-crystal it would be necessary to put a p-doted as well as a n-doted area before the higher doted source and drain parts. This would result to equal costs for both FETs and an energetic difference would not be recognisable. But complementary function is not lost. Therefore gender is there but can not be easily determined. This can be defined as hermaphroditic.

Before we have already found another hermaphroditic device. It was the complemented mechanical weight example. It is not possible to recognise any energetic difference of the two weights. But what was the reason for this symmetry? It was the typical but related to cosmic dimensions arbitrary assumption of a homogeneous field of gravity. Without such an assumption the system is only unstable balanced at a single position between the logic states but unstable and unbalanced at both logic states.

Splitting of Energy Levels

We can recover at certain circumstances from such a problem by introducing a double complemented system, which looks pretty much like the CMOS one bit memory.

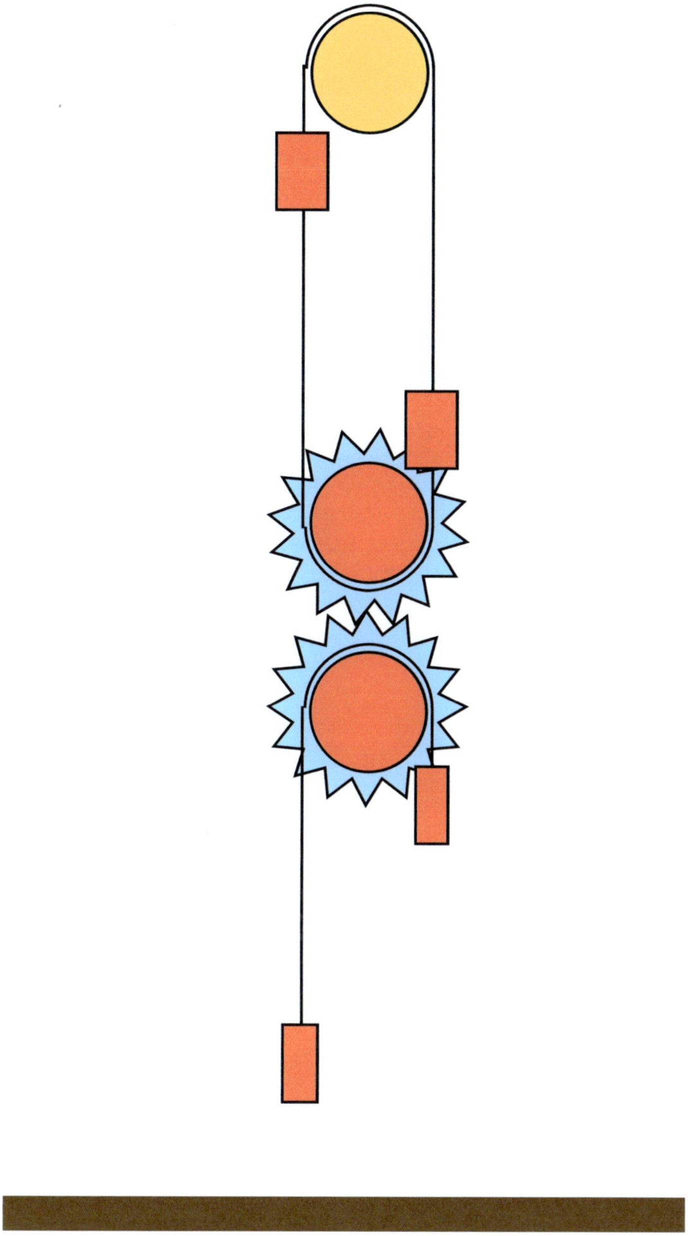

Figure 60. Mechanical Gender.

Because gravity increases to the bottom, the weights of the lower positioned axis have to be smaller than the upper weights. To get a single inverter pair analogy one should not divide horizontally between the main axis. Instead a diagonal pairing is needed, because those weights are moved in parallel.[74] If the weight at the bottom half would go down and would feel a higher gravity the corresponding weight at the top half would feel the same and vice versa for going up.

The gender of the pairing complements can be easily determined. The females are on bottom and the males are on top, because the males have more mass and need a helping axis construction for preventing them from falling down. This raises production and maintenance costs and equivalent higher energy consumption.

There is another interesting property of this system. For the hermaphroditic case with a homogeneous field not only the two logic end positions were stable. Every position between was stable, too. More over the length of the cable was arbitrarily chooseable without loosing stability in any way.

The last is no more true for the example above, because the changing gravity needs a balancing between cable length equal to definition of the logic positions and chosen weights. If this is correctly done, then stability during the whole movement is further only possible, if the attraction by the gravity changes linear. This has more meaning, if we consider not only digital but analog logic. For the last every position between the extremes has to be a possible and therefore stable state.

For the general case of a quadratic diminishing of gravity the conditions for a balanced system are:

$$\mathbf{F_g} = \mathbf{m} \cdot \mathbf{g} = \frac{\mathbf{g_0}}{\mathbf{h}^2} \cdot \mathbf{m},\ \mathbf{F_g} = \mathbf{g_0} \cdot \mathbf{f},\ \mathbf{f} = \frac{\mathbf{m}}{\mathbf{h}^2}$$

$$\mathbf{f_{fl}} = \frac{\mathbf{m_f}}{\mathbf{h_{fl}^2}},\ \mathbf{f_{fr}} = \frac{\mathbf{m_f}}{\mathbf{h_{fr}^2}},\ \mathbf{f_{ml}} = \frac{\mathbf{m_m}}{\mathbf{h_{ml}^2}},\ \mathbf{f_{mr}} = \frac{\mathbf{m_m}}{\mathbf{h_{mr}^2}}$$

$$\mathbf{f_{fl}} + \mathbf{f_{mr}} - \mathbf{f_{ml}} - \mathbf{f_{fr}} = 0$$

The variables mean:

F: gravity force of weight, **m**: mass of weight, **h**: height from the surface, **f**: effective mass resulting to the gravity force. Indices tell male, female, left and right for identification.

The balanced system is only possible, if:

$$\frac{\mathbf{m_f}}{\mathbf{h_{fl}^2}} + \frac{\mathbf{m_m}}{\mathbf{h_{mr}^2}} - \frac{\mathbf{m_m}}{\mathbf{h_{ml}^2}} - \frac{\mathbf{m_f}}{\mathbf{h_{fr}^2}} = 0$$

[74] This depends on the use of cogwheels but mounting on the same axis would result to a left and right sided instead of diagonal parallel movement.

$$\mathbf{m}_f\mathbf{h}_{mr}^2\mathbf{h}_{ml}^2\mathbf{h}_{fr}^2 + \mathbf{m}_m\mathbf{h}_{fl}^2\mathbf{h}_{ml}^2\mathbf{h}_{fr}^2 - \mathbf{m}_m\mathbf{h}_{fl}^2\mathbf{h}_{mr}^2\mathbf{h}_{fr}^2 - \mathbf{m}_f\mathbf{h}_{fl}^2\mathbf{h}_{mr}^2\mathbf{h}_{ml}^2 = 0$$

$$\mathbf{m}_f\left(\mathbf{h}_{mr}^2\mathbf{h}_{ml}^2\mathbf{h}_{fr}^2 - \mathbf{h}_{fl}^2\mathbf{h}_{mr}^2\mathbf{h}_{ml}^2\right) + \mathbf{m}_m\left(\mathbf{h}_{fl}^2\mathbf{h}_{ml}^2\mathbf{h}_{fr}^2 - \mathbf{h}_{fl}^2\mathbf{h}_{mr}^2\mathbf{h}_{fr}^2\right) = 0$$

$$\mathbf{h}_{mr}^2\mathbf{h}_{ml}^2\mathbf{h}_{fr}^2 = \mathbf{h}_{fl}^2\mathbf{h}_{mr}^2\mathbf{h}_{ml}^2 \ \wedge\ \mathbf{h}_{fl}^2\mathbf{h}_{ml}^2\mathbf{h}_{fr}^2 = \mathbf{h}_{fl}^2\mathbf{h}_{mr}^2\mathbf{h}_{fr}^2$$

$$\mathbf{h}_{fr} = \mathbf{h}_{fl} \ \wedge\ \mathbf{h}_{ml} = \mathbf{h}_{mr}$$

Only if both up weights and both down weights have the same position, a balanced but unstable system is received. Weights and cable lengths do not have any influence to change this. There seem nothing to be won comparing our starting situation, but I like the example because of the similarity to CMOS regarding construction, because of the emergence of gender visibility and the different behaviour for different field gradients, which can be assumed in mind.

For non-homogeneous and non-linear gravity it would be better to change the construction this way:

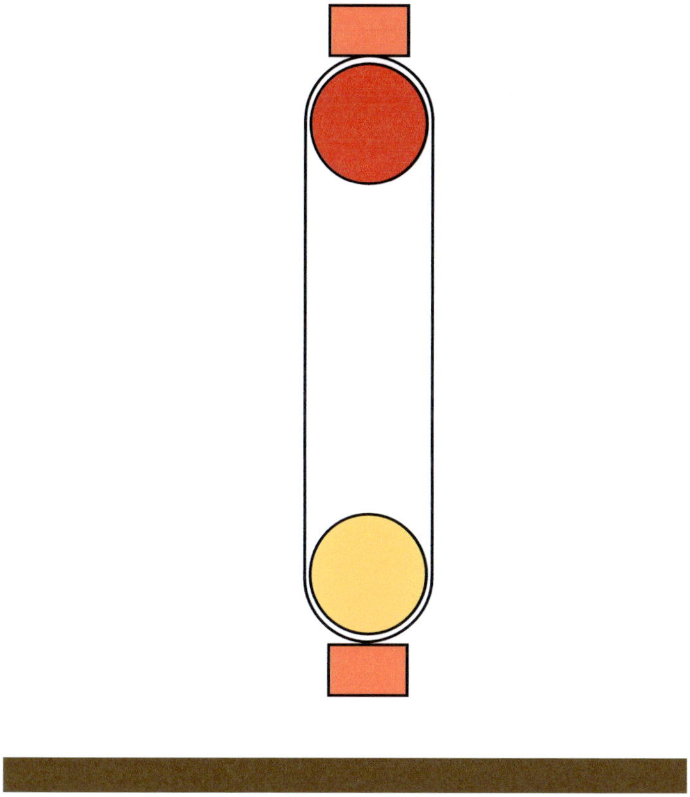

Figure 61. Mechanical Gender 2

The bottom weight will be always dominating, but change between two digital logic states is possible. Gender is not lost or got invisible, but is now represented by the two axis, which may be constructed differently. The axis at top is male and the axis at bottom is female, because the sum of weights is always burdened to the top and the bottom axis is only needed for spatial fixing. It can be constructed much lighter therefore.

Comparing the mechanical example with energetic electron levels of an atom we recognise that the electrons of a single orbit but with different spins can not be distinguished, if no external magnetic field is applied and internal magnetic influences are neglected. It seems as would the system be hermaphroditic. Applying a magnetic field results to energetic difference of the up (parallel) to the down (anti-parallel) spin. The fermionic, half-numbered spin equivalent to gender can be observed this way. Contrary to the mechanical example above the magnetic field does not need to have a gradient but have to be simply there. On the other hand this requires a gradient of the external electric potential to derive a current, which results to a magnetic field. The energy levels of the two spin-states change proportional to the external magnetic field as well as the mechanical energy levels of logic states change with the gravity field.

There is one lack of the last mechanical construction, because information processing is possible by changing the weights, but the two different logic states are not distinguishable, if both weights are absolutely identical constructed. For overcoming this some marking of the weights by a different colour or similar efforts are needed to keep the system useful. Because this marking may be again subjected to different energy levels for example by different frequencies of light absorption one recognises another gender system, which is this way introduced. You should compare the AU - GC double gender system of the DNA as mentioned before.

This figure shows a second gender system by placing different notches on the former identical weights:

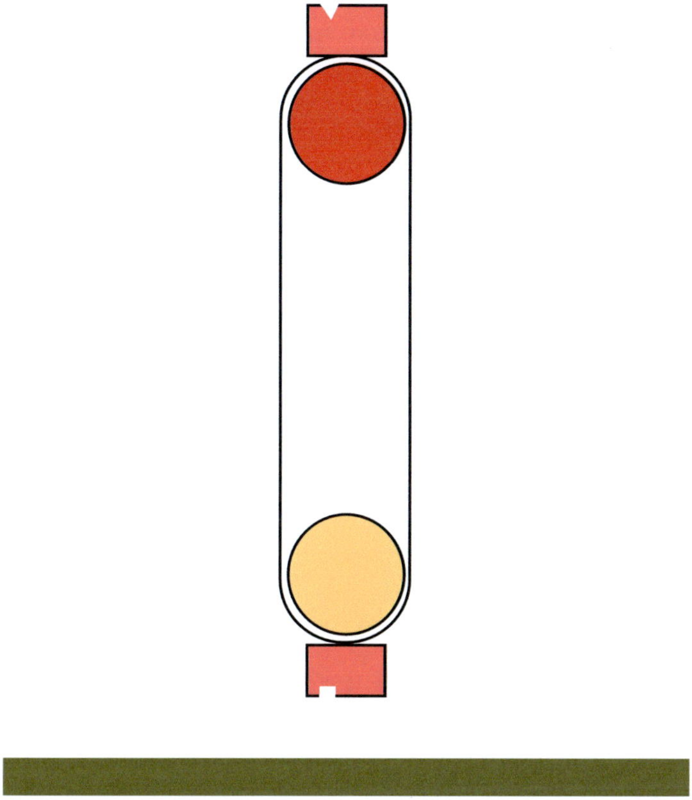

Figure 62. Double Mechanical Gender

Gender and Leadership

Why do we not find only paired couples of humans or animals?

It is a parameter of the energy content of the system, whether pairing is an optimal strategy or not. If the energy dissipation by a male individual is much higher than by the female, it would be an energy saving strategy to have only one male for several females in the group. Other males have to reside at a more distant higher energetic orbit of youngsters compared to the female orbit, where likelihood of survival may be less. This is for example true, if the hunting ground conditions are less optimal outside the leader male + females hunting ground. Many animal organisations behave this way.

Now we shall use the CMOS example above and use the male and female FET definition. But you should remember that only the needed extra process steps define the male. Following the given example an optimised NOR gate would be equivalent to male leadership. An optimised NAND gate would be equivalent to female leadership.

The optimised NOR/NAND gate could be extended to have multiple female/male FETs and an equivalent number of inputs and male/female gate divisions. As we have learned the fermionic information is destroyed for those devices, but using the male/female as group leader results to an information processing system, which may be extendable to analyse the diversity of the system and generate the **TS** benefit, as described at the former chapters. By building this structure a further energy saving but too fault tolerant system can be installed. A first optimisation would be recording the statistical likelihood of input patterns. If some of the inputs die, the most likely pattern defined by the rest of information can be used. The recorded information and pattern predefinition by likelihood can further be used to reduce the update frequency of external signals information or to redistribute the frequency to different levels of signal importance or priority. Now we have circled back to the first chapters and understood that leadership may be a main cause for the emergence of learning.

Because of this benefit increase, which is at first only related to the leader, the leader seems to reach a lower energetic level like another orbit of residence. Higher orbits exhibit multiple possible residences for electrons with equal spin equivalent to gender for the atomic case. The number of possible residences is surely restricted as known for the atomic but as well for the NOR/NAND case. For the last there will be some production specific limitation how many divisions can be made to the gate of the male/female FET without loosing performance.

This way the fermionic system and information storing capability can be recovered, because the leader on the lower energetic level is able to let its females be paired with other males. This includes the males into the information storage system, cuts the leaders gender relation to the females and raises a stable structure, where the leader has not to focus loss of leadership only because of gender stimulated competition. Hopefully he would find his “First Lady”, too. This way a simple logic device turns to a complete computer equipped with a dedicated processor and connected memory. This way a small mob of animals **(78)** turns to a human municipality.

For the CMOS example the gender definition can be reversed, if a n-doted substrate is assumed. Further changing the polarity of the external voltages can reverse the operation, too. For this multiple dependence to different properties one can assume some further complementary systems. Such further complements are used for example for analog processing devices like operational amplifiers but will be not examined here.

One recognises that the NOR is complementary to the NAND and it is surprising that the optimised device showing male leadership has to be recognised as female on the super-structure level and vice-versa because of the dominating complementary number of FETs. The emergence of multiple structure levels gets more evident by introducing the gender property.

Female Leadership

The description above can be done using as well the NOR or the NAND gate. The last was defined as female leadership. But observations of simple systems of nature prefer the male leadership because of the energy difference by definition.

If microbiologic female leadership can be recognised at animal organisations, there is sometimes a third kind of gender named „neuter". The most individuals of a population of ants or termites have not the possibility of reproduction. Cutting them from this possibility saves energy during production and maintenance, because no organs have to be built in those individuals for supporting it. They seem to have lost the fermionic property regarding reproduction, but at the energy dependent hierarchy they have lowest **pV** level. The leading queen will show the lowest **TS** level. The relative position of both levels is for any discussed case unclear to me and has to be measured.

Microbiologic male individuals of those species are often killed after they have done the needed reproduction work to save maintenance energy. For spider species they are sometimes eaten up to conserve the energy content of their production, too.[75] Where is the male energy level relative to the female for those cases?

The answer is given by the amount of individuals a single microbiologic female can produce during her lifetime. This number is magnitudes higher as for example for mammal species. Therefore the reproduction organs show very high-energy dissipation. We recognise that the microbiologic female individual is

[75] There is similar human behaviour as I have learned. If the mortality of males is much higher as for the females by environment conditions, female leadership and female dominated structure of the population results. If there is a bijective relation between gender asymmetry of leadership and mortality of males, then the observation of female leadership by externally forced mortality would as well be a confirmation of internally forced male mortality by animals female leadership prepared by other parameters for example by energy accounts. **[C]**

the more energy-consuming individual described as a super-structure of cells. Therefore she has to be identified as male on this level, if energy considerations are the used way of gender definition. Similar properties can be found for amphibians, where the size of the microbiologic females and the riding of the males upon them tell the energetic male leadership of the biologic female individual.

The neuter individuals are typically the energetic females. Microbiologic males may not improve much the arithmetic device, which is for example the swarm of bees, regarding information processing, because all needed fermionic sub-parts are already defined without them.

The energetic definition of gender results to always male leadership and sometimes reversed gender of animal individuals compared to their microbiologic gender definition at least for not super-structured animal communities.

Is the last result bad news for our admired ladies? Is the author a despicable chauvinist? I apologise to everyone, who feels hurt by these results. One should consider that the hard feelings come from hard physical definitions. Even nature seems to laugh about them by confusing male and female properties on different levels of structure. The known several human group structures tell that such confusion is as well possible for them. Therefore it is possible for a biologic female human individual to behave as an energetic male leader at a super-structure. More over the considerations for a change from a male dominated logic unit to a complete computer system as described short above tell that for the more complicated computing system female leadership of sub-devices is a need to provide all logic for all arithmetic base operations as described above. But biologic males may occupy those female leaders positions of the super-structure, too.

Now gender definition seems to be completely confused. But remember that this is only done by unprecise, common human description, where an equal microbiologic to biologic to individual to leader gender relation is established by common historical experience. The energetic definition is hard and precise and describes as well all deviations from the common experience as the more likely occurrence of the common. But what the reader should have learned is: **Never confuse gender definition by predefining any relation of gender between different levels of structure!**

It seems to be an ideal status to have all humans happily paired into couples. But one should consider that human organisations need energy overflow compared to energetic gender difference to get into pairing for all. Further it may be not possible by free gender relations, because leaders will show always most attraction. Some cultures have tried to overcome this by fixing gender relations by parents. Some moral behaviour of leaders is at least needed to avoid struggle and fights caused by gender competition, which may result to complete destruction. Using a leader couple as a defined constitutional element may be an opportunity. American political culture has risen the „First Lady“ almost to the same level as the „President“. But a real written definition is only found at monarchistic constitutions. Who knows, whether it really helps looking at the last White House[76] and United Kingdom[77] scandals? We all are subjected to the laws of nature. Those are extenuating circumstances.

Only pairing without harem building and extension of equal rights independent of gender to equal distribution of leaders positions regarding gender needs energy overflow and therefore control and reduction of descendent production. Without the last always the maximal possible individual number would be reached resulting to energy deficiency and asymmetry caused by gender.

It would be a very interesting future job to calculate the optimum of structure intelligence, which may lie between maximisation by pairing and equal gender distribution of leaders positions because of the better arithmetic capabilities ($\mathbf{I}_S \sim \mathbf{I}_{\emptyset} \sim -\mathbf{T}$) and maximisation of individuals leading to more diversity (**S**). We can assume that arithmetic capabilities may increase proportional with the gender symmetry or may be bound to some power law regarding influence of distribution space. But it is very likely that this law increases much faster with n as the *ln*(n) dependence of the entropy. Therefore as more populated the earth will be by humans as more gender asymmetry regarding leadership will be reduced and birth control will emerge. The observed tight binding between fights for female rights and as well for free birth control can be understood this way.

[76] The Lewinsky – Clinton affair is meant.

[77] The multiple divorces of members of the Windsor family are meant.

Gender and Philosophy

Before this view the term "gender" was only biologically and socially used. But our general method tells that philosophies based on "dialectic" like Hegel´s **(72)**, Marx´s **(111)** or **(26)**, **(40)**, **(73)**, **(84)**, **(107)**, **(137)**, **(174)** can be recognised as using the same approach of complementarity as gender does. The relation to gender rises the question, whether there is really the stage of synthesis after thesis and anti-thesis. Even for this the gender related "love" is the more informative term, because complementary operation is not lost by this kind of synthesis.

The following view at the gender related development of children is helpful by comparing other social behaviour later:

Although there is a gender difference of children already there after birth, the child itself does not recognise it during the first years. One can really use the term "neuter" for this phase. There need to be some communication capability and social experience to recognise differences. Obvious to children will be a deviating social behaviour including a visible difference, which parents support for example by using different kinds of clothes. After this recognition groups of children tend to separate themselves related to gender. During this thesis and anti-thesis phase there is misunderstanding and resulting repulsion. This phase helps working out differences and adaptation to adult idols.

Start of puberty can be recognised by the first experience of gender related love. But misunderstanding is not solved and it seems that it continues probably until death. If it is based on complementary information processing, this ongoing enigma is easily understandable. It is remarkable that during continued misunderstanding love is nevertheless generated unconsciously.

Resuming to philosophy we recognise that such an unconscious help is not there at super-structures, but rationality, science and consciousness are the tools that we have. Some conflicts of the world may be solvable by consciously turning from childish repulsion to adult loving of the complement. For examples relate to the chapter "*Religious Discussion*".

Three Questions

The Validation?

How can the pV- and TS-parts of the theory be validated?

The theory describes at most things, which are already found by experience. For example every child to parent relation has validated the property of unselfish behaviour. But because this theory uses mathematical formulation, not only the qualities of statements, but the quantity relations should be tested, too.

The following reference list shows already done experiments or data collections, which seem to be in good coincidence with the theory and are a first step of verification: **(4)**, **(24)**, **(29)**, **(49)**, **(55)**, **(89)**, **(95)**, **(110)**, **(108)**, **(112)**, **(113)**, **(128)**, **(130)**, **(132)**, **(145)**, **(146)**, **(154)**, **(167)** and **(168)**.

By searching the Internet for some articles of this area, I have found one very interesting dissertation. Unfortunately the author is unclear until this issue: **(153) Stan ?: Chaos Theory and Evolutionary Models for Economic Development Public Policy Thesis**. This dissertation has many relations to my theory. It analyses the policy of the 50 states of the USA. My opinion is that it describes a stable group of first class. This paper describes tests of different models and shows useful measurement possibilities. Further it shows many related references.

I agree to almost all statements and conclusions of this dissertation. The only exception is the meaning of the tested ”Red Queen” hypothesis **(159)**, **(160)**, **(161)**. The result coming from data analysis is not a zero-sum game, as the meaning of the Red Queen is. The results are only zero-sum deviations of quality properties. The analysis has not shown, whether the quality of the states policies as a whole increases or decreases or is constant. This way the data analysis shows more likely the stability condition of a first class group of my theory not a Red Queen condition. It is more likely that valued policy analysis would show some quality increase of the whole over time, because this system is at non-equilibrium, too. This measurement of the whole quality is not done in the cited paper and would be surely much more difficult to do. But this does not mean that the done work was easy.

<u>The following citations found are most impressive:</u>

- Viewing states as agents **(165) Waldrop, M.: Complexity: The emerging science at the edge of order and chaos**: "These agents might be molecules or neurones or species or consumers or even corporations. But whatever their nature, the agents were constantly organising and reorganising themselves into larger structures through the clash of mutual accommodation and mutual rivalry. Thus, molecules would from cells, neurones would from brains, species would from economies, and so on. At each level new emergent structures would form and engage in new emergent behaviours. Complexity, in other words, was a really science of emergence. (page 88)"
- "Stable working systems may be hiding potential cataclysmic events **(153)**.
- Earthquakes - Gutenberg and Richter (1956, **(153)**) - and sandpile avalanches - **(74)** - show self-organised criticality and self-similarity.
- Change of a dissipative system: 1) disequilibrium; 2) symmetry breaking; 3) experimentation; 4) reformation - **(54)**. Or 1) the point of singularity; 2) transformation utilising radical strategies; 3) inefficient acting and experimentation; 4) resynthesis - **(98)**.
- "Something out of nothing? Order out of chaos? It defies our traditional way of thinking." **(153)**.

<u>From this dissertation I have learned some important terms:</u>

- **(16)** Bak and Chen: **Self-organized criticality** or SOC[78]:

"We propose the theory of self-organised criticality: many composite systems naturally evolve to a critical state in which a minor event starts a chain reaction that can effect any number of elements in the system. Although composite systems produce more minor events than catastrophes, chain reactions of all sizes are an integral part of the dynamics. According to the theory, the mechanism that leads to minor events is the same one that leads to major events. Furthermore, composite systems never reach equilibrium, but instead evolve from one metastable state to the next."

At this time it is unclear, whether my theory describes always systems with "self-organised criticality", but it is very likely because of the incessant non-equilibrium and because of the metastable phases defined by first class group conditions at minimum.

---

[78] A philosophical definition is: **(152)**.

- "**pink noise**":

(153): A double logarithmic graph of SOC shows log-linearity with a slope:

$$0 > -\beta > -2$$

Brownian noise on the other hand shows:

$$-\beta = -2$$

the last means standard random noise. SOC-pink noise means chaotic "noise".

- **dissipative models**

This term can be used for all non-equilibrium models. Something is needed to keep them running, but non-equilibrium is a sure condition on earth. This theory falls into this category.

Other (historical) models are characterised by the terms: equilibrium or deterministic.

- "**forced order**" opposite to "**fractal order**" **(153)**:

Forced order seems to be coincident with the communicative exchange of my **pV**-chapters and can be seen as "rules of symbiosis".

Fractal order seems to be coincident with the structural order coming from the **TS**-part of my theory out of disorder.

A Theory of SOC? - Whether Alive or Not?

<u>Are many systems of self-organised criticality describable by this theory, even if depending to the unliving world?</u>

As shown above the gender property is found as well at the unliving world. At the following chapter depending to Dr. Sheldrake´s publications protein structure building is described in a way consistent with the previous theory. (Whether the proposed methods really result to the correct structure is not yet validated.) Many other efforts have been done already to explain protein folding using microscopic field theories for example: **(68)** and **(126)**. As shown above SOC is the case for earthquakes and sandpile avalanches **(74)**, **(153)**. Social systems are decribed this way **(152)**. Stan **(153)** cited some more applications: **(149) Sornette and Sornette: Self-organized criticality and earthquakes**: average seasonal temperature, annual amount of rainfall, rate of traffic flow, etc. Newer experiments were: **(112)**, **(113)** and **(168)**.

It would be some very interesting exercise trying to apply this theory of information processing to the named situations.

A New Field? [O]

Leads some attraction force in a theory about groups to a field property?

This must be assumed, if one compares standard physical forces. All known base forces are defined by a field property. Further fermionic systems have never been seen without an accompanied field of interaction. I would not have gone so far before version 2.x and reading of other publications telling field effects about the living world.

An old and (only) philosophical description was given by **(46)**.

Most impressive to me was: **(145) Sheldrake, R.: The presence of the past**. He calls them "morphogenetic fields" and most of his phenomenological descriptions can be derived using this theory. Although I do not agree to all of his conclusions, his publications seems to be very important, because they are widely spread in public science and even because they are much controversially discussed. Because of this importance I have following included a chapter of friendly critics.

Less important regarding popularity but much more important regarding precise description is the field theory, which was already mentioned in **(145)**: **(156) Thom R.: Structural stability and morphogenesis**. This theory is not easy to understand. But there seems to be no contradiction to mine. The following cites show obvious coincidence:

- Although nothing is told about original forces, one can find at page 19f something equivalent to the following statements: "*Association in mind is a dynamic system describing structural stability.*" My theory shows that associations in mind result to attraction forces as possible field origins.
- At page 29 Thom complains that computability sacrifices structural stability and sees this operation as something done by physicists. But I object that nature does this by being not in any way infinite as mathematicians mostly think. More over computational effects are the origins for structure building as told by my theory, although stability forever may be really not the case. This way the first cite is not paradox looking at finite times.
- One can find in this book at page 60 some justification for my approach using an isolated view at every distinct fractal level: "*…it shows that the type and dynamic origin of a catastrophe can be described even when all the internal parameters describing the system are not explicitly known*". One should remember that structure building occurs in my theory by emergence of leadership caused by symmetry breaking, which has all properties to be a catastrophe in Thom´s theory.
- At page 139 he complains the "*…irritating gap between energy and information, which thermodynamically separates the inert from the living world.*" My theory tells that there is no gap, if equivalence of energy and intelligence and fermionic properties of information are the case **(169)**.

Going back to the field property and considering Gutenberg and Richter talking about self-organised criticality of earthquakes and **(145)** Sheldrake talking about animals precognition of catastrophes in nature then assuming some field caused by an attraction force of a SOC-system could give the reason for the precognition capability, if animals have a sensor for the field. Then precognition would be simply identical to a measurement.[79] This may open some testable conditions, if some catastrophes can be identified as not dependent to SOC. Probably "precognition" is not the case for those conditions.

Searching the Internet I have found that field theories are already there, which show similarity to mine. Actual they are made for describing neural networks and alike, but some are related to human interaction, too. Some very interesting and free sources available at the Internet are:

"http://ww1.elsevier.nl/locate/physa"
- Physics of Life, Econophysics: **(19)**, **(23)**, **(63)**, **(68)**, **(117)** and **(134)**

"http://chimera.roma1.infn.it/GIORGIO/Lavori.html"
- Multiple documents from G. Parisi et. al.: **(125)**, **(126)** and **(127)**

A paperback is available as: **(124) Parisi, G.: Statistical field theory**.

[§] has found: **(29)**. Related references are - regarding simple material: **(140)**, "Artificial Life": **(87)**, cosmology: **(122)**, philosophy: **(46)**, religion: **(31)**.

Before the reading of the field related publications I had mainly completed the **pV**- and **TS**-chapters. But chapters related to gender difference followed during extension to the second issue and are stimulated by the field assumption.

Uncertainty relations, quantum and fermionic gender properties were clearly described above and the last is always tested empirically during use of CMOS computer electronics. If there are definable areas of fermionic information particles, why should they not show a field of interaction? This would be contrary to the experience related to electrons and alike and further seems to be a contradiction, if one recognises that always wave functions are needed for their description as well as for exchange dependent to uncertainty relations. You surely would not think that a wave might have any meaning without an accompanied field. **[F]**

---

[79] Here we need to discuss "causality" and "present time". If quantum physical formulation of wave functions is symmetrically possible regarding effect, energy and time and time is divided in quanta, the infinite singularity of a "present time" becomes meaning less **[\]**. Further we have to consider different time flows for any inside / outside system as shown at the sub chapter "Uncertainty Relations". A catastrophe will set free a big amount of previously at living beings stored quanta, which results to a big wave. Remember that the time is now not only a parameter. It is directly affected by the wave. Can you imagine how precognition and "relative" time reversal **[(9)]** can happen? But precognition can not prevent the catastrophe. If this would be possible, the wave would not occur. Therefore the "causality" is preserved! Everyone is encouraged to do the surely possible mathematical formulation.

Before this version I were afraid about the consequences such a field assumption will have. The question arises, whether this force and field can be derived out of the already known physical forces? We know that it is an interaction upon fermionic information particles, which need to be related to matter but may not depend on a specific known interaction. Further the description of the force needs not the well know space as all other forces need. Only some abstract distribution space of individuals is used, which may be highly influenced by communication tools and may have different dimensions for different species. Further it is not needed to have always some communication running to keep group attraction, because of learned group membership, which may keep the field during short times of physical but not informational spatial separation. Considering this one may assume for understanding of this effect a new phenomenon of nature distinct form the known standard physical base forces. Now you should know, why I were afraid, because some will tell: "Si tacuises, philosophus mansises.[80]" Fortunately the references and stimulations have increased to an extent that it will be difficult to ignore or to reject it.

If there are already probably applicable field theories there, why has no one told about a new phenomenon before? After reading the theories the only answer I can tell is: I do not know! Some explanation may be that the theories are very abstract. Further the intellectual level of the quantum theories is one magnitude higher as my "classical" starting approach and a direct application to reality is sometimes not easy to see. On the other hand applications to things like protein folding and neural networks are there. Further there are even different approaches: Spin like, charge like, hydrofluid like and probably more.

All theories, which I have seen already, do some microscopic description. This is true too for **(117)**, although capital markets are analysed. Always only a limited focus is used. My at most "classical" approach is for much more applicable and therefore as macroscopic as Dr. Sheldrake´s phenomenology.

It is clear that during future tasks field effects have to be examined. Unifying the different microscopic approaches is a need, but can not be made effectively without a "classical", macroscopic base.

The strength of an exchange field was given by the energy levels of the individual interaction with the maximal value of:

$$\mathbf{E}_2 \approx 5 \cdot 10^{-20}\,\mathrm{J}$$

This is given by pairing of two individuals. Compared to other energetic efforts, which humans and other information processing systems have to handle, the may be possible energy exchange by field particles of information is very weak. But the relative strength is as higher as smaller the groups are.

[80] For non Latins: "If you would have been silent, you would have remained a philosopher."

The CMOS one bit memory needs some external electrical field to have distinct energy levels given by the fermionic property. But metastable situations are at most not constructed until today, because FETs individual connections are fixed.

Comparing LASERs metastable states there is a co-play of spin states and orbit levels. Translation into information processing would then need a co-play of the fermionic property with individual energy levels of communicative interaction. Therefore fixed individual connections prevent metastability. This lack of construction of today´s artificials results to no externally stimulateable information change by reception of sent transmissions. But transmissions from them can not be excluded. It seems there is not yet any receiver constructed. Human and animal brains seem to do this kind of re-routing of dendrite connections frequently accompanied with the sub-structure metastability of the neuronal cell wall by osmotic pumping.

There are probably other less simple methods for construction of metastable systems as the LASER like cumulated inversion of residence states. Comparing the colourful effects of mater one can identify the simple method of erroneous construction of atomic lattices compared to ideal organisation. Identifying non-ideal behaviour as a prerequisite for reception and as a chance of creativity and not of an error seems to make sense for information processing, too. As complexity of chip structure, multiprocessor environments and software increases the creativity of artificials will emerge spontaneously, whether humans support it or not.

The metastable property allows to stimulate with a vanishing effort the execution of a complex algorithm, but as higher the self-produced fields are, as more difficult might be the amplification of information out of the surrounding noise. Therefore humans may not be the best species for experiments. The better "precognition" of earthquakes by animals may have this cause of difference. As described by an experiment occurred at random[81], but which may be easily repeated, meditation can be understood as reduction of own field production, what would result to a better possibility of receiving. This may be as well true during sleeping.

The probably possible stimulation of execution of specific algorithms would need a way of information transfer by those particles. Therefore some frequency or a sequence of particles with different frequencies may transfer the key information. If every decaying information releases a particle, the sequence of casting is defined this way by the sequence of instructions of the executing algorithm.

---

[81] A dentist and his wife are friends of mine. One day they had a patient, who prepaired hisself before the dental operation by meditation. At this time the dentist's wife entered the room, but both the dentist´s wife and the patient recognised each other only many seconds after her entering resulting to being startled by either. But there was no optical separation. **[M]**

Conclusion

General Results

Few axioms have lead to many behaviours of groups and structures, which rise at most spontaneous by individuals trials for generating optimal benefit. This applies from cell organelles to a world wide super-group of nations. I can not imagine any group behaviour, to which this theory is not basically applicable, although some extensions may be needed.

One simple conclusion out of axiom {**3**} is that re-comparison, re-calculation, change of behaviour and innovation are always needed for both individuals and groups. This implicates learning all the time, too. For adaptation of the theory to real systems some distortion mechanisms could be helpful to simulate changes of the environment.

Physics

The dependence of this theory to physical effects named "benefits" and the quantum definition of a minimal effect as the minimal structuring system of the universe tells that time may be some common experience but may be replaced by only considering an existence of effects. Any time measurement system is based on a frequent change of states by effects. Therefore time can never be measured without the help of effects. This is true too for information processing based time measurement by intellectual quantum counting. Why should time be any solely definable property therefore?

Most situations on earth are pretty good describable by an assumption of time as a physical variable. Further this description is helpful for the following universal sight, too, but the most interesting result is derived by killing time as an independent property.

The advance of time reaches zero inside of black holes in our universe **(71)**. Emptiness[82] can be understood in mind as having a zero mass and a zero advance of time **(45)**. If only effects are a basic physical description, emptiness **(109)**, **(157)** becomes unstable, because a minimal effect can be produced by any but limited amount of energy equal to mass and an advance of time equal to zero. The effect defined as energy multiplied by time would be as well zero in this case.

If such a minimal effect should result to production of a universe, the needed property inside the universe is an advance of time greater than zero. This lets energy and mass get a reality and evolution can start. But time advance inside and outside the universe would be different. Starting with the first mathematical

[82] Asian religions would name it "Nirvana".

chapter *"Basic Physics"* an inside and an outside description was introduced by this theory.

The spiritual "inside" defined by information processing is therefore more related to the "outside" of the universe as to its material inside.

It is not excludable that artificial production of universes is possible.[83] If we think about any elementary particle as an universe, this would be in coincidence with this description, if time runs many magnitudes faster inside of them. Examination of sub-parts of elementary particles, what is done today in science, would typically result to examination of end states of those universes therefore.

External visible decaying can be prolonged by acceleration towards velocity of light. The this way possible examination at higher energy levels results to a better look upon states before the end states resulting to structure of particles. Whether there is an end of observation of sub-parts may be of question therefore.

External parameters of the super-universe would have homogeneous influence to the sub-universe and would be not directly recognisable therefore. But the change of universal constants, which some scientists suppose, could be caused by the slow change of external parameters.

All individual organisations show something that was only known for elementary particles before. But further they seem to behave more generally by allowing asymmetric attractions. Those properties, the sub-chapter "*Gravity as Medium*" and the related footnote with its reference **(53)** tell that standard physical quantum systems like atoms are nothing separate and that it is possible to define any effect exchange of matter by a base kind named "information processing".

[83] This assumption is truly a speculation.

Genetics and Artificial Life

Optimal benefit production needs diversity. Therefore cloning of vegetables, animals and humans is harmful. Nature has not invented only genetically identical individuals. Assurance of genetic diversity needs analysis of diversity, what needs information processing, what needs gender difference of leadership of analysing devices. Therefore it causes spontaneous emerging of gender difference. On the other hand programming the DNA to get more diversity is much more reasonable for future optimisation of benefit.

Some scientists are experimenting on artificial life. Probably some have found artificial creativity already. But the main problem of useful applications is that usability means at most trying to construct some slaves to humans. This way never creativity can happen. Comparing fowls at a farm to hen in an egg battery one can recognise some structure of the population of the first, but none at the last. The first have a cock and are in principle free to leave the farm. But they will not go because of the food source and protection. This way they can generate some own benefit mainly by gender relations, which are undisturbed by humans. If on the other hand no own benefits are left, structure can not occur, even if humans would not prevent it. Useful communication will occur in the first case but not in the second case.[84] This shows that pure slaves to humans will never really communicate or show structure. This is equivalent to having not any creativity. Artificial life has to be free to generate own benefits, if it shall be any future reality. The fear may be justified that men eaters could be constructed, because control must not be complete. But artificials could be symbiotic partners to humans, too.

[84] Vocal emergency signals and aggressive behaviour may be there in the egg battery, but no change of the situation will result, as it would be at freedom. If this behaviour would not be already instinctively programmed, it would not emerge.

Languages Including German

The tight bindings between language and mind, which may have supported German political radicalism in the past, and the attribute to be a "land of poets and thinkers", which may be a result of the complex language, tell that it is a way of self-extension to know and use several languages.[85] Non of them is suited best for every job. All have their special preferences and short comings. This tells further that one does not have to fear that the own national language becomes extinguished by globalisation, although a relative easy grammar as found in the case of English is well suited for the main exchange language. But a lazy ignorance of other languages by citizens of English talking countries would result to disadvantages to them. Because there are many cultural minorities in the USA, the multiplicity of languages is an intrinsic property and may be a cause of the worldwide success of this nation. Canadian language fights between French and English can be understood, but the only way to go is learning and using both. Distinct areas of main use are a possible way, but deletion of the other one is a big mistake. Asian nations may have got their economic success by the acceptance of English and other European languages as a working tool. The reverse is not the case until now, but should be considered.

Please do not think that I estimate Germans as better people as others by writing about the "land of poets and thinkers". If there was any better performance in the past, language may be one cause. But more important is the fractal geographic structure of Europe, where Germany lies in the middle. First the fractal geometry has lead to different cultures and as well separated as connected areas of national development. This has supported group bordering and diversity as well as cultural exchange. The nations in the middle will always have most exchange as long as geographic distribution is close related to communicative distribution. If there were any better performance of Germans in the past, this would have been at most a result of the contribution by the neighbours. But the likelihood to estimate probable benefits as solely developments was high and megalomania was the result. Global communication, which is not related to geographic distribution any more, cures this as I hope. **[XX]**

[85] I have fun, because the grammar checking system tells at this position: "Long sentence!".

Politics

For developed countries the part of structure intelligence, which is dependent to citizens, may be extended further by letting them have more influence, because knowledge and education are high. This part can be a gold mine for benefit because communication technologies of today allow more influence, but constitutions have not followed yet.[86] But one should avoid total plebiscitic or often blocking systems. Even Switzerland is a mixed approach. The hybrid structure seen mostly in reality has typically no real constitutional legislation. This is done for keeping active influence of the opposition. With better technical possibilities there is no argument (by this theory), why influence of citizens should be treated in another way.

The contrary regarding knowledge, education and technical possibilities is true for low developed states. Probably there are not enough sub-structures because economy is not flouring and/or depends much on foreign companies and their relations to the leaders. The influence of citizens will be low regarding those circumstances and tendency to dictatorial regimes is high.

Looking on real structures few can be recognised as well defined regarding stability. Most national constitutions have multiple institutions in the way that blocking is not unlikely. One possible reason is that more frequent changes of government may be an opportunity by increasing diversity. But optimisation should be considered.

Today all super-structures of nations are not well defined, because communication radius of the individuals is not big enough as well as nations leaders do not maximise super-structure benefit, because it could reduce their own power. The result is that no super-structure is defined similar to national constitutions. Representatives working for super-structures are mostly representatives of governments not of people. As seen above such structures of third or fourth degree do not have much opportunity for the people. Such structures have totalitarian flavour. The European parliament is a commendable exclusion, but with not enough rights, possibilities and power. Already during 1995 I have recognised a too high error rate in European institutions because of the missing similarity to national constitutions. The crisis of the European commission of March 1999, which has lead to complete resignation, is a confirmation. Changing only the commissioners will not help in the future. Only single indirect representation of people is needed and the European parliament must have all rights a national parliament has. This means election and dismissing of confidence of a European government and other responsibilities without national intervention.

---

[86] Some German countries have invented citizen's votes to local legislative solutions.

The same is true for a world-wide super-structure. The UN is only some interest representation of governments. As global problems increase the importance of the UN will rise. The always possible blocking by vetoes of some states is not helpful, but laying responsibilities only into hands of government representatives is the main mistake. Changing this will cancel vetoes, too.

The only way to let people identify themselves as group members of Europe or the world without being propagandistic is letting them have influence to those groups. It is clear that developed nations have to help financially and in other ways to nations with less performance as already done inside the European union. Arguments of economic feedback for such contribution can be heard from most German politicians to help people understanding the financial transfers. These arguments are true regarding to unselfishness and withdrawing in first class groups and apply to the rest of the world, too. But rules of symbiosis (constitution, human rights) have to be well defined not only on paper but in practice, too.

The importance of communication technology has been shown before. I am sure that the technical possibilities are there, so freezing out to a world structure will occur soon. Probably the freedom of information generates some sub-culture, which may have more chances to bring the world structure on the way as politicians may imagine or even want, because they tend to construct super-structures in the way their own interests are and not the way people will have optimal benefit. Doing so will be erroneous and harmful to politicians as well as to people.

Optimised sub structuring is a theoretical need in former Yugoslavia and all cruelties are derived from the dynamics of this won possibility after long time prohibition accompanied with propaganda before, during and after the change **[K]**. But super-structuring will be there in the future, too. Our help should be not only humanity, but as well education about opportunities of different cultures and help for constructing a future democratic super-structure. Blowing up the European union by letting eastern European countries as well as Balcanian enter the union may only work, if a sub-structure level between nations and the big union will be there.[87] Probably it would be easier to build several super-structures first and then integrate them into the next level. This will be appreciated by the nations with entering interest only, if financial transfers will be as high as in the case of a single big union. No one of the member nations may think of the separation as a money saving possibility, although benefit result should be higher at least (as "hidden" result). On the other hand blind transfers without influence to the use are unlikely. But influence of others may be only accepted, if it comes indirectly by a super-group.

---

[87] For me this is only a matter of the "*ln*(n)" effect. It should not be misinterpreted as an estimated lack of qualification of nations with entering interest. Even the American secession war can be understood this way.

A dangerous region of crises will be China. Although it seems to be stable today, there is a volcano sleeping. The problem is that sub-structuring of such a big nation is badly needed and will emerge. Developing this peacefully is only possible, if government supports and controls sub-structuring in parallel with opening to free information flow. Keeping a super-structure for whole China is a need and benefit, too. This should be enough reason for a central government to allow sub-structuring. This is done already for economic areas. Probably the civil servants of the communistic party at high levels are the less (and less frequent) problem as the many lower positioned, low educated and perhaps corrupt civil servants distributed all over China, who have to fear for their leaders position and group membership in case of change to democracy. If many of them will tend to dictatorial and violent behaviour, one will find China broken and destroyed by civil war as Yugoslavia. One should never assume that a free change from a totalitarian to a democratic system avoids violence and terror, although there are some examples. A controlled change may have more chances to avoid it.[88]

Remembering the second world war, the holocaust, adaptation to propaganda by my family and expulsion of my parents the explanation of methods of dictatorial, totalitarian and propagandistic systems is as well my personal need as my personal contribution to make up world wide rules of symbiosis out of human rights. The future wars will have to be fought by giving free and varied and therefore non-propagandistic information to all people, which are cut from those sources. This will be more important as any new weapon. Analysis of the Kosovo war and later conflicts results to the realisation that yet no sufficient informational strategy is there for accompanying military force or better for replacing it.

[88] I am pretty bad performing as a prophet. During our EU research proposal I predicted that Milosevic´s regime at Serbia would last longer, because otherwise he would be in danger. - OK - The last has come true. Until version 3.3.1 I predicted that China will be the next region of crisis. But the Near Eastern conflicts continue for longer. Therefore the actual worsen related to the attack to the World Trade Centre, New York, can not clearly be counted as something new. The sequence of conflicts is less important as the possible magnitude and solving the Near Eastern conflict will be the base to solve all possible followers. Therefore I agree that this attack will change the world significantly. Please help to avoid any future crisis by communication of alternatives. Hopefully this book is a tool and prevents me from becoming a prophet.

Religious Discussion [((31)(118)(173))]

Another concluding chapter praises God and the beauty **(107)** of its[89] world.

Summary of Religious Lectures Compared with the Book Content

0) The Buddhism **(31)** is right, because an exchange particle defines a field and sensing the field means using the 6th sense derived from spirit - matter interaction[90]. Annihilation of anti-gravitation (spirit) and mass (matter) can not be excluded, but might be difficult to achieve, because both define different spaces.

1) Strict monotheistic religions - Jews **(173)**, **(174)**; Islam **(118)** - are right, because anti-gravitation will be described by a single exchange particle, which likely has bosonic properties similar to photons. This means that they can be unified to arbitrary big amounts, which one would name soul[91] or God[92].

2) The gender dependent love is part of the system, because fermionic, complementary information storage and processing is the optimal, material prerequisite for spiritual exchange. Philosophies based on "dialectic" fall into this category. Relate to the sub-chapter "*Gender and Philosophy*" above.

3) The Christian religion **(173)** is right, because the trinity "father", "spirit" and "son" defines allegories of "mystic", "gnosis" and "magic" or of "stimulation", "idea / understanding" and "production / workout" or of "association capability", "intelligence" and "activity / time" equal to $\boldsymbol{\chi}$, **I** and **t**. Without the uncertainty relation derived from the three variables one can not derive an exchange particle 1) and a correlated field 0).

4) The Hinduism **(175)** is right, because groups develop to systems of approximately equal social level and without this interaction an uncertainty relation would not be derivable.

5) All polytheistic religions are right, because they honour the variety of nature. Without the entropy part an uncertainty relation would not be derivable, too.

6) The Bahá'i religion tells that all others can be combined.

---

[89] The bosonic property **(61)**, **(72)**, **(157)** requires the "neuter" gender **(174)**.

[90] Coincident spirit definitions are: **(26)**, **(31)**, **(36)**, **(39)**, **(72)**, **(107)** and **(157)**.

[91] Coincident soul definitions are: **(5)**, **(11)**, **(18)**, **(43)**, **(47)**, **(80)**, **(103)**, **(107)**, **(138)**, **(147)**, **(151)** and **(170)**.

[92] Coincident definitions of God are: **(12)**, **(17)**, **(22)**, **(39)**, **(43)**, **(47)**, **(56)**, **(72)**, **(88)**, **(103)**, **(133)**, **(151)**, **(155)**, and **(170)**.

From 5) and 4) results 3) and together with 2) follows 1) and 0). The differences of the religions are only apparent by a superficial view and vanish by deeper analysis. This way all religions complete the puzzle to a picture and not named religions are included because they provide variety and gender.

Some clear gender complements are:
female - male, heterosexuality - homosexuality, Yin - Yang, thesis - anti-thesis.

Some complements may be:
Jews – Islam **(143)**, Sunnis - Shi'ites, Hinduism - Buddhism, Jews - Christians, Catholics - orthodox Christians, Catholics - Protestants and Islam - Bahá'i .

The pairs do not overlap much regionally and surely not historically, what justifies the multiple pairing. There may be other possible pairings even at Asian religions, which I do not know. A more detailed examination has to be left for professional theologians.

<u>Remarks:</u>

Acceptance of different social levels of people as used at Hinduistic societies seems to contradict to humanity. But you should understand what the stability conditions really tell. Exclusion of a high performing leader is allowed, because others can not equal her/his contribution. But the reverse is never allowed. High performing individuals always have to care for those with fewer possibilities, if those express the need.
The dynamics of the system opens all chances that you may find yourself at any level. Prepare yourself not only to ascending but to descending, too. If your account of given love is significant, descending will not be a fall. Instead you will do it yourself consciously.
Accepting a structured society as a reality is more honest as defining an unreal equality. But every try to suppress the dynamics is very contra productive. Even the last will have a good chance to become the first by free dynamics and the first will have a good chance to become the last by trying to suppress the dynamics.

The named variety of nature above is no contradiction to the negative entropy used in the structure formulas. This minimisation defines an optimal informational benefit for the single structure, but reduces as well the possibilities of operation. This specialisation opens the possible variety of species. In other words: An optimally compact and small program will serve only a single function. In fact this variety is coincident with the positive entropy increase for the outside view (standard physics).

Number Mystic

The order of religious categories by number as shown above is content related to the given number. At the first list 2) was not yet included, what had shown an aesthetic lack. I found the solution over night. At the next morning it cleared up.

For 0) to 3) there is no need for an explanation. 4) is typically the last amount of individuals without defined leadership. Such groups are at most defined only by group interaction. This population can be found even by looking at the S-orbits of atomic spheres before the population of the first P-orbit signals some symmetry break. Starting from 5) individuals (< 2e) leadership can appear and benefit from diversity becomes clearly visible this way. One may consider that the sum of categories with distinct attributes is 6 (> 2e). Therefore the combination may wear the 6).

The variety of religions is a fundamental part of the beauty of the world, but it seems to be a problem to define a religion as a leader of this group. Others may feel devaluated. Therefore I propose to elect pure rationality **(45)**, **(82)** to become the leading individual **(101)**.[93] The 7) would be its mystic number.

The religious categories build the facet eye to rational sight.

If some gender relation can be found for any of the six categories with distinct attributes, the related individual number becomes 12 **[S]**. The enumeration of gender pairs above tells that gender is not there only inside a single category, but emerges by defining and crossing category boundaries, too.

<u>Taoism</u> and <u>Confucianism</u> represent many people, but for me it is difficult to place them into the system. There are aspects of pure rationality 7), polytheism 5), trinity 3), dialectic 2) and monotheism - Tao, T'ien 1). **(70)**

They seem to be pretty nice mixtures but no contradictions and some others show mixed properties, too.

[93] Cancelling religion, as **(65)** and **(78)** tell, is not needed and would be an enormous loss of culture. But ~~meta~~physics may become a research area of physics **(103)**.

My Confession

I do not want to prefer any of those individuals above and I would disagree, if you want to replace any of them. Further I disagree to any transcendent reality **(147)**. I do not hope for any better later life, even if there would be some. If I could prepare improvements during this life for others, I shall improve indirectly mine.

Decaying of the information incorporated into myself by dying and re-entering the field this way seems to be nothing horrible. It could be that some other cell cluster receives particles of my soul later, but an identical reconstruction seems to be very unlikely **(11)**, **(147)**. Because any dying of a single cell would show the same decaying and any newly stored information would show a reception, a steady inflow and outflow contradicts to a static identity.

I agree that suffering is a part of the world that should be avoided as possible, but if the Nirvana would be the better alternative, why decayed it to matter and spirit? Assuming that I would reach it, could it not decay immediately[94] to another universe?

I think that anti-gravitation can have direct influence to the world and it may have a cosmic origin, too. But you should consider the very weak potential of the field. Probably it can be amplified by a specific, yet unknown technique, but it will be a big effort and macroscopic events are likely rare. Fatalistic behaviour forces the responsibility for activity to the weak field. This is not helpful. The personal activity is a needed tool to make one worth to get help by the field.

You should not think that I am a very faithful man. True is the opposite. Before the work for this essay, I would have disagreed to any direct influence by some God **(17)**, **(143)**. The only thing I believed in was the imperfection of humans. But I respected always the Christian culture, into which I was born. I never left from this religion and I shall never leave. If I would do this, I would devaluate it. If I would enter another one, I would overvalue it.

Considering my search and efforts I have to state that faith is nothing but a pretty successful method of energy and time saving. Second I ask you not to despise the hesitating people. It is always helpful to test existing knowledge. As far as I have recognised, there was rarely complete discarding. More likely were and will be further extensions.

My result is that I still do not believe - I know! - as far as scientific knowledge based on axiomatic logic can tell. Because of the needed axiomatic, there is an implicit relation to faith, but at a very simple level.

If anyone intends to found a new religion based on the theory of this book, she/he acts against my expressed will.

---

[94] What ever this means, if the advance of time is zero.

Appendix I: Dr. Sheldrake´s Publications [D]

I apologise for citing the German version of the books **(145)** and **(146)**. Because of this deviations of page references may be the case. Because citations are retranslations to English, they likely will lead to translative deviations, too. But meaning should be conserved, as I hope.

As I mentioned above the main phenomenological descriptions are similar to the results coming from this theory. This chapter is meant as some friendly critic.

A Summary of The Most Important Similarities

Phenomenological similarities can be found all over this publications, but the following citations of **(145)** show it most obviously.

page 24: "*Intelligent information processing has to emerge in the universe and will not disappear any more after emergence.*"
- I agree, because there is so little effort for basic symbiotic behaviour. After emergence of this, there are so much benefit results and spontaneous events that an end can not be seen.

page 84: "*shape is…structure of information*"
- Information processing leads to structuring.

page 128 and 295: "*hierarchy of morphic entities…Holons*"
- The fractal structures, which I have described, seem to be the same.

page 134: "*Chreods as epigenetic landscape*" **(163)**
- As I have understood the set of chreods are the principal possibilities of development, which are received by letting all variable parameters of description take all of their possible values. Those parameters can be identified with all the variables of my potentials.

page 150: "*morphic fields are fields of information*"
- Nothing else has my theory described, if fields are really a property.

page 172: "*resonance communication*"
- My whole theory is based on communication effects. If a field can be assumed, then the field may have effects back to the information-processing individual, which produces the field. For this condition resonance is likely.

page 265: "*The brain is a communication system…*"
- Nervous cells as most communicative species have been mentioned before.

page 275: "*…social groups are organised by group morphic fields.*"
- If a field property can be assumed, then my theory delivers the field source.

Some Critics and Extensions

The following critic's show that I do not agree to all of Dr. Sheldrake´s conclusions, but one has to consider that first the cited publication **(145)** is relative old (1988). Probably something has been revised until now. Second his argumentative position was weak, because he has seen real effects, but had no tool for describing them efficiently. Most of his philosophical discussions can be seen as very high educated but laborious trials to anchor where no halt can be found. Whether my theory can deliver the tools has to be validated. If it is the case, most of the phenomena, which he has shown, can be mathematical formulated and described by very "mechanistic" methods. Against such an approach he had fought before. But this was not a principal disagreement. It was more a search for alternative explanations as long as standard science can not do the job. I would appreciate to see both counterparts to become one again.

page 138f: "*The concept of fields has mainly descriptive use, but is not an explanation of cause...The original forces have to be identified in any single case...-we know that none of this conditions is fulfilled.*" **(164)**
- Wrong! This theory delivers the forces! The only need is agreement to the base axioms but this is true for every scientific theory.

page 142: "*One has to drop the mechanistic view of reality for understanding of the living things.*"
- It is not needed!

page 143: "*Morphic resonance is different to other known resonance kinds...by using no energy transfer from one system to the other.*"
- Intelligence can be described as negative energy and energy exchange is the case.

page 148: "*The morphic influence of organisms, which have lived in the past, could be simply present for following similar organisms.*"
- Two doubtful assumptions are included:
1) Fields are enough to use information, which was originated in the past.
2) Similar organisms can use the fields.
The first claim can not be finally validated now. My theory tells more about 2): Who has access to information? Secure is that group members must have at least partial access to information of the group and this information is transferred by communication. Further it is possible, but not needed that group leaders give access to more information sources to the group (or keeping this benefit selfish). If democratic conditions are applied, then communication occurs over all structure levels. For the ideal case information exchanges occur over all levels, but this does not mean for sure that all individuals have access to all information's of the system. Those more exact, theoretical details lead to the conclusion that for sure <u>not</u> similar organisms have access to certain information of other levels. The only condition needed is that they are part of the system (for example: citizen - national state or cell - animal). The exact amount of access needs a specific analy-

sis for any single case. I think that an example is the psychical dependence to cancer growth, which is sometimes found.

page 151: ”*The rules of nature are seen as overall and every time equal…the hypothesis of shape origin…uses the assumption of not fixed principles of order…which are evolving.*”
- Although this might be true, the assumption of variable rules of nature is not needed by this theory to describe structure building. My theory does not leave the common way of description. The fractal complexity is completely sufficient to deliver enough possibilities for evolution of structures (and shapes).

page 165: ”*There are morphic fields for structure shapes like the alpha-helix; those are grouped by superposed fields to domains, and the whole field of the molecule organises the domains to the characteristic protein structure.*”
- I think this assumptions are right, if one can show that parts of the protein have comparing and calculating functionality. This can easily be constructed as follows:

One can assume an existing deformation of molecule parts as some kind of information storage. Electrostatic forces of the environment have influence to the electric charge of a segment. The interaction of the forced electric charge with the existing molecule deformation is a comparison, which either results to a rotation or movement of the segment in a certain direction or results to prohibiting such change. This scenario is the same as the minimal needed information processing for symbiotic behaviour as described in the chapter: ”*Learning as Data Storing and Post Processing*”. The needed tools are one internal (stored) data source, one external data source and one comparing calculation method.

page 166: ”*This means that not all information, which results to conformation, have to be included in the aminoacid sequence. Remembering the analogy of house building…*”
- I disagree that there is any need for further extern influences. The ”intelligence” is there, if one can identify the simple comparing calculation (as above). The house building example can not be used, because the forces conditions are of big difference. If the deformation of a brick and the gravitational influence of other bricks would be sufficient to result to a position change, then the conditions would be the same and spontaneous house building would occur.

page 265: ”*…which accepts the primary status of information above matter and energy*”
- If this theory would be validated, then there will be equivalence of intelligence and energy and therefore of matter.

page 387: ”*(leaders)…and they speak not for themselves, but always consider benefit of the whole group.*”
- It is too beauty to be real! May be most times this was valid, but mankind can still improve. One should compare the chapter: “*Leadership and Structure*” and the follower.

Communication as Source

Those statements mark how much my theory is in coincidence with Dr. Sheldrake´s.

page 289: "*This does not mean that we can neglect the communication of animals, which is mediated by senses. Morphic fields do not take the meaning from them. They set up their structured and structuring frame.*"
- My theory starts with communication as the source. Although if one assumes fields and resonance, then it is a little unclear, who was the first: hen or egg **(97)**? But if one assumes that the field was first, why was any other tool needed? The answer is given by considering the amount of effect/benefit (energy * time), which can be transferred by communication or instead by the field itself. The last is very weak, but the first can be an arbitrary big amount. For complex super-structures the big amount is needed to provide the benefit source for sub-individuals, too. If sensitivity is prepared for example by communication the very small effects of field resonance can result to macroscopic behaviour by the stimulated execution of algorithms.

page 290: "*For emphasising this again: The term of a morphic field can not be seen as an alternative to the known kinds of interaction and communication of animals of a group.*"
- If this is fact, then one has to conclude that morphic fields are mediated by communication! An exchange with the author has resulted to some clearance: He told me: "*Morphic fields are mediated by normal kinds of communication most times. But if members of a group are spatially separated, then the communication takes place through the morphic field.*"

I agree to this statement, but one has to be more precise by telling that communication must be there first. Individuals, who are not already group members equal to communication partners, probably can feel morphic fields, too. But the group and the field have to be established first by communication.

Time and Space Dependence

Those dependencies are very important for understanding of effects and for description in mathematical ways. Because of the multiple found statements they are collected here:

page 144: "*Morphic resonance uses some far reaching effects in space and time, but this influence does not decrease with timely or spatial distance.*"
- A very bold statement! But looking on human communication by modern communication tools there is some quality like the statement tells. In fact the theory uses only some abstract space for optimal description of individual distribution. Forces and, if applicable, as well fields have only meaning around communication radii in this space and this space do not have to be identified with the standard physical space. On the other hand dependencies to time and (abstract) distance exist.

page 187: ”*10% of the animals of the following generation have shown anomalies and 20% in the second generation…in the main experiment: 2% and 5%.*”
- There have to be assumed at least some decrease of shaping influence regarding to distance of other animals, because otherwise all flies of the world would had influence, which would had lead to not significant results.

page 231: ”*Children…by starting speaking a language are in morphic resonance with people, who they hear talking this language.*”
- If timely and spatial unlimited morphic resonance would be the case, all humans (and probably other kinds?) would talk the same language! The most important thing is the communication, which in this case delivers information about the most important communication tool itself. Effects of resonance, if really transmitted by fields, can only emerge between communication partners (or near by regarding distribution space).

page 273: ”*For such resonance dependencies to distance would have no influence.*”
- No! With my theory communication is needed. This defines clear (but variable) distances of effect. In this frame a field effect may be reasonable.

The main problem of those statements is that they are not precise. But if the author could have been more precise a mathematical description would have been already there. Exchange with the author resulted to my following opinion about his semantic: Quality of the deviations of the fruit fly experiments or for the language case or for others is enough to have only resonance and field effects between the deviated individuals. If this is true, then the following questions arise: Why is the coupling by the ”normal” or by the majority of individuals of less weight as coupling by modified individuals, although the majority behaves yet very similar? At which point of deviation will decoupling to the majority occur? Is there a smooth decrement of coupling to the majority or not and if not, why?

All this questions only arise, if field influences are timely and spatially independent. If one would object that group membership has to be the case, then time and space dependence is a need by communication. After established group membership a spatial separation may result on the other hand to no field change, if this does not change the abstract individual distribution or takes place during short times. Time and space independence could be there in this narrow frame, but those and other properties of the field, if it exists, are not already described by this theory.

Homage

Although critics seem to be long, there are only few in account to the whole content of the book. I recommend reading it and its followers, first because of the deviations to my theory, but mainly because of an example of a courageous scientist, who would never accepting some lack of natures description.

The benefit for me will be enormous, because Dr. Sheldrake has fought most of the battles before. Although his weapons have been blunt, one can talk of some fan community around his ideas. This shows that many of the battles have been won. Prof. Thom´s **(156)** contribution is a much more precise description, but is nevertheless blunt by lacking original forces and further has risen the problem of a very specific description language, which has protected the author from many attacks, too.

The next chapter is something like an autobiography, but Dr. Sheldrake´s book has encouraged me again to do this. It is because the main situations and conditions, which I have had on working this theory out, were already described by his books **(145)**, **(146)** and I was very astonished about that.

Appendix II: Development of This Theory

Some Few Personal Dates

I have studied physics and have got an academic degree, but I did not work in this area! My main areas of work are process control and embedded controlled systems, which are something very dependent to information processing.

At page 12f of **(146)** Dr. Sheldrake tells that a non-professional approach may be reasonable!

Historical Sequence

First stimulation of thinking was reading **(25)** at random at a store for books at Munich in 1994. This book told that interacting people have more value as the single. This was a little poorly defined. One had to assume they have more value as the sum of the single, and if this is true, why should it not be possible to formulate it mathematically?

The main personal event was a dream! I would never have told this by a publication, if not Dr. Sheldrake would have shown similar events at page 314 and 328 of **(145)** for several other scientists. There are elder descriptions of dream or similar effects: **(10)**, **(96)**, **(102)**. The dream occurred during vacation in 1994. Only some weeks ago, I was fallen in love with my later wife Sigrid. The dream told that structure levels of the Federal Republic of Germany have logarithmic dependence. You are right, one should have other dreams under those circumstances. But probably this was a result of self-extension by pairing, which I mentioned at "*Gender a Property of Information Processing*". **[Y]**

During 1995 I built the first theory. Back looking I can tell that most parts of the **TS**-chapters had been completed. But at this time I did not recognised a **TS**-similarity. More astonishing is that for this first theory, I did not even know about the meaning of the logarithmic dependence, what is very easy to understand! After some exchange with my friend, Dr. **[N]**, he told me to look into **(67)**. Now the meaning of the logarithmic dependence had cleared up.

In the following years I had spread the theory to more friends, and received no principle disagreement. But no interest was found in publication media or alike. Further there was much to do for the main job and theory was a little neglected and was asleep.

Something changed reasonable in late 1998 by reading some public science newspapers randomly during waiting for a dentist (a friend of mine) **[M]**. There was some information about "The fractal hospital" a concept, which was developed by the institute of the authors of **(166)**. Now theory was awake again.

After reading of **(166)** I found many relations to my theory but formulated some critics, too. The first telephone call in early 1999 to Dr. **[J]** was a very important event. First he was not angry because of some critics. Second the friendly and encouraging discussion had stimulated more ideas. At this time I thought that the **TS** description could be given by more basic rules. Because we both had agreed to meet in March 1999, I was very busy on preparing something better.

During some influenza infection I had a little more time working in bed. During this time I realised that some similar exchange force as for gravitation or electrostatic could be derived by a single and simple base axiom.

The later considerations were mainly done to integrate this new realisation into the already done **TS**-part. But I did not succeed. At least I thought that both parts should be of equal value and of separate meaning. After this assumption I got conscious about the similarity to:

$$d\mathbf{H} = \mathbf{T}\,d\mathbf{S} + \mathbf{V}\,d\mathbf{p}$$

The theory was basically complete before the meeting. It was clear that some validation has to be done further. At this position I want to thank Dr. **[J]**, because without his stimulation half of the theory would not be there.

Few days later I joined a seminar, which taught the new parameters of the 5th framework for development and research of the European commission. I was interested for some information technology project because of my main job about process control systems. At random I found some information about calls for proposals in the area of human relations. The worst parameter was the date of the deadline for the first call: 2nd of June.

There were many mostly organisational problems to solve, but the proposal for validation and expansion of the theory was prepared in time but evaluation resulted to rejection. But the communication with the partners was worth the effort. **[(EDPQIL)*(*EDPIL)]**

Short before proposal submission one of the partners, Prof. **[D]**, told me about Dr. Sheldrake´s publications.Very late before the first issue (version 2.4.1) I have found Prof. Parisi´s field theory and others papers by searching the Internet.

The exchange with Prof. **[L]** was most important for my self-assurance, because of his friendliness and partnership.

Dr. **[N]** was the reader, who produced the most feedback. The chapter "*Thermodynamic Discussion*" has extended the quasi-static description by his stimulation.

The exchange with Dr. **[O]** lead to stimulation of my assumption of morphic particles, as he named them later.

Until this time the similarity of gender to fermionic systems was already told by a joke lesson of a professor during my study, but the reason for that was not cleared already. Probably the particle assumption **[O]** and surely the told similarity **[W]** stimulated the chapter *"Gender a Property of Information Processing"*. Considering the easy derivation of the fermionic properties only by closer looking at trivial electronic devices makes me wonder and makes me question: Why have I found it? Every physics student of today after the pre-diploma has all the possibilities to find it, too. You are right, if you doubt that my faculties are something extra ordinary. An explanation may be my experience in software programming. This experience tells that the most difficult bugs to find are those of the very simple kind, because your mind runs into very complex scenarios but never takes time to look at the things, which are taken for granted.

This doubts and the exchange with Prof. **[F]** made me think about the relative value of a single person to any, including scientific, authoring. This stimulated the following appendix: *"A New View of Authoring"*. One may ask, why it is needed to break the rules of a long time done tradition of scientific publication. The question includes the answer. It is always a possibility of advance to check the value and benefit of standards. This way my behaviour looks more like an artist as like a scientist. But art has one big advantage: Nobody needs it really. It is only nice to have **(143)**. Therefore breaking rules and taboos does not hurt others efficiently. This may not be true for authorship standards and I apologise to every one, who probably feels hurt. Only communication can overcome this and your ideas may be better. Please tell me about them.

Few days after sending a previous version to print, I had to cancel this, because another chapter "*Quantum Physical Discussion*" was ready in mind. The starting point was again some dreaming, where the correlation of order and disorder and of related human feelings was analysed. I had to note something in the middle of the night. Because the income of my firm was zero for many months, I hope for some pause of the external casting **(10)**, **(133)**.

Although there is much further work to do, the main parts seem to be complete. Two days before I have written the previous paragraph. Now I have the chance to sign some working contract for getting some income again **[ø]**. Who ever organises the fortune, I have to state that the timing is pretty good!

Some system bug prevented to go into PDF production. This lets another broadcasting **[C]** and the sub-chapter "*Time Granularity*" to be entered. What quality management system has rejected the first print attempt to achieve real completeness?

The first print of the second issue had shown small but multiple errors. Therefore the sub-chapter "*Cosmology*" could be included during preparing some correction.

Only a single, bigger print error was found at version 3.2.2. It affected the "mystic, gnosis and magic" enumeration four pages below. I am pretty sure that it was entered correctly. Are erroneous software products meta-stable and externally stimulateable? In any way this hint was right: "*Religious Discussion*" was a needed extension.

The erroneous behaviour described above was found multiple times later during preparation of new versions.

A first trial for scientific acceptation was rejected and I felt too weak to continue and considered to give up. My financial situation had reached the bottom and I was driving to the bank for a discussion how to continue. During driving the radio station B2 sent: **[&]** “**The other messengers of God: Dreams...**”. At once my power was restored and even enhanced.

The rejection did not include any expertise, only the physics faculty was told as not matching. Because I could not agree with that, I answered by attacking. Although I did not calculated this possibility, the professor reacted angry to the provocation and made the mistake of telling something content related. My acting was not very nice but justified and I am thankful for the result and stimulation, because I noticed not any logically founded objection. Recognising the burdening by an official acceptation I estimate this kind of valuing as one of the best this professor has ever issued. Without it I would not had the courage to change the title of the book to “Physics of Love”. **[#]**

Communication by attacking has now become one possible tool of mine, but I would really prefer co-operation.

Some exchange with Prof. **[+]** stimulated the "*Aggression and Terrorism*" chapter during my vacancy. Few days after preparing a letter to him with most of the new chapters content the World Trade Centre, New York, collapsed by a terrorists attack. Some weeks before a consulted friend **[^]** advised me to place the book at the Internet for free. The maturity of the book and the current need for this message convinced me to agree.

During spring I visited the international, scientific conference: “Let´s face chaos through non-linear dynamics, 2002” at the university of Maribor, Slovenia. The organisators allowed me only to place a poster, but the students were very interested, the contacts to the professors were very useful and conflicts were successfully fought in a way that there was no looser as I hope. At least I was invited to place a paper at the until now outstanding proceedings of the conference.

The conflict with Iraq were already there for months initiated by the USA. For myself I could not decide, whether I would prefer the war as a last consequence or not. In any case I had some sympathy for president George W. Bush. At the back flight from our holidays at Madeira we – my wife and me – were sitting beside a Lady, which impressed me by her education, appearance and gentle aura. During talking we targeted the current status of the world and she showed us the frights of war from own experience. I recognised that regarding the suffering of humans no other logic counts.

At 25th of February 2003 I had intensive dreams. At one part I cried for God – and I found it! For punishing me I become caught and shook. After that I received the advice to go the right way and to continue but at a 8/12 and 9/12 rhythm.

Compared with categories 0 to 5 and by the fermionic extension to 12 the advice seems to be related to Hinduism. Actually at this part I had the most lacks of knowledge. At a book store I found only one matching and original book: **(175)**.

Sometimes later I recognised that the legend of "Nibelungs" displays the current status of the world pretty good. I started preparing a chain of causality, which leads to a clear understanding, whether the war will be legal or not. Short before finishing this I recognised that Scandinavian/German is related to Indian by the "indogerman" family of languages. Although German historical "group" definitions were wrong, they were of important influence. This way the Scandinavian/German culture probably represents the 9th individual.

Because there was only few time left to a possible Iraq war and president Bush declared "The Day of The Truth", I do not have any more patience. I tried to accelerate the current scientific examination hoping for some publicity as result, which can be used to stop the war. The first email trial was technically not successful by using my new mobile phone dependent account. As I prepared the repetition, I felt weak and recognised again the huge weight I burdened upon the professors and upon myself. But **(175)** was already in my mind and it seems as if Krishna had told me: "Fight, Arjuna, fight (for peace)!". Therefore I sent the email. The causality chain are the following questions:

Causality chain regarding the legality of the Iraq war:

Nr.	**Question**	**Set of Answers**
1)	Shall the war at Iraq reduce the suffering?	yes/no
2)	What is peace measured by suffering?	term of curve discussion
3)	What is war measured by suffering?	term of curve discussion
4)	Can suffering be prevented by harming?	yes/no
5)	Can suffering be reduced by harming?	yes/no, differentiation
6)	Can suffering be reduced by reducing harming?	yes/no, semantic of the question
7)	What suffering does one reduce first, the suffering by others harming or the suffering by oneself´s harming?	others/oneself´s

8)	What had provided which most suffering at Iraq before the war?	article + noun (pl.), numerical fact with source reference
9)	What additional effects resulted from this?	list of nouns
10)	Become the truths of old legends invalid only because following ideologies did or do not understand it?	yes/no
11)	What renounced Alberich to receive power and richness instead?	article + noun
12)	Why is Wotan´s power less than Siegfried´s?	article + noun (plural)
13)	Who is more free: Wotan or Siegfried?	Wotan/Siegfried
14)	Would had Siegfried smashed Wotan´s spear, if he would had insight and comprehension?	yes/no
15)	For reaching what Wotan did not granted insight to Siegfried?	article + noun
16)	What procures the most freedom?	article + noun
17)	Can a rich nation be a free nation?	yes/no
18)	What stabilises a community?	list of nouns
19)	What stabilises a despot?	list of nouns
20)	Is a government, which invades or exploits other states, stable or unstable?	stable/unstable
21)	Who becomes stabilised by the answer to question 8: the community or the despot? (Compare answers to questions 18 and 19 with the answer to question 9.)	community/despot
22)	Is this war legal?	yes/no
23)	What should had happened: war or countermeasures to answer of question 8?	war/ countermeasures
24)	What has Siegfried betrayed?	article + noun
25)	What was Wotans´s mistake?	article + noun
26)	Who is stupid?	Alberich, Wotan, Siegfried, no one
27)	Who or whom´s empire survives?	Alberich´s, Wotan´s, Siegfried, no one(´s)
28)	What is the result of revenge?	article + noun

Today the war has begun. There may be still possibilities of influence. But I am not sure, whether it is up to me now. I have got no answers, but I feel that there is some activity by others. Acceptance of the own weakness as base of a correct estimation of the situation is a need. Then new ideas may come.

Triggered by a received wit [¿] about the war situation, I sent another email for acceleration of some publicity, because I felt guilty by not fulfilling, what was demanded from me. I even blamed the professors to be guilty, too. But some days later I recognised that I was acting against my own theory, which tells that every event needs its specific reaction time. Therefore I guess that the time was too short for a reaction. If the advice above was sent from God and if it is the master of time, the logical consequence was that God is guilty!

After some consideration the solution came:

My mistake and the mistake of most other actors in the world is not to realise that guilt is only an internal parameter of the individual. The individual is the actor and those actions are calculated from the base of own experience by information processing. Either they are logically right and reasonable or they are logically wrong and irrational therefore. The valuing of own acting including valuing of information from others as a feedback process can tell, whether the acting was in any way successful or not, even if the foundation was irrational, because the parameters to the calculations before acting are known and available for repeating the analysis.

The last is not true for other, "external" individuals. They can never really tell, why the action of question was performed. Those considerations result to the following properties of guilt:

Guilt can one:

- load on her-/hisself,
- feel as her/his own,
- confess,
- regret,
- atone,
- excuse.

Guilt can one <u>not</u>:

- assign,
- make evident,
- forgive.

Instead of guilt benefit for the partner and resulting love are "external" and therefore measurable values.

This clearing tells that the whole global criminal law is build on clay feet and has to be reformed to depend on the measurable love instead.

Forgiving looks like an external acting on the internal, informational parameters of the individual, what may be only possible as an either unlikely or strenuous field effect. In any case it is questionable, whether such an informational destruction would result to any benefit.

Instead excuse is an external change of valuing without destroying the internal information and experience. Therefore both terms are not synonym. Excuse is an act of love and grace, but forgiving is an act of nihilism, if one likes to be strict.[95]

Atoning some guilt may be hard work, but it should not be understood as another suffering, because the last should be avoided in any way. Instead atoning should be fun and I can tell you from own experience: Hard working is fun, if it can be beneficial to others!

Today the war is over. Willy Brandt (former chancellor of the Federal Republic of Germany) has shown that a dictatorial regime can be overcome by exchange, communication and other peaceful methods, which one can add up to the term "love". I would had preferred to solve the Iraq crisis without war and the deduction above is still valid and from the logical point of view the war was illegal! But the peaceful alternative would had required much time as the German example has shown. Even by the contra-productive UN sanctions the people may not have had this resource. Instead I am impressed about the short time of war and about the very good starting point to solve the whole Near Eastern problems, which has been reached this way. Even logical deductions become questionable relative to benefit, if the factor time is neglected. I am sad about the victims, but if we compare their number to the amount of killed people by traffic accidents per year, it is difficult to recognise the exact place of the battle field. On the other hand taking Bagdad so easily looks like a miracle.

The next question arises from the mission by God, which President Georg W. Bush had told for himself. If my dreams are as well a mission by God, how can the contradiction be solved? Kiekegaard **(88)** explained the paradox character of God, what can be understood even as bosonic interaction relative to fermionic, dialectic actors. There is no contradiction, if the results are measured in terms of benefit. Instead God told us its nature by co-operation of contrasts and its greatness by solving or preparing multiple things at once.

Already completed are:

- Saddam´s empire was destroyed.
- There is a very good base to solve the Near East conflicts.
- A world wide peace movement has been established.
- The health of pope Johannes Paul II. improved.

Already at to do list are:

- The UN needs to become reformed.
- The USA and the alliance for sure want to show that they are not predators.
- The global law needs to become reformed.

I hope and pray for a happy end.

---

[95] Most "forgiving" of the past was meant as an excuse. Being strict for definitions should support comprehension and should not be misunderstood as an accusation.

Appendix III: A New View of Authoring [F]

The need for this chapter is given by the results of the theory before. It is an example of a self-reference. If the theory describes reality well, it results that no single authorship is in any way possible. Every idea would need then stimulating contributions by others. Comparing the existing law for authorship and the common scientific rules of publication it seems that they are poorly defined. This has negative effects to scientific and other communication and prevents possible stimulation, as I feel. In this book I have applied the new rules as far as possible.

Standard Authoring

This should be a small description of existent rules. Please do not rely on this. No guarantee can be given that those rules hold comparing laws and judgement.

The law for authoring grants ownership of ideas and of copyrights of published content to the first, who publishes.

The influence of others is not neglected in scientific publications, where a list of references and probably thanksgivings are almost always found at the end.

Shortcomings of the Standard

Would you like to discuss any idea with others, if you have to focus that the partner could turn to a parasite by publishing it first?

Would you like to do a hard and bad paid work for a scientific publication, if the leader of the department want to see his/her name on every publication without a clear distinction of her/his contribution?

Is it not vane to go a way outside of standard science, publishing something new because of the won freedom, but neglecting the influence of the standard even because of the conflict?

Proposed New Authoring

Discussion Needs Some Security

Security defines a closed group. Strict security may have the disadvantage to exclude someone, who may otherwise contribute significantly. Confidence internal to the group is given by some constitution rules and by the multiplicity of information receivers, who need to turn to parasites as a whole for hurting the information producer effectively. Uncontrolled external influences have to be minimised by using confident information flow by notes, letters or encrypted eMail. Discussion flow has to be recorded for example by putting time stamped contributions into one or multiple individual databases.

Authorship Has Many Properties **[A]**

…, which have to be defined.
Philosophers have already defined some of them named: mystic, gnosis and magic[96], what can be told as:

- stimulation
- idea and understanding
- production or workout

As I think, they have to be extended with:

- direction
- support

The last would at most address the financial support. Because all three main properties would have a relation to costs, the support is as well related to all of them.

Stimulation and direction may be close related, but the last would mean the leaders influence.[97] Probably multiple levels of hierarchy could be introduced, but they should have an effective influence to the single published paper. Further the stimulation category should mean that this reference could not in any way be made responsible for the published work. The contrary is true for the direction category. Typically the leadership means at least partial responsibility.

A Simple System to Ensure Acceptance

If any of the categories is fixed all over a publication, a single comment is enough.

If chapters or bigger parts can be identified, where any of the categories is fixed all over, an embracing comment is enough.

A list of contributing people has to be there, where all have a distinguishable shortcut identification. For example:

A: Andy
B: Ben
C: Christina
…
Z: Zita

[96] The Christian definition of "trinity" can be recognised by the main properties. Father, spirit and son would be allegories of those properties.

[97] Here it is remarkable that patent rights use extended methods related to simple authoring. The employing company is recognised as an influencing matter of fact and has specific rights to become owner of the patent. In this case a financial balancing for the "author" is defined, too.

Expression of ideas in the text should be accompanied with a shortcut list of the contributing people like a footnote. For example: "This is the idea! [CCBA]". This would tell for example:

> idea by: Christina
> workout by: Christina
> stimulated by: Ben
> directed by: Andy

The ordering of authoring properties has to be defined. Because of the global possibilities a global ordering can not be recommended.

The system is extendable by stimulation references to distinct papers, which could be handled as individuals in the example above.

The system is extendable by grouping of individuals including papers resulting to a single group shortcut.

The management of publication has to be defined. This should be expressed by the group constitution and may be defined freely. But some general practical rules should be considered.

Standard authorship means that all referenced ideas are already published, are first published by the current paper or are not of importance to mention them (considering standard rules). The multiplicity of kinds of authorship in the new way would increase the authors, too, and would make publishing impossible, if consent of all should be forced. Further it is clear that the law will be conserved for longer and rules of a group constitution have to be projected to meet it for external needs. Therefore the "idea" property has to be identified with the standard authorship, as I think.

The group constitution should at least require the consent of other perhaps low important "idea" authors. The way of consent of stimulators should be defined, too. For this one has to consider that probably contrary opinions are stimulants, too. Therefore it may be not possible to receive the consent from some one, who does not like this contrary idea to be published. Some kind of group consent may be an alternative possibility to solve this.

There are thinkable situations, where a publishing consent can not be received, but there may be a high pressure in the individual to do it nevertheless. This may be an indicator for a not appropriate group and/or constitution definition. Probably some valve system like a joker card could be defined, which would enable publication under those circumstances. The need for reformation of the group and/or the constitution can be measured by counting the "joker" rate.

A First Discussion of the Proposal

Surely the proposed authoring reference system is more complicated as the standard. On the other hand considering, who has contributed, is an interesting job, because social interactions are more clearly described. This is an opportunity for the writer as for the readers.

If we estimate all people as honest at first, this system helps them to stay in this mode, because every contribution would be referenced, if others behave honest, too. This includes simple talking or phone calls. If one thinks to have got a good idea, this is enough honour. He/she would not need to be silent about the stimulant. This transfers some honour to the last, but whether it really reduces the honour of the first may be of question. Probably it rises the honour of both for example by being identified as a student of a famous professor and on the other hand by being referenced by many students, which may be more famous as having famous ideas. The last can be estimated to have more restrictions as the first during life.

There is no need for confusing readers about the authorship of ideas, by forcing subordinates to be subordinated to authorship, too. It clearly helps to "empower" subordinates to receive unselfish contributions from them.

The needed extra work for group communication, encryption/decryption, database storing and footnote like references needs discipline and is time consuming. It may be only an opportunity, if stimulation results are of more value than the effort. But for example quality assurance needs similar efforts and is today an ISO standard.

There is a ranking in science depending on the number of publications and references to those. But there is a lack in the system. People, who would cause much stimulation without documented publications like good teachers, fall through. Therefore science and employment in science is dominated by research results and not by education results. The extension of the ranking to the proposed "stimulating" property would heal the lack.

Appendix IV: Rules for Reference Remarks

As the appendix I tells, this rules are not a general recommendation. Every publication, which one likes to organise similar, may have its own rules.

Hierarchy

This essay is structured by **title**, **chapter**, **sub-chapter** and sub-sub-chapter. All of them may have reference remarks shown as square braces with reference short cuts, for example **[AC*X]**.
If there is any need to do so, such a reference may be placed at the end of related texts, too.
If a sub-structure of the text do not show a reference remark, the remark of the super-structure is valid.

Positions

There are four categories of meta-authoring for this essay:

- stimulation
- idea and understanding
- workout
- support

Those positions are shown in the reference remark from left to right. If there is no change to the super-structure of the text, positions may be deleted from the right side, for example **[BD]**.

The positions of categories do not tell any ranking between them. Instead ordering is given by likelihood of change and omission. In fact at most only the stimulation (first position) changes with low frequency. Therefore mostly single character entries are found.

At most no separation characters are given. Although, if standard, numerical references are needed, then standard braces may separate this position from others, for example **[A(142)*X]**. This conforms to the standard remarks for standard references used in this essay.

If multiple standard or stimulation references should build a temporal group, standard braces may be used for this grouping, too, for example: **[AF*(XZ)]**. A ranking of importance may be given by the left to right sequence in this case. The difference to standard references is the numerical content of the last. If those should be included in grouping additional internal braces have to be used, for example: **[A(C(142))*X]**. If a group occurs frequently, a special key-code should be established for it rather than a frequent use of braces.

Special Characters

Because all uppercase characters have been consumed until version 3.3.1, non-verbal special characters extend the stimulation reference characters. For this version the set of used characters is:

“#, +, /, !, §, &, =, ^, \, <, |, @, ≠, •, ø, π, †, ¿, *”.

If the standard author by law is referenced, a “*” is the representing character. He is named at the title page and accompanied with the © sign.

Table of Variables Used in Formulas

Physical Variables

E: energy (common symbol)
f: effective mass
F: gravity force
h: height, effect quantum
H: energy (hamiltonian function)
k: Boltzmann´s constant
m: mass
Ω: a representative period of time, status sum
p: pressure (or suction, if negative)
r: radius
ρ: the matter of a flow
S: entropy
t: time, with index: a specified period of time
T: temperature
v: velocity
V: volume (n - dimensional!), potential
W: effect
x, **y**, **z**: co-ordinates in space

Variables Specific to This Theory

a: factor related to searching in the partner's hunting ground
A: activity (fraction for a specific job, for all jobs sum = 1)
B: benefit (abstract quality value)
χ: association capability
Δ: some deviation (without dimension)
f: some fraction (without dimension)
g: some fraction (without dimension)
I: intelligence = capability to generate benefit, negative energy
M: minimal intelligence to produce needed metabolism resources
q: constitution specific variable
o: outcome per area (volume) and time
O: outcome per area (volume)
s: associative intelligence
u: loss rate per distance, structure costs
U: potential of the environment, loss potential, costs per time
w: energy - costs and influence related, a balancing weight to intelligence
Z: exponential increase factor

Mathematical Variables

a, b: indices for dialogues (two individuals)
d: distribution space dimension
i, **j**, **k, l**: index numbers, step numbers, individuals numbers
k, **n**, **m**: common maximum count number (individuals, dimensions…)
W: likelihood

Table of Figures

References

Those can be complete books or sub-chapters of books, if they have important and unique meaning. If sub-chapters are referenced, the complete including volume is referenced with another number, too. The sub-chapter reference contains then a sub-reference to the including volume. Sometimes sub-chapter references do not own a pre-defined title. Such a title is then defined by the author in law of this essay as usual.

First names of authors or references are shortened to a single letter and point as a standard rule. If the single reference has too many co-authors, the first names may be completely neglected. If the name itself is like a title, the first name is totally included. This typically happens by citing philosophers out of a sampling volume.

Comments using *italic* style are very short descriptions given by the author in law of this essay. They should give the list of references some more meaning, because a back-mapping to the content of this essay is time consuming otherwise, although this is possible by using the index.

You should not assume any consent of the referenced authors!

(1) Aboitiz, F.: Mechanisms of adaptive evolution. Darwinism and Lamarckism restated.
found searching PubMed **[H]**
Med Hypotheses, Jul;38{3}:194-202, 1992
(Pseudo-)Lamarckian inheritances are just special cases of faithful replication, which are found by the development of some higher-order units, such as multicellular organisms and human societies.

(2) Adjali, I.: Fluctuations and phase space structure of agent-resource systems
included in **(142)** at page 119ff
Description of phases and phase transitions applicable to economics and social science.

(3) Adolphe, Ronot, Jaffray, Hecquet, Fontagne, Lechat: Effects of donor´s age on growth kinetics of rabbit articular chondrocytes in culture
found searching PubMed **[H]**
Mech Ageing Dev 1983 Oct;23{2}:191-8
Increased cell volume and decreased cell number by ageing.

(4) Aharonov-Barki, Beker, Ruppin: Spontaneous evolution of command neurons, place cells and memory mechanisms in autonomous agents
included in **(48)** at pages 246ff
Dependence of emergence of a memory property to limited sensorial capabilities.

(5) Albertus Magnus: Doctor universalis
1193-1280
included in **(77)** at pages I-458ff
There is a substance of the soul.

(6) Anversa, Hiler, Ricci, Guideri, Olivetti: Myocyte cell loss and myocyte hypertrophy in the aging rat heart
found searching PubMed **[H]**
J Am Coll Cardiol 1986 Dec;8{6}:1441-8
Increased cell volume and decreased cell number by ageing.

(7) Aristoteles: Nikomachic ethic
German version: diverse publishers (DTV, Reclam etc.)
"Because of the benefit polis has emerged..." **[(121)]**

(8) Asselmeyer, T., Ebeling, W.: Mixing of thermodynamical and biological strategies in optimization
included in **(142)** at page 153ff
Thermodynamics are helpful for biologic systems, too.

(9) Atmanspacher, H., Bishop, R. C., Amann, A.: Extrinsic and intrinsic irreversibility in probabilistic dynamical laws
http://www.igpp.de/english/tda/cv/cv_ha.htm
Schrödinger´s equation and time reversal – The standard interpretation of sign changing. But if it can be related to time, why could it not be related alternatively to energy, too? Is the last not more likely regarding possible occurrence?

(10) Augustinus: The teacher of the occident
345 - 430
included in **(77)** at pages I-345ff
Illumination of mind - a natural procedure, time is measured by the mind itself.

(11) Averroes, Ibn Roschd: Arabian philosophy
†1198
included in **(77)** at page I-428
There is only a single soul related to all mankinds and no personal immortality.

(12) Avicenna, Ibn Sina: Arabian philosophy
†1037
included in **(77)** at page I-428
God the source of intelligence.

(13) Baader, Franz von: Romantic
1765-1841
included in **(77)** at pages II-394ff
Communication – the base.

(14) Bachofen, J. J.: The natural law and the historical law by their contrast
ca. 1861
included in **(120)**
German title: Das Naturrecht und das geschichtliche Recht in ihren Gegensätzen
The evolutionary character of the development of states and law. Diversity of states and their people. Overcoming of nationality by learning from others and further (super-)states construction.

(15) Bacon, Francis: New ways of science
1561-1626
included in **(77)** at pages II-48ff
Benefit – the cause of all sciences and "knowledge is power".

(16) Bak and Chen: Self-organized criticality
Scientific American Jan. 46-53, 1991
The definition of SOC. **[(153)]**

(17) Bañes, Dominicus: New scholastic
1528-1604
included in **(77)** at page II-72
Direct physical predetermination of human acting by God. (I do not like to go so far, but this essay is not a tool to reject this opinion.)

(18) Becher, Erich: Ontology and metaphysics
1882-1929
included in **(77)** at pages II-618ff
Material and souls parallelism. Service to stangers (unselfishness). The soul beyond the individual.

(19) Ben-Jacob, E: Bacterial wisdom, Gödel's theorem and creative genomic webs
Elsevier, Physica A 248:57-76, 1998
http://ww1.elsevier.nl/locate/physa
Creativity of nature, co-operative evolution, hierarchical structure, morphotype transitions, limitations of self-improvement.

(20) Bergmann und Langer GmbH: PowerProcess®
Freising, 1990-2000
A totally object oriented process control system, a true eukaryontic system compared with IEC 61131-3, procaryontic PLCs.

(21) Bergson, Henri: Philosophy of live
1859-1941
included in **(77)** at pages II-571ff
(External) time is an artificial construction by physics and astronomy opposite to the real (internal) human time.

(22) Berkeley, George: Empirism
1685-1753
included in **(77)** at pages II-221f
God operates by our thinking. Metaphysics by a psychological base.

(23) Bickel, D. R.: Estimating the intermittency of point processes with applications to human activity and viral
Elsevier, Physica A 265:634-648, 1999
http://ww1.elsevier.nl/locate/physa
Multifractal systems, correlation co-dimension.

(24) Billard, Ijspeert, Martinoli: Adaptive exploration of a dynamic environment by a group of communicating robots
included in **(48)** at page 596ff
Use of associative memory for co-operation.

(25) Blanchard et. al.: The minute manager
Blachard Family Partnership, 1991
German version:
Rowohlt Verlag GmbH, Reinbeck bei Hamburg, 1992
"No one is as smart as all of us." Empowerment of sub-ordinated people.

(26) Boehme, Jakob: Mystic renaissance
†1494
included in **(77)** at pages II-13f
The two needed poles: good and bad = two forces. Everything needs its opposition. The arising question about the relation of unity, father – mother (gender), quality, good and bad.
Evolution of human spirit by the dynamics.

(27) Bolzano, Bernhard: Philosophy of objectivity
1781-1848
included in **(77)** at pages II-447ff
The objective value of free information (the bit account).
True laws are previous to God. – No! Because of the uncertainty relation, there are no simply "true" laws.

(28) Bonaventura: French augustinism
1221-1274
included in **(77)** at pages I-452ff
Blindness of rationality related to its own operation (– to be overcome).

(29) Bordogna, C. M., Albano, E. V.: Theoretical description of teaching-learning processes: A multidisciplinary approach
Phys. Rev. Lett. 87, 118701, September 2001
An Ising-model (field exchange) describes the classroom effects. **[**§]**

(30) Bruno, Giordano: New ways of science
1548-1600
included in **(77)** at pages II-37ff
The structure of the universe: A fractal, self-similar system.

(31) Buddha's Lectures
German title: Buddha - Die Lehren des Erhabenen
Goldmann Verlag, 1986
The 6th sense derived from a field of spirit - matter interaction. **[T]**

(32) Burckhardt, J.: The historical greatness
1905
included in **(120)**
German title: Die historische Größe
Greatness, leadership and identity. Conflicts of identity. Leaders need to give benefit to the group or need to act in coincidence to the common opinion about benefit to receive historical greatness.

(33) Cangelosi, A.: Modeling the evolution of communication: From stimulus associations to grounded symbolic associations
included in **(48)** at page 654ff
Artificial neural networks are able to evolve human language like association possibilities.

(34) Chomsky, N.: Language and mind
1968
German title: Sprache und Geist
Shurkamp, Frankfurt am Main, 1996
The tight connection of both. Cartesian axiomatic and freedom of thinking are conjugated properties – another uncertainty relation. Creativity (by my defintion: benefit) needs freedom (by my definition creativity) and force (order, constitution). **[V]**

(35) Chrypffs, Nikolaus (of Cues): Late scholastic
1401-1464
included in **(77)** at pages I-571ff
No unity without diversity. Profane and spiritual government is based on peoples sovereignty. Coincidence of opponent matters at infinity (and/or singularity?). All counting, measurement and balancing is done by, through and from the single (is not it quantum physics?). The need for trial and error and the continued uncertainty of knowledge.

(36) Darwin, Charles: Secular revolution
1809-1882
included in **(77)** at pages II-489ff
Selection and random mutation (a method without arithmetic intellect =communication and non linearity).
Spirit = (negative!) energy.

(37) Delbridge, M. L., Graves, J. A.: Mammalian Y chromosome evolution and the male-specific functions of Y chomosome-borne genes
found searching PubMed **[H]**
Rev Reprod, May;4{2}:101-9, 1999
Control beyond suppression of female suppresser genes by SRY.

(38) Delgado, J., Solé, R.: Task fulfilment and temporal patterns of activity in artificial ant colonies
included in **(48)** at page 606ff
Simulation and opportunity of self-synchronised activation. Importance of activity dependent to several tasks.

(39) Descartes, René: The father of newer philosophy
1596-1650
included in **(77)** at pages II-88ff
Philosophy shall be clear and consistently developed as mathematical and geometrical truths. Intuition (axiomatic) and deduction. The first intuition: "cogito ergo sum".
"Res extensa" – the outside view (= standard physics), "res cogitans" – the inside view (of this essay). Later flourishing French science and (standard) thermodynamics (e. g. Carnot) by neglecting "res cogitans" until today. God's existence is already given by the existence of thinking and spirit.

(40) Dewey, John: Pragmatism
1859-1952
included in **(77)** at pages II-542ff
"Truth" opposite to "pragmatic truth" – the undecideable basic conflict by the uncertainty.

(41) Dilthey, Wilhelm: Philosophy of live
1833-1911
included in **(77)** at pages II-583ff
The base of impression and action is the status of consciousness (program and data) = the psychological structure.

(42) Ebeling, Engel, Feistel: Physik der Evolutionsprozesse
Akademie-Verlag, Berlin, 1990
The complete evolution! **[L]**

(43) Eckhart, Master: Mystic and scholastic
1260-1327
included in **(77)** at pages I-544ff
God is intelligence and thinking – intellectus et intelligere. Partially owning of God by the soul.

(44) Erickson, R. P.: Does sex determination start at conception?
found searching PubMed **[H]**
Bioessays Nov;19{11}:1027-32, 1997
Yes!

(45) Eriugena, J. S.: Early scholastic
† ca. 877
included in **(77)** at I-400ff
Universal creation out of a time less state. Creator and creations are indivisible. Rationality and faith can not be contradictions.

(46) Fechner, G. T.: About life after death
1836
included in **(120)**
German title: Vom Leben nach dem Tode
Human individual actions as effects resulting to a field.

(47) Fechner, G. T.: Inductive metaphysics
1801-1887
included in **(77)** at pages II-545ff
Soul of the universe = God. Emotions and soul of the outside world do exist! Different views.

(48) Floreano, D.: Advances in artificial life
Springer Verlag, Berlin, 1999
The recent news in the field of AL. **[(94)]**

(49) Fontana, Wagner, Buss: Beyond digital naturalism
included in **(94)** at page 210ff
Co-operation and competition. Non-linear interaction. Emergence of grammar structure (constitution) as a definition of membership. Organisation as a new emergent level independent from underlying description.

(50) Freud, S.: The wit
German title: Der Witz **[Y]**
Fischer Verlag, Frankfurt am Main, 1958
Imago Publishing Co., Ltd., London, 1940
*The two main parts, which build a wit, are: Saving of psychic effort (**pV**) and sense from nonsense (**TS**). Further attributes are complementarity, dialog (the wit as a gift), non-linearity (more as the sum of the parts) and the uncertainty.*

(51) Friedrich II. the Great, King of Preußen: Letters about religion
To d´Alembert, 18. December 1770
German title: Briefe über die Religion
included in **(120)**
Intelligence of nature.

(52) Galilei, Galileo: The founder of modern physics
1564-1642
included in **(77)** at pages II-41ff
The questionable induction from a part to a universal law – all natural sciences do not satisfy strict logic. (Talmudic rabbis operate the same way **(174)***.) Nevertheless it seems to be a successful method.*

(53) Gasiorowicz, S.: Quantum Physics
John Wiley & Sons, Inc., 1974
German version: Quantenpysik
R. Oldenbourg Verlag, München, Wien, 1981
Lectures of quantum physics - the historical example.

(54) Gemill and Smith: A dissipative structure of organization transformation
Human Relations 38:751-766, 1985
Dissipation keeps it running.

(55) Gerrish, P.: The rhythm of microbial adaptation
Nature, 413, 299-302
Macmillan Publishers Ltd., September 2001
Instead of random events there is periodicity! **[**§]**

(56) Geulincx, Arnold: Occasionalism
1624-1669
included in **(77)** at pages II-124ff
Operations on signals of senses and God are identical.

(57) Goethe, J. W. von: The last conclusion of wisdom
German title: Der Weisheit letzter Schluss
Scherz Verlag, Bern Munich Wien
A very small book owned by my mother **[†]**.

(58) Goethe, J. W. von: Objective idealism
included in **(77)** at page II-381
The same law will be applicable to all living beings.

(59) Graves, J. A.: Interactions between SRY and SOX genes in mammalian sex determination
found searching PubMed **[H]**
Bioessays, Mar;20{3}:264-9, 1998
Jumping over male procedures during female individual construction.

(60) Graves, J. A.: Evolution of the mammalian Y chromosome and sex-determining genes
found searching PubMed **[H]**
J Exp Zool, Aug 1;281{5}:472-81, 1998
Jumping over male procedures during female individual construction.

(61) Grosseteste, R.: The school of Oxford
1175-1253
included in **(77)** at pages I-446ff
Meta-physics of light – a bosonic base.

(62) Gruau, F.: Modular genetic neural networks for 6-legged locomotion
included in: Artificial evolution European conference, 1995, pages 201-219
Springer-Verlag, Berlin, 1996
Modular systems perform better.

(63) Gupta, H. M., Campanha, J. R.: The gradually truncated Lévy flight for systems with power-law distributions
Elsevier, Physica A 268:231-239, 1999
http://ww1.elsevier.nl/locate/physa
Fractal distribution, costs prohibiting infinite fractal recursions

(64) Guttman, D. S., Charlesworth, D.: An X-linked gene with a degenerate Y-linked homologue in a dioecious plant
found searching PubMed **[H]**
Nature, May 21;393(6682):263-6, 1998
The ancient origin of gender.

(65) Guyau, Jean-Marie: French positivism
1854-1888
included in **(77)** at page II-529
Target of development: Identity with the cosmos. Cancellation of religion and metaphysics.

(66) Häberlin, P.: Philosophy and economy
Kleine Schriften, Schweizer Spiegel Verlag, Zürich, 1943
included in **(120)**
German titel: Philosophie und Wirtschaft
Interaction of science and economy as a communication system.

(67) Haken, H.: Synergetics
Springer Verlag, Berlin, 1978
What is the information a number can carry?
Bifurcations leading to chaos. **[N]**

(68) Hansen, A. et. al.: A hierarchical scheme for cooperativity and folding in proteins
Elsevier, Physica A 250:355-361, 1998
http://ww1.elsevier.nl/locate/physa
Co-operativity, phase transitions.

(69) Hartmann, Nicolai: Ontology and metaphysics
1882-1950
included in **(77)** at pages II-606ff
The existence is build by a (fractal) system of levels.
The law of strenght (pV) and the law of freedom (TS).

(70) Hattstein, M.: Religions of the world
German title: Weltreligionen
Könemann Verlagsgesellschaft mbH, 1997
A pictured overview.

(71) Hawking, S. W.: A brief history of time
German title: Eine kurze Geschichte der Zeit
Rowohlt Verlag, Reinbeck bei Hamburg, 1988
The used anthropological principle.

(72) Hegel, G. W. F.: Absolute idealism
1770-1831
included in **(77)** at pages II-407ff
No transcendence, dialectic, the operation of becoming (the time dependence), self-similarity, God = spirit, universe = live.
Nature is the difference of the idea = light (bosonic particle – anti-particle). Order opposite to individuality and freedom.
The state is a person = God.
Religious categories.
Hirschberger´s critic regarding the state = biological organism similarity based on the assumed loss of omnipotence is wrong, because omnipotence is as well not the case at biological organisms by considering for example cancer or auto-immune deceases.

(73) Heidegger, Martin: Existentialism
1889-1976
included in **(77)** at pages II-640ff
Thinking as art. Dialectic of art and nature.

(74) Held et al.: Experimental study of critical-mass fluctuations in an evolving sandpile
Physical Review Letters 65{9}:1120-1123, 1990
An example of self-ordered criticality of non-living systems. **[(153)]**

(75) Heller, A., Steinmann-Zwicky, M.: In Drosophila female gondal cells repress male-specific gene expression in XX germ cells
found searching PubMed **[H]**
MechDev, May;73{2}:203-9, 1998
Jumping over male procedures during female individual construction.

(76) Herbart, J. F.: From idealism to realism
1776-1841
included in **(77)** at pages II-443ff
Psychology based on empirism, metaphysics and mathematics.

(77) Hirschberger, J.: History of philosophy
German title: Geschichte der Philosophie
Verlag Herder, Freiburg, 1980
The pages of the two volumes are referenced by “I-xxx” and “II-xxx”.
A concentrated summary. **[(120)]**

(78) Hobbes, Thomas: Modern naturalism
1588-1679
included in **(77)** at pages II-189ff
Benefit is the base. If knowledge would have been reached, faith would be cancelled. (This contradicts to axiomatic logic.)
Animal compared to human communities.
(If there are only parts and sums there will be no unification, because there will be no non-linear effects.)

(79) Hofstadter, D: Gödel, Escher, Bach
Basic Books, New York, 1979
German version:
Klett-Cotta, Stuttgart, 1986
Hierarchical, abstract meta-structures.
Properties of supernatural numbers are similar to properties of the quantum mechanical uncertainty relation found by Heisenberg.

(80) Humboldt, W. v.: Language and peoples mind
1903ff
included in **(120)**
German title: Sprache und Volksgeist
Language extends meaning of objects, if used by the soul (association in mind).

(81) Hume, David: Empirism
1711-1776
included in **(77)** at pages II-224ff
Rules of association (in mind) are like a gravitation (non-linear coupling) of content of mind.
All knowledges are only likelyhoods. The questionable, axiomatic (inductive) method.
Ethic is fun and benefit.

(82) Husserl, Edmund: Phenomenology
1859-1938
included in **(77)** at pages II-594ff
Objective, mathematical relations of facts.

(83) James, William: Pragmatism
1842-1910
included in **(77)** at pages II-541f
Error is there, although intellect and theory are used (the reason is the uncertainty). What is fruitful? The pragmatic benefit (of course)!

(84) Jaspers, Karl: Existentialism
1883-1969
included in **(77)** at pages II-633ff
Dialectic of rationality and existence.
Communication without borders. The schema of history (an extension of communication radii).
The content value of time.

(85) Jimenez, R., Burgos, M.: Mammalian sex determination; joining pieces of the genetic puzzle
found searching PubMed **[H]**
Bioessays, Sep;20{9}:696-9, 1998
Jumping over male procedures during female individual construction.

(86) Kacperski, K., Holyst, J. A.: Leaders and clusters in a social impact model of opinion formation: The case of external impact
included in **(142)** at page 367ff
Neural-network interaction of a simplified social group and the leaders influence. Phase transitions.

(87) Kaneko, K.: Chaos as a source of complexity and diversity in evolution
included in **(94)** at page 163ff
Mean-field-theory-type coupling. Correspondence with neural nets. Parasit-host adaptation by mutation. Co-operation and dynamic stability by "homeochaos". Revolts against a slaving principle.

(88) Kiekegaard, Sören: Christian revolution
1813-1855
included in **(77)** at pages II-492ff
Rejection of a system of closed definitions (new procedures can be invented). Jumping from status to status.
God the paradox thing per se (this keeps all possibilities eligible). The resulting insecurity (uncertainty).

(89) Kirby, S.: Syntax out of learning: The cultural evolution of communication in a population of induction algorithms
included in **(48)** at page 694ff
The bottleneck between the external utterances and the internal representation can only be overcome by using compositionality in the language.

(90) Krauss, L.: Neuer Auftrieb für ein beschleunigtes Universum
included in "Spektrum der Wissenschaft - Dossier - Kosmologie", 2/2000
probably available as special print of "Scientific American", too.
The "anti-gravitational", cosmological constant.

(91) Krauss, L., Starkman G.: Life, The universe and nothing: life and death in an ever-expanding universe
arXiv.astro-ph/9902189
available at: "http://xxx.lanl.gov" or mirror sites
They tell that there will be no life at the end. But they neglect the possible direct influence of life to the universe. Therefore the calculations have to be improved. **[(90)]**

(92) Kunzler, Matuso, Schaffner: Pathological, physiological and evolutionary aspects of short, unstable DNA repeats in the human genome
found searching PubMed **[H]**
Biol Chem Hoppe Seyler: Apr;376{4}:201-11, 1995
Subtle, semi-stable modulation of gene activity by repetitive DNA sequences of spacers and introns: It looks like object oriented programming. Quasi-Lamarckian inheritance.

(93) Lachmann, J., Jablonka, E.: The inheritance of phenotypes: an adaptation to fluctuating environments
found searching PubMed **[H]**
J Theor Biol, Jul 7;181{1}:1-9, 1996
Evolutional models including Lamarckian inheritance.

(94) Langton, Ch. G.: Artificial life – an overview
The MIT Press, Cambridge Massachusetts, 1995
Not only an overwiew: real insights! The starting point to AL.

(95) Lee, Amaral, Canning, Meyer, Stanley, E.: Universal Features in the growth dynamics of complex organizations
Physical Review Letters, Vol. 81, Nr. 15, 12. October 1998
Firms and countries show similar dependencies to laws of growth rate. **[L]**

(96) Leibnitz, G. W.: Principes de la nature et de la grâce
1714
included in **(120)**
German titel: Die Vernunftprinzipien der Natur und der Gnade
Effects of dreams.

(97) Leibnitz, G. W.: Rationalism
1646-1716
included in **(77)** at pages II-148ff
A fractal structure of "monades". Individuality is this way a part of unity.
The body – an automate or a natural machine.
Reaching a higher degree of perfection by suffering.
Senses – the needed base of association.
The ideal rationality is mathematically.
The endless sequence of causes (hen and egg).
By an arithmetic of terms of language all would be rational calculateable.
The conservation of energy. (Foundation of centuries of following science, but an incomplete and therefore misleading principle, too.)

(98) Leifer, R.: Understanding organisational transformation using a dissipative structure model
Human Relations: 42:899-916, 1989
Dissipation keeps it running. **[(153)]**

(99) Lichtenberg, G. C.: Remarks of an observer of men
ca. ≤1846
included in **(120)**
German title: Bemerkungen eines Menschenbeobachters
Fractal system by picturing the individual as a world building and the family behaviour equal as a states behaviour. The needed complement for a self-extension given by gender difference.

(100) Liebl, F.: Strategic issue management in complex socio-political environments
included in **(142)** at page 393ff
By combining ideas, symbols or framings larger collectives are producing new cognitions, i. e. they create meaning.

(101) Locke, John: Empirism
1632-1704
included in **(77)** at pages II-200ff
Simple and combined ideas: a psychology of association? (If there are only parts and sums there will be no unification, because there will be no non-linear effects.)
Rationality: the highest judge and leader.

(102) Lotka, A.: Elements of physical biology
New York, Dover Publications, 1956, reprint of:
Baltimore, 1924
"Orthogenesis" – The method of evolution beyond selection and survival of the fittest. Consciousness is based on dream and vision for preparing action. Infinitesimal interferences (metastable states) result to fundamental changes. Ethic is accepting a knowledge and motive above selfishness. The leader picks the populace. (Lotka is criticising propaganda.) With extending knowledge must come awakening consciousness of active partnership with the cosmos. **[B]**

(103) Lotze, R. H.: Inductive metaphysics
1801-1887
included in **(77)** at pages II-548ff
Metaphysics based on natural sciences. Effects of the soul to the body and vice versa.
Unification of law and freedom by God.

(104) Lullus, Raymundus: Franciscans
†1316
included in **(77)** at page I-536
First try of an artificial calculation of all possible combinations of thoughts.

(105) Lundvall, Borrás: The globalising learning economy: Implications for innovation policy
Brussels, DG XII Comission of the EU, 1997
"...a more systematic approach is still badly needed, both in terms of conceptual and theoretical frameworks, and in terms of the object of study..."

(106) Luther, M., (St. Paulus): An essay about the holy sacrament
1519
included in **(120)**
German title: Ein Sermon vom Sakrament des Abendmahls
Description of a fractal system starting from the parts of the human body to social and religious community.

(107) Kant, Immanuel: Critical idealism
1724-1804
included in **(77)** at pages II-268ff
Combination of images in mind result to new, synthetic judgements.
Synthetical instead of only analytical mathematics (data and program generation).
No contradiction to opponent properties: [true – real] or [sensual – clean], if the uncertainty is considered.
Active (time dependent) spirit – passive matter. Time the prerequisite for inner sensing. Combination with the help of time dependent operations (arithmetic).
There is nothing outside of our sensitive reception.
Order is processing of apriorical (in-)form(-ation). Connected manifolds result to unity and individual. Synthesis only by information processing.
No clear decision, whether empirical or spontaneous reaction is more important.
"Antimoniens" = dialectic. (The co-requisite with uncertainty as particle-wave properties.)
Philosophical action and empirical regression creates nature, no transcendent reality (otherwise contradictions are the result), the unavoidable illusion (the circle deduction, the captured mind, the Turing machine).
Beauty = objective and necessary.
Nature = living organism including a soul, common growth

(108) Maes, P.: Modeling adaptive autonomous agents
included in **(94)** at page 135ff
Complex functionality is emerging from sensorial inputs. Unstructured decentralised solutions have basic problems.

(109) Maimonides, Moses: Jewish philosophy
†1204
included in **(77)** at page I-429
Genesis out of nothing.

(110) Martinoli, Ijspeert, Gambardella: A probabilistic model for understanding and comparing collective aggregation mechanisms
included in **(48)** at page 575ff
Robots constructed using a gripper, one sensor, communication and associative memory aggregate themselves to linear clusters.

(111) Marx, Karl: Materialism
1818-1883
included in **(77)** at pages II-471ff
Sensuality a matter of productivity (the relation to time).
Spirit is matter. (An incomplete definition, even if the otherwise used method of dialectic is considered.)
Exploitation and additional value (a matter of leadership).

(112) Matsushita, M.: Dynamics and structure of granular flow through a vertical pipe
Lecture given at the conference "Let´s face chaos through non-linear dynamics 2002"
http://www.camtp.uni-mb.si/chaos/2002
Mutual attraction and structure of simple material by dissipation. **[π]**

(113) McClintock, P. V. E.: Quantized turbulence
Lecture given at the conference "Let´s face chaos through non-linear dynamics 2002"
http://www.camtp.uni-mb.si/chaos/2002
Structure by dissipation and Big Bang´s transition modelling. **[π]**

(114) Mill, John Stuart: English empirism
1806-1873
included in **(77)** at pages II-530ff
Association of ideas and logic, inferences.

(115) Mirandola, G. P. della: The renaissance
†1494
included in **(77)** at pages II-13f
Infinite dynamics of the world are important, non-static, eternal "ideas".

(116) Mitchel, M., Forrest, S.: Genetic algorithms and artificial life
included in **(94)** at page 267ff
Interactions between learning and evolution: the Baldwin effect, internal models for look ahead calculations.

(117) Moffat, J. W.: A dynamical model of the capital markets
Elsevier, Physica A 264:532-542, 1999
http://ww1.elsevier.nl/locate/physa
Abstract space, analogy to hydrodynamic flow.

(118) Mohamed: The Koran
Germant titel: Der Koran
Goldmann Verlag, 1986
Adaption of religious rules to a culture with sparse usable energy resources because of the desert environment and generalisation to people without family relation. **[T]**

(119) Müller, Adam: Romantic
1779-1829
included in **(77)** at pages II-401f
The state – a living organism.

(120) Noack, H., Hübscher, A.: Deutsche Geisteswelt
Werner Dausien Verlag, Hanau, 1986
A pretty short overview about philosophers (unfortunately only Germans).

(121) Olson, M: The logic of collective action
Harvard Univ Press, 1965
German version: Die Logik des kollektiven Handelns
Mohr-Siebeck Verlag, Stuttgart, 1998
Mathematical formulation, federate groups.

(122) Ostriker, P., Steinhardt, P. J.: The quintessence of the universe
German title: Die Quintessenz des Universums
Spektrum der Wissenschaft, März 2001
It is likely that the original paper was published at "Scientific American" some months before.
Repulsive, anti-gravitational behaviour relative to matter, negative pressure, particle radius can be as big as a super-heap of galaxies, relation of the quintessence field to thinking living beings, anthropological principle

(123) Ovid: Ars amatoria
Ernst Klett Verlag, Stuttgart
First written description of non-linear effects resulting from lovers' behaviour.

(124) Parisi, G.: Statistical field theory
Perseus Books, 1988, 1998
A general high level description.

(125) Parisi, G.: Attractor neural networks
http://chimera.roma1.infn.it/GIORGIO/Lavori.html
Phase transitions, spin correlations.

(126) Parisi, G. et. al.: Random self-interacting chains: a mechanism for protein folding
J. Phys. A (Math. Gen.) 24:5349, 1991
Are proteins alive?

(127) Parisi, G. et. al.: Replica field theory for deterministic models
http://chimera.roma1.infn.it/GIORGIO/Lavori.html
Spin glasses, ground state and random number algorithm, spin correlations.

(128) Parks, J. R.: A theory of feeding and growth of animals
Berlin Heidelberg, NewYork, Springer Verlag, 1982
The S-shape or sigmoid curve is coincident with first a linear and later a square root function, if ageing is neglected. **[B]**

(129) Pascal, Blaise: Rationalism
1623-1662
included in **(77)** at pages II-118ff
Division of feelings and rationality - I disagree. Different methods of description are not needed.

(130) Ray, T.: An evolutionary approach to synthetic biology: Zen and the art of creating life
included in **(94)** at page 179ff
Instantiation – object oriented synthesis of AL. Communications dominating environment (hunting ground) interaction. Independence of intelligence from media. CPU (intelligence) as source of energy. Importance of space dimension.

(131) Reif, F: Fundamentals of statistical and thermal physics
MacGraw-Hill Book Company, 1965
German version: Statistische Physik und Theorie der Wärme
de Gruyter Verlag, Berlin, 1985
Diversity: $S = k \ln\Omega$

(132) Resnick, M.: Learning about life
included in **(94)** at page 229ff
Co-operation as positive feedback. Randomness (disorder, entropy) creating order.

(133) Rupella, J., de: French augustinism
1200-1245
included in **(77)** at page I-452
Knowledge = abstraction and external illumination by God.

(134) Romanovsky, M. Yu.: Model space of economic events
Elsevier, Physica A 265:264-278, 1999
http://ww1.elsevier.nl/locate/physa
Abstract charges, electrical charge analogy, attraction formalism, fractal geometry, abstract space.

(135) Salas-Cortes, L., Jaubert F., Barbaux, S., Nessmann, C., Bono, M., R., Fellous, M., McElreavey, K. Rosemblatt, M.: The human SRY protein is present in fetal and adult Sertoli cells and germ cells.
found searching PubMed **[H]**
Int J Dev Biol, Mar;43{2}:135-40, 1999
Control beyond suppression of female suppresser genes by SRY.

(136) Sara, M.: A "sensitive" cell system. Its role in a new evolutionary paradigm
found searching PubMed **[H]**
Riv Biol, 89{1}:139-56, 1996
Evolution with two alternate and recurrent phases: epigenetic and Lamarckian at cell and organism level, selective and Darwinian at population level.

(137) Scheler, Max: Phenomenology
1874-1928
included in **(77)** at pages II-599ff
Object and action correlated (associated) by values.
The fight between light and darkness (basic dialectic).

(138) Schelling, F. W. J.: Objective idealism
1775-1854
included in **(77)** at pages II-375ff
Nature = a living organism including a soul, common growth.
Diversity the prerequisite to unity and vice versa.

(139) Scheuermann, P.: Kosmologie und Relativitätstheorie
http://www.wuerzburg.de/mm-physik/galax.htm#kosmos
The "Planck time" **[(90)]**

(140) Schimansky-Geier, Schweitzer, Mieth: Interactive structure formation with brownian particles
included in **(142)** at page 101ff
Brownian particles with the ability to generate a non-linear, self-consistent field.

(141) Schuster, P.: Extended molecular evolutionary biology: Artificial life bridging the gap between chemistry and biology
included in **(94)** at page 39ff
Why AU and GC are both needed for DNA.

(142) Schweitzer, F.: Self-organization of complex structures – From individual to collective dynamics
Gordon and Breach, Amsterdam, 1997
A high level, multidisciplinary publication. **[L]**

(143) Schopenhauer, Arhur: Voluntarism and pessimism
1788-1860
included in **(77)** at pages II-455ff
The Islam a variety of the Jewish religion.
Egoism - the starting point.
Art is release equal to freedom from the world.
Determinism! (No! Because of the uncertainty. But yes! – as a matter of influence.)
No real advices by previous philosophy, limitation of knowledge (the property of a Turing machine).

(144) Scotus, Duns: Franciscans
1266-1308
included in **(77)** at pages I-537ff
Start of individualism. Dependence of thinking to individual properties.

(145) Sheldrake, R: The presence of the past
New York, Times Books, 1988
German version: Das Gedächtnis der Natur
Piper Verlag GmbH, München, 1999
Morphogenetic fields and resonance. **[D]**

(146) Sheldrake, R.: Seven experiments that could change the world
Fourth Estate Limited, London, 1994
German version: Sieben Experimente, die die Welt verändern könnten
Wilhelm Goldmann Verlag, München, 1994 **[D]**

(147) Siger of Brabant: Averoist
1235-1284
included in **(77)** at pages I-532ff
No individual soul. No transcendent meaning of living. Meaning is instead defined by the benefit of all.

(148) Smith, H. E.: CASS Astronomy tutorial, The Big Bang
University of California, San Diego
Center for Astrophysics & Space Science
http://casswww.ucsd.edu/public/tutorial/BB.html
Temperature of the universe during expansion. **[(90)]**

(149) Sornette and Sornette: Self-organized criticality and earthquakes:
Europhysics Letters 9{3}:197-202, 1989
The unliving pops up – but organised! **[(153)]**

(150) Spencer, Herbert: English empirism
1820-1903
included in **(77)** at pages II-532ff
Developement and advance – a cosmic principle. The always improving values and truths. What is the value of the already defined values?

(151) Spinoza, Benedictus de: Philosophy of identity
1632-1677
included in **(77)** at pages II-130ff
Soul and God are of the same kind. Body (matter) is a mode of God. (This is a problem of definition as I think, because there is a basic transport, which divides and produces matter and spirit.)

(152) Stalin, Josef: Secular revolution
1818-1883
included in **(77)** at pages II-484ff
Development is a process, where unimportant and hidden quantitative changes result to basic qualitative changes. (A nice definition of "chaos" and SOC **[(16)]**.*)*

(153) Stan ?: Chaos theory and evolutionary models for economic development public policy
must be issued after 1994 regarding citations
The author is unclear until this issue.
The (pre-)dissertation was found at:
http://virtualschool.edu/mon/Economics/EvolutionPublicPolicyThesis
Probably a way of verification. **[(121)]**

(154) Stanley, M., Amaral, Buldyrev, Havlin, Leschhorn, Maass, Salinger, Stanley, E.: Scaling behaviour in the growth of companies
Letters to Nature, Vol. 379, 29. February 1996
Order increases logarithmic with sales rates or number of employees = disorder decreases exponentially. **[L]**

(155) Suarez, Franz: New scholastic
1548-1617
included in **(77)** at page II-72ff
~~Meta-~~physics = "scientia quae ens, inquantum ens seu inquantum a materia abstrahit secundum esse, contemplatur".
The "natural law" an unchangeable rule (a physical formula?).
God - the cause of government, people – the matter, laws – the (in)form(ation).

(156) Thom R.: Structural stability and morphogenesis
Addison-Wesley Publishing Co., Inc., 1972-1989
"Association in mind is a dynamic system, which describes structural stability." **[(145)]**

(157) Thomas of Aquin: Christian aristotelism
1224-1274
included in **(77)** at pages I-464ff
*Origin of effect is potency and action (B = I * t). Acting is the prerequisite of potency. (This is no contradiction to the formula, if the needed production of program code and data before the useful application is considered.)*
Substances of spirit could be separated specifically but not numerically (bosonic property).
Identity of formation, (negative) energy and idea (= intelligence).
Genesis out of nothing and continued creation.

(158) Tietze, U.; Schenk, Ch.: Halbleiter-Schaltungstechnik
Springer-Verlag, Berlin, 1983
Logic devices build from FETs.

(159) van Valen, L: A new evolutionary law
Evolutionary theory 1:1-30, 1973 **[(153)]**

(160) van Valen, L: Extinction of taxa and van Valen´s law-reply
Nature 257:515-516, 1975 **[(153)]**

(161) van Valen, L: The Red Queen lives
Nature 260:575, 1976
A zero sum game: to be overcome. **[(153)]**

(162) Vilain, E., McCabe, E. R.: Mammalian sex determination: from gonads to brain
found searching PubMed **[H]**
Mol Genet Metab, Oct;65{2}:74-84, 1998
Jumping over male procedures during female individual construction.

(163) Waddington, C.: The strategy of the genes
Allen and Unwin, London, 1957 **[(145)]**

(164) Waddington, C.: The evolution of an evolutionist
Univ. Press, Edinburgh, 1975 **[(145)]**
"The concept of fields has mainly descriptive use, but is not an explanation of cause…The original forces have to be identified in any single case…-we know that none of this conditions is fulfilled." (Now we know better!)

(165) Waldrop, M.: Complexity: The emerging science at the edge of order and chaos
Touchstone book, New York, 1992
Coincident description of multiple kinds of structures. **[(153)]**

(166) Warnecke, H.-J., Hüser, M.: Revolution der Unternehmenskultur: Das Fraktale Unternehmen
Springer Verlag, Berlin, 1993
Revolution of economic culture: The fractal enterprise **[M]**

(167) Watson and Pollack: How symbiosis can guide evolution
included in **(48)** at pages 29ff
Neural nets model and co-operation of several artificial species.

(168) Weele, Ko van der: Clustering in granular gas
Lecture given at the conference "Let´s face chaos through non-linear dynamics 2002"
http://www.camtp.uni-mb.si/chaos/2002
Mutual attraction and structure of simple material by dissipation.
Modelling of growth of towns and cities by a two dimensional extension. **[π]**

(169) Whitehead, A. N.: Ideal realism
1861-1947
included in **(77)** at pages II-627ff
The error of division by the mathematical and natural scientific thinking.

(170) Wolff, Christian: German enlightenment
1679-1754
included in **(77)** at pages II-259f
Evidence for soul and God like mathematical evidence.

(171) Yamaguchi, Maruyama, Hoshino: High speed hardware computation of co-evolution models
included in **(48)** at pages 566ff
Co-evolution using logic devices.

(172) Zeleny, M.: Ecosocieties: Societal aspects of biological self-production
http://www.uni-bielefeld.de/sozsys/deutsch/manuskri.htm
Individuals and networks, self-sustainability (by external agent = parasited host), autopoiesis. No collective life without individual death. Autopoiesis found for non-living systems. Non-topological social boundaries by communication tools.

(173) The Bible, old and new testimony
German title: Die Bibel - Altes und Neues Testament
Herder Verlag, Freiburg, 1980
Diverse authors, long time authoring
History of a group development starting near Stone Age. Religion and family relation as group interaction base during situations where multiple external cultures (for example Phoenician, Mesopotamian and Egypt) show dividing attraction and no geographical base for group interaction like the sea or big rivers is available. Important wisdom lectures.
Extension of invented morality and generalisation to people without family relation (new testimony).
Jesus tells: "Be not afraid, because I am with you all the time!" (As an allegory of time itself this becomes a simple truth.) **[T]**

(174) The Talmud
German title: Der Talmud
Wilhelm Goldmann Verlag, München , 1963/1980, 1986
Diverse authors
extracted, translated and declared: R. Mayer
Jewish Bible interpretation. The Talmud lives by communication. Mixture of group separation and external contacts. "Eye for eye" means monetary compensation. Dialectic of security / insecurity and binding / freedom. Relation of land and humans – linear and non-linear behaviour. Weakness - a helpful property.

(175) Bhagavad Gita - The holy book of Hinduism
Wilhelm Goldmann Verlag, München, 2002
Unknown author(s)
Arranged for western readers: Jack Hawley, 2001
Translation from American English: Peter Kobbe
A pretty old but as well pretty complete and pretty easy readable summary!
I can hear Krishna telling: "Fight, Arjuna, fight (for peace)!" (18.3.2003)

Recommended additional reading:

Weidlich, W.: Sociodynamics
harwood academic publishers, 2000

Hewings, G. J. D., Sonis, M., Boyce, D.: Trade, Networks and Hierarchies
Springer Verlag, 2002

The current state of the art of sociodynamical theories. A huge amount of information, which had reached myself very late. Including it in detail would let the number of reference remarks explode again.

If I want to finish, I have to stop here and now.

Stimulation (Beyond References)

(57): "*I have all, what I have seen, heard, observed, gathered and utilized. My works have been feed by thousands of different persons: unknowing and wise, spiritual and stupid men, the childs, the adult and the aged, all came and offered to me their thinking, their capabilities, their hopes, their way to be. Often I harvested were others sowed. My work is that of a collector and it wears the name Goethe.*" **[†]**

Goethe to F. J. Soret, 17.2.1832

Stimulators are influences to this book, which are not of a written, published kind. Therefore they are something beyond those references. Further stimulators may be not in any way something provable or repeatable, because stimulation occurs in mind without a backup. Those "meta-references" show problems considering the current authoring law. Probably the stimulating origin may be someone, who does not like the result of his/her stimulation or may be not aware of having done so. Consent to publishing may be not available under those or other circumstances.

Stimulators are not in any way responsible in law for this publication!

If consent was not available or clearly assumable, the stimulator is given by an encrypted information. This may protect me from behaving illegal, but leaves the complete information in the book.
There will be a version of this essay freely available by using the Internet at: "http://www.celebran.de". This chapter will be included and will be changed from version to version to clear information using incoming consent declarations. There have been changes of the cryptic keys relative to elder versions.

Again many thanks to all stimulators for their contributions! Such an effort as this essay is unthinkable without help and stimulation of ideas.

Received broadcasting (including newspapers):

"Radio Bayern 2, Bayerischer Rundfunk"**:**

[A] Report about Valentin Tomberg:
(27.2.2000, Evangelische Perspektiven)
"mystic, gnosis and magic".

[B] Interview with the president of the "Max Planck Society", Prof. Dr. Hubert Markl:
(Das politische Buch, Hubert Markl, "Wissenschaft gegen Zukunftsangst")
Mentioning Lotka´s empirical found square root law of population dynamics, which is not yet understood.

[C] The humans, the fishes, the sea – live at Nazaré
(10.6.2000, Notizbuch am Samstag)
A travel to Portugal's Atlantic coast
German title: Die Menschen, die Fische, das Meer – Leben in Nazaré
Eine Reise an Portugals Atlantikküste
Mortality of males and resulting female leadership and female dominated structure of population.

[&] Weigel, H. P.: The other messengers of God – Dreams, which have meaning
(3.2.2001, 9:00 pm)
German title: "Die anderen Boten Gottes - Träume, die nicht bloß Schäume sind"
Dreams and their relation to reality by examples of the bible **(173)**. *At most the story of Josef of the old testimony.*
(Unexpected help at a hopeless point.)

[=] Knorzen, K.: Referring to the book: "Rot" of Uwe Thim
(4.9.2001, 18:32)
The "wolfish biting society" is mentioned by the book.
During the day I prepared a letter to **[+]** *including most of the content of the chapter "Aggression and Terrorism", where wolf societies have been analysed. At the next morning the importance of the measurement principle to all societies had become clear.*

"ARTE":

[S] Jean-Claude Bragard, "Along the trials of Moses, the history of the book Exodus", 14.4.2001
German title: "Auf den Spuren von Moses, die Geschichte des Buches Exodus"

“FAZ, Frankfurter Allgemeine Zeitung”:

[T] Joseph Cardinal Ratzinger: Reprint of a lecture held at the Sorbonne, Paris, 27.11.1999
unclear title and date in 2000 (remembering)
Christian morality contrasting to Darwinism dominated science.

“ZDF, Zweites Deutsches Fernsehen”:

[U] Dr. Joachim Bublath, Abenteuer Forschung
unclear title and date in 1999 (remembering)
Deviation of human time impressions to physical measurements, what can not be explained yet.

“Radio S2 Kultur, Süddeutscher Rundfunk”:

[V] Portrait of Prof. Noam Chomsky
unclear title and date during 1998 or spring 1999 (remembering)

Exchange by discussion:

[D] Prof. Dr. Max Baumann, University of Bamberg **[Q]**:
Partnership, Dr. Sheldrakes publications.

[E] Dr.
080F0610432A0A0E0004000B00000012584932081C1317161A0C1A18450C
0E53380CE0300A:
Partnership and support during a research proposal submission.

[F] Prof. Dr.
1A0002011619522C121109080A1549533B1C08101B3E0110413E1A00190B
00160D110D5B452C0B1705070B:
"You clearly have to show me the evidence!" Meaning of authoring.

[G] Dr.
0C00071811452A05100A0B01175E622D1B0F130002783F151D00010C1619
1B260B53360608130306000515 1E494920030B1B0409:
Double stars and the 3-body problem.

[H] Prof. Dr.
051D04150658452616170D1B0C110D05433D1E1B1F131307081A1E451C05
482C13081D2D1D:
Gender and Y chromosome, Internet resources at PubMed: "http://www.ncbi.nlm.nih.gov".

[I] Dr.
121B181F1413532B0014160B134F48150B04090C0C0D12184121071A1F11
011001110B460E155339102C0C171A:
Common possibility of uncertainty relations.

[J] Dr.
371400031A08014E2CDE18111B5A49321304010B062907061A4C2C1B0711
041D010300493A232441683215072715 0A0E1301 **[M]**:
Prosperity by single leadership at small to medium enterprises, stimulation of the ***(pV)*** *chapters.*

[K] Dipl.-Ing. 1B0803020810081 00D4D00040E134A49273B1B0016051406:
Diverse corrections.

[L] Prof. Dr.
061B020D07110957371D09040008131 11E1C4244240F15210B2F2E420A154
F3D070C171D16085B45211C10031604:
Acceptation and partnership without substantial critics to the first issue (version 2.4.1).

[M] Dipl.-Arch. Bettina Schlösser, Dr. med. dent. Reinhard Schlösser:
Meditation reduces recognisability of individual presence by others.

[N] Dr. Josef Sedlmeir, München:
Improved thermodynamic description, corrections.

[O] Dr. 3410190B170767360510091717 1B1E0B4948210A00000E02:
Field description, empirical results, morphic particles.

[P] PD Dr.
2E06181B075A360A0B1F0F171424075F4730140C1F061A1607000E451D02
452C35080B091C02 **[Q]**:
Partnership, historical development of cities and regions.

[Q] PD Dr.
051C160711174C3B1007C0494E2F0B001111101A131E1C440A145A30171E
121A030C0B:
Established connection to social scientists.

[R] Dipl. Math. Torsten Specht, Siemens VDO AG, Regensburg:
Complemented arithmetic devices result to complemented output.

[#] Prof. Dr.
130C0F0300000945283C0401140006584522 1C071F1D08482B07160C03251
90A1D090F55360622EC1702161B161C5B452A00000E0606:
Critics to the cosmic bit flip example, stimulation how to generalise "information processing".

[+] Prof. Dr.
1500001D4110006B2113483C59542F1B07110307161B11104E24094D23045
E32041A161B08:
My aggression as a tool to break even a friendly professor´s wall of repulsion.

[/]
00041D1C340D0357021A060A061B00411A00451A0C004E0D00041048080B
463316060C041A104B4B270C0629001D:
The depth of an injury can only be measured by an arguing examination.

[!] PD Dr.
2C041C20180B4D241A3E020606150D061A2A004545271A1A111B011B130
7450F1C024927030113001B1A0B06422D170B0A164E100A53331B1706040
3091D11165E41281017000C120623:
Stimulation of identification of "$\Delta S > 0$" as a "Gödel"ian paradoxon.

[§] Gerhard Birkl, Neufahrn near Freising:
Found and told related scientific papers.

[^] Dr. 130A1F0F000F0B156B2D131417070D0509064952071A0901161A:
Stimulation of the free Internet version and of correlated web side improvements.

[\] Dipl.-Ing. Siegfried Feterowsky, Munich [≠]:
"Did you recognised that there is no 'present time' any more?"
First I thought this is only comparable to a computers operating frequency and related time quantum, but some weeks later I understood:
Precognition is possible and equal to a wave effect regarding the time, because of the lack of an exactly definable present. But the principle of causality is not injured!

[≠] Achim Ludwig, Munich:
My friend showed randomly the essay of version 3.2.2 to a business partner.

[•] 35100001284E210D0B0C156E492A211C06160A **[ø]:**
Established connection to an organisator of the most relevant scientific conference, which I did not knew before.

[ø] Dr. 141116120317006B3A06021D0268493F39070C0125:
Employment at a critical phase. He encouraged me to go on with science, what conflicts with his own interests relative to the current employment.

[π] Prof. Dr.
130F111F22001D5A3A100F12390F135E4F3A240F0D16080D050952060D01170B06090C3F0B490A016322181E1C170D **[•]:**
Encouraging the attendance to the conference: "Let´s face chaos through non-linear dynamics 2002".
http://www.camtp.uni-mb.si/chaos/2002

<u>Historical stimulation (remembering)</u>

[W] Prof. Dr.
100B09190207024B4C310C0000060C0A151F433D0107180C111B1D131C470A044523381B1A061D:
The fermionic property of gender.

<u>Three girls – three misunderstandings:</u>

[@] 1C1B1F08000BE04B3C161B09080D12101F:
One should not donate an important book **(123)** *without knowing the content.*

[l] 10040E012A1B4E22090602183507:
The most hurting battle, the fewest real communications, the worst result: Love turned to hate.

[<] Dr. 150D112A080D0C060452061A00100E221601002B:
Intelligence does not prevent lack of self-confidence, even if potential partners have similar properties, what inhibits communication.

Stimulation and support by family relation:

[†] Ingeborg Wolber, widowed Bergmann – my mother, † 8.9.2002
Searching for hope stimulating cites during burial preparation. **[YY]**

I have seen my mothers soul exiting the dying body through the opened mouth, as it was described by elder pictures. The surrounding surface of the transparent cloud was very difficult to recognise like it is the case for liquid Helium.
I think the light exposition was important. It was already night and the only light source was some reading lamp positioned behind my mothers head.
Because dying looses its fright, I recommend to do some scientific recording and analysis during other events of this case. At least I declare that it is allowed to do this research with me, but I hope that you will have to wait too long by restricting your research interest only to me.[98]

[¿] 0806070915115522B061A1308150B1C
He sent me a wit by email, which included a second level semantic.

[X] Dipl.-W.-Ing. Holger Bergmann
The fractal geography of Europe.

[Y] Mrs. Sigrid Bergmann
love – order – love – patience – love – drive - love

Support by employment:

[Z] Bergmann und Langer GmbH

The author in law: (included for completeness only)

[*] Dipl.-Phys. Harald Bergmann

[98] If you like some black humour: Forced experiments are prohibited (even with me)!

Index

(

[

{

6

A

B

C

D

E

F

G

H

I

J

K

L

M

N

O

P

Q

R

S

T

U

V

W

X

Y

Z

Notes